Corporate Hegemony through Sustainability

Corporate Hegemony through Sustainability

A study of sustainability standards and CSR practices as tools to demobilise community resistance in the Albanian oil industry

Sara Persson

Södertörns högskola

Subject: Business Studies
Research Area: Politics, Economy and the Organisation of Society
School of Social Sciences
Baltic and East European Graduate School

Södertörns högskola
(Södertörn University)
Biblioteket
SE-141 89 Huddinge

www.sh.se/publications

Cover image: *Patos-Marinza Oilfield*, Sidonie Hadoux (© 2014)
Graphic form: Per Lindblom & Jonathan Robson

Stockholm 2020

Södertörn Doctoral Dissertations 179
ISSN 1652-7399
ISBN 978-91-89109-31-5 (print)
ISBN 978-91-89109-32-2 (digital)

Till Farmor

You said: Your grandfather died of cancer, and so did the rest of his colleagues at the factory.
I said: Why did you not sue the company?
You said: It was a hard time. I took long walks all over the city.

You said: When I finished school I had three options – factory worker, shop worker or secretary.
I said: I am so grateful for the opportunities that I have been given.
You said: I am so proud of you.

I whispered in the dark: I miss you.

Abstract

Many critical business scholars have disregarded sustainability standards and corporate social responsibility (CSR) activities as mere window dressing, operating as a smokescreen to hide illegitimate corporate practices. Others have pointed to these activities as hegemonic articulations, as a way to strengthen corporate alliances with and dominance over other actors in society. In this PhD project I investigate how corporate hegemony and the implementation of sustainability standards and CSR practices are linked at the local level, focusing on the Canadian oil company Bankers Petroleum Ltd. (Bankers) and their operations in Patos-Marinza, an area in south-central Albania with residences in close proximity to oil extraction activities.

Between 2010 and 2015, I was involved as a consultant and staff member working in Bankers' Community Relations Department at Patos-Marinza. In this dissertation I take an autoethnographic approach, meaning that I write about and analyse my own role in the subject I am studying. Through the lenses of the Gramscian concept of hegemony and Political Discourse Theory, I examine two competing discourses in Patos-Marinza. The discourse describing company operations as an 'investment' was Bankers' hegemonic narrative, giving meaning to company activities and incorporating various groups in Albanian society into a corporate alliance. The 'investment' was a narrative aiming at closure, of incurporating 'all' as beneficiaries of the oil industry and thus trying to reduce grievances and requests from society by satisfying them. However, the remaining demands from the communities of Patos-Marinza endangered this all-encompassing vision; the constant appearance of grievances interrupted the corporate narrative, threatening to create an antagonistic frontier between the company and local residents. During this period, a counter-hegemonic discourse describing company activities as an 'invasion' began to emerge: grievances were filed, protest groups formed, oil deposits vandalised, and roads blocked.

To deepen my analysis of this antagonistic dynamic I study three specific grievances raised by the communities of Patos-Marinza and Bankers' response to these complaints. These three grievance areas highlight how Bankers' implementation of international sustainability standards supported the extension of a corporate alliance, breaking potential chains of equivalence between various community demands and controlling truth claims through dialogues, technology and experts. My conclusion is that rather than disregarding compliance to sustainability standards and CSR activities as window dressing, it is important to examine what these do in specific empirical contexts and how grievances, which could otherwise be mobilised to demand improved corporate practices, are isolated and silenced in the name of sustainability and corporate responsibility.

Keywords: hegemony, Gramsci, Political Discourse Theory, autoethnography, community grievances, sustainability standards, CSR, Albania, Patos-Marinza, oil industry.

Përmbledhje (*Summary/abstract in Albanian*)
Disa studiues të biznesit i kanë shpërfillur standardet e qëndrueshmërisë dhe aktivitetet e përgjegjësisë shoqërore të korporatave (PSHK), duke i konsideruar ato thjesht si dekorues vitrinash, që shërbejnë si një perde tymi, për të fshehur praktikat e paligjshme të korporatave. Të tjerë i kanë parë këto aktivitete si artikulime dominuese, si një mënyrë për të forcuar aleancat e korporatave me aktorë të tjerë në shoqëri dhe dominimin ndaj tyre. Në këtë punim doktorature unë kam trajtuar lidhjen midis fuqisë së korporatave me zbatimin e standardeve të qëndrueshmërisë dhe me praktikat e PSHK-së në nivel vendor, duke u përqendruar në kompaninë kanadeze të naftës "Bankers Petroleum Ltd." (Bankers) dhe operacionet e tyre në Patos-Marinëz, një zonë në Shqipërinë Jugqendrore, ku zona naftënxjerrëse është shumë pranë asaj të banuar.

Gjatë viteve 2010-2015, kam qenë e përfshirë si konsulente dhe pjesë e stafit të Departamentit të Marrëdhënieve me Komunitetin në kompaninë Bankers në Patos-Marinëz. Në këtë disertacion unë kam përdorur një qasje autoetnografike, që do të thotë se unë shkruaj rreth rolit tim dhe e analizoj atë në çështjen që po studioj. Përmes lenteve të teorisë së Antonio Gramsci-it dhe të ligjërimit politik, unë shqyrtoj dy qasje konkurruese në Patos-Marinëz. Qasja që i përshkruante operacionet e kompanisë si një "investim" ishte rrëfimi dominues i Bankers-it. "Investimi" ishte një rrëfim që synonte mbylljen, që i përfshinte "të gjithë" si përfitues nga industria e naftës dhe duke u përpjekur në këtë mënyrë të pakësonte ankesat dhe kërkesat nga shoqëria duke i plotësuar ato. Sidoqoftë, kërkesat e tjera nga komunitetet e Patos-Marinzës përbënin një rrezik për këtë vizion gjithëpërfshirës. Filloi të artikulohej një qasje tjetër kundërdominuese, që e shikonte aktivitetin e kompanisë si një "pushtim". U bënë ankesa, u formuan grupe protestuesish, u dëmtuan depozita nafte dhe u bllokuan rrugë.

Për ta thelluar analizën time të kësaj dinamike konfliktuale, unë jam ndalur në tri ankesa specifike të ngritura nga komuniteti i Patos-Marinzës dhe në përgjigjen e Bankers-it ndaj këtyre ankesave. Këto tri fusha të ankesave nxjerrin në pah se si zbatimi i standardeve ndërkombëtare të qëndrueshmërisë nga Bankers-i ishte faktor mbështetës për zgjerimin e aleancave të korporatës. Përfundimi im është që, në vend që të shpërfillet pajtueshmëria me standardet e qëndrueshmërisë dhe aktivitetet e PSHK-së e të konsiderohen si dekorues vitrinash, e rëndësishme është të shqyrtohet se çfarë bëjnë këto në kontekste specifike empirike dhe se si, në emër të qëndrueshmërisë dhe përgjegjësisë së korporatës, izolohen dhe "u mbyllet goja" kërkesave, që në të kundërt, mund të përdoren për të ushtruar presion për përmirësimin e praktikave të korporatave.

Fjalë kyçe: Gramsci, teori e ligjërimit politik, autoetnografi, ankesa të komunitetit, standarde të qëndrueshmërisë, PSHK, Shqipëri, Patos-Marinëz, industria e naftës.

Sammanfattning (*Summary/abstract in Swedish*)

När företags hållbarhetsarbete diskuteras inom den företagsekonomiska forskningen så har vissa forskare påpekat att det ofta inte är mer än vackra ord, medan illegitima och skadliga företagsverksamheter tillåts fortsätta. Andra forskare har beskrivit företags hållbarhetsarbete som maktverktyg som på lika sätt stärker företags dominans över andra aktörer i samhället. I denna avhandling undersöker jag hur företags hållbarhetsarbete påverkar maktrelationer på lokal nivå, genom att fokusera på oljeföretaget Bankers Petroleum Ltd. (Bankers) och deras verksamhet i Patos-Marinza, ett område i sydcentrala Albanien där oljebrunnar och hushåll ligger sida vid sida.

Mellan 2010 och 2015 arbetade jag som konsult och senare som anställd på Bankers avdelning för samhällsansvar i Patos-Marinza. I avhandlingen använder jag mig av autoetnografisk metod, vilket betyder att jag skriver om och analyserar min egen roll i ämnet som jag studerar. Genom Gramscis teori om hegemoni och politisk diskursteori, så undersöker jag två konkurrerande diskurser i Patos-Marinza. Den ena var Bankers dominerande narrativ som beskrev företagets verksamhet som en 'investering' och skapade en allians mellan företaget och olika grupper i det Albanska samhället. 'Investeringen' var ett narrativ som syftade till att begränsa klagomål och krav från samhället genom att gå dem till mötes och således inkludera 'alla' i den sociala kontexten som oljeindustrins vinnare. Återkommande klagomål från samhället i Patos-Marinza var ett hot mot denna fulländade vision och riskerade att skapa splittring mellan företaget och lokalsamhället. Ett konkurrerande narrativ som beskrev företagets verksamhet som en 'invasion' formulerades, klagomål framfördes, protestgrupper bildades, oljedepåer vandaliserades och vägar blockerades.

För att fördjupa mig i denna konfliktfyllda dynamik så har jag analyserat tre specifika klagomål från lokalsamhället i Patos-Marinza och Bankers svar på dessa. Dessa tre klagomålsprocesser understryker hur Bankers implementering av internationella hållbarhetsstandards gynnade företagets allians med övriga samhället, skapade splittring i lokalsamhället och förstärkte företagets sanningsanspråk genom samhällsdialoger, teknologi och experter. Min slutsats är att det är viktigt att inte avfärda företags hållbarhetsarbete som tomma ord utan istället undersöka vad hållbarhetsdiskurser 'gör' i specifika kontexter. Eftersom tal om hållbarhet är ett dominerande inslag i stora företags kommunikation idag är det viktigt att kritiskt granska om detta leder till förändring bort från skadliga företagsmodeller eller om det endast fungerar som legitimerande mekanismer som ger företag större makt.

Nyckelord: hegemoni, Gramsci, politisk diskursteori, autoetnografi, klagomål från lokalsamhället, hålbarhetsstandards, CSR, Albanien, Patos-Marinza, oljeindustrin.

Contents

Thank you…

Residents of Patos-Marinza
For sharing your stories again and again
For meeting me as a fellow human being even when I represented oil
For continuing to fight for the children growing up next to oil wells

Colleagues in the oil industry
For teaching me that laughing is a way to stay sane
For making my days tolerable even when I lost hope of humanity
For showing care in an industry that hopefully soon will be replaced

Interviewees
For honouring me with your trust
For speaking openly and honestly about complexities
For meetings that will stay with me long after this book is printed

…

Malin Gawell and Peter Dobers
For your deep wisdom, joyful engagement and caring leadership
For having my back when I hesitated and for being my shield when I needed peace
For giving me courage and confidence to tell my own story and find my own way

Ann-Sofie Köping and Johanna Fernholm
For your encouragement and generous reading of my first academic words

Birgitta Schwartz and Noomi Weinryb
For your supportive and critical questions that reorganised this text to the better

Jenny Helin
For inspiring me to write differently and engage deeper with autoethnography

Sverre Spoelstra
For your generous engagement, insightful comments and advice

Bengt Jacobsson
For valuable comments, kind words and encouragement

Staff, fellow doctoral students and postdoctoral researchers at CBEES
For creating a supportive and happy environment at CBEES during my first year

Jenny Gunnarsson Payne
For lectures and advice that inspired my engagement with discourse theory

David Payne
For inspiring lectures and detailed comments that brought my work to a new level

Simon Lilley
For your warm welcoming to Leicester and for insightful advice

Eda Ulus
For your heartfelt support and generosity

Roland Hartz
For inspiring and encouraging conversations

Andreas Diedrich and fellow students at UFIS
For hands-on seminars that taught me new ways to discover and present my 'field'

Sidonie Hadoux
For beautiful pictures and inspirational chats

Merita Xhediku
For generously accepting a last-minute translation mission

...

The Foundation for Baltic and East European Studies
For providing the possibly to read and write for four uninterrupted years

The School of Social Sciences and the subject area Business Studies
For accepting my funding applications for conferences and an exchange period

Helge Ax:son Johnson Foundation
For several grants that supported my visits to Patos-Marinza

...

Mamma and Pappa
For your love, unconditional support and inspiring curiosity

Hannis
For being my life long companion and for your online activism to save our planet

Lisa, Kerstin, Jessica, Samya, Sofie and Hana
For your sisterhood, encouragement and generosity

Johan
For your everyday love and companionship
For being a feminist in practice and when it really matters
For an ongoing private seminar that continues to expand my horizons

Alfons
For your smile that brightens up every morning
For your determined resistance against our regime
For forcing me to stay optimistic about the future

List of abbreviations and acronyms

AAP	Anglo Albanian Petroleum
AGS	Albanian Geological Service
AKBN	National Agency for Natural Resources
bopd	barrels of oil per day
CAO	IFC's Compliance Advisor/Ombudsman
CEO	Chief Executive Officer
CI	Community Investment
CMS	Critical Management Studies
CO_2	Carbon Dioxide
CSR	Corporate Social Responsibility
DIDR	Development-Induced Displacement and Resettlement
EBRD	European Bank of Reconstruction and Development
EITI	Extractive Industries Transparency Initiative
ESAP	Environmental and Social Action Plan
ESIA	Environmental and Social Impact Assessment
H_2S	Hydrogen Sulphide
HSE	Health, Safety and Environment
HR	Human Resources
IFC	International Finance Corporation
MNC	Multinational Corporation
MNE	Multinational Enterprise
NGO	Non-Governmental Organisation
NSI	National Seismological Institute
NO_2	Nitrogen Dioxide
OMV	OMV Aktiengesellschaft
SIA	Social Impact Assessment
SO_2	Sulphur Dioxide
WHO	World Health Organization
UNEP	United Nations Environmental Program

Prologue

Autobiographical tales from Patos-Marinza[1]

Dear reader. This is a story about a field in south-central Albania called Patos-Marinza. It is a vast agricultural area divided into thousands of small land plots, with multiple villages spread across dusty gravel roads. On a clear spring day, the sky is high and intensely blue, the fields green from bourgeoning crops and the snow-capped Mount Tomorri rests proudly on the horizon. I call it a 'field' but most people would add 'oil' to its description. The area is thus most often defined, neither by its people nor by its crops, but what it hides from sight over one thousand metres underground. Oil was first extracted from the abdomen of Patos-Marinza in the 1930s and since then people have worked intensively on its surface to unearth its treasures.[2] Iron towers known as derricks have been raised to drill holes deep into the ground and pipelines have been laid out over great distances to transport the oil into tanks where it has been stowed and treated. During the Albanian communist regime led by Enver Hoxha, oil extraction was carried out by the state-owned company Albpetrol. Later, when communism collapsed in the 1990s, multinational corporations took over oilfield operations. In this process, some people became rich from Patos-Marinza's resources while others, living on top of its black gold, remain in poverty. Those who became rich were often brief visitors; they took what they wanted and left. I am one of those persons.

The stories I will tell you in this dissertation take place between 2009 and 2016, when the Canadian oil company Bankers Petroleum Ltd. (Bankers) implemented an ambitious Corporate Social Responsibility (CSR) program in Patos-Marinza, guided by international sustainability standards. During this period I was a consultant, and later, staff member in Bankers' Community Relations Department, and was running around the villages of Patos-Marinza on behalf of the company, trying to make

[1] Persson (2019). Part of this text was first published in the AOM CMS Division Newsletter.

[2] Albpetrol (no date).

residents with grievances calm down. Residents would complain about issues such as poor air quality, blocked drainage canals and noise disturbances but rarely could I do something to ease the negative effects that the oil industry had on their lives. I left Patos-Marinza at the end of 2015, just as all the foreigners before me had done, but the conflicts between residents and the company continued.

In this dissertation I take an autoethnographic approach, which means that I write about and analyse my own role in the subject I am studying. Carolyn Ellis, one of the pioneering advocates of this approach, describes autoethnography as "an opening to honest and deep reflection about ourselves, our relationships with others and how we want to live".[3] My dissertation project started when, as a company representative, I found myself standing on a road in the middle of Patos-Marinza, with oil trucks lining up in both directions as a group of angry men blocked the way. The men had decided to form a barricade as part of their strategy to make the company act, and this was one of many protests I encountered during my years in Patos-Marinza. My research is built around these pivotal moments in order to investigate how the relationship between corporate dominance, community resistance, CSR and sustainability can be understood. These 'impressionistic' tales from the field[4] are a way of making my experiences from Patos-Marinza come to life for you as a reader and through these stories I will discuss the local struggles which are the building blocks of globalised capitalism and sustainability regimes.

Local compliance to global sustainability standards

Let me start by diving right into the process that brought me to Patos-Marinza. In the following autobiographical narrative[5], I describe how global sustainability standards[6] were introduced to Bankers in order to guide the company's CSR strategy.

> I came to Patos-Marinza as part of a consultancy group that implemented Bankers' social baseline study and social impact assessment during 2010 and 2011.[7] These processes consisted of individual meetings and focus group discussions with over 500 stakeholders in Patos-

[3] Ellis (2013/2016), p. 10.
[4] Van Maanen (1988/ 2011).
[5] Autobiographical narrative, written in 2016.
[6] IFC (2012b); EBRD (2014).
[7] Bankers Petroleum (2011a); Bankers Petroleum (2011b).

Marinza including local authorities, village leaders and local residents. It was a hectic period during which our team held one meeting after another where we got to hear community members' frustrations with oil industry activities. Participants in the meetings brought up a lack of jobs, environmental pollution, dust from heavy traffic and earth tremors, all issues which they felt were directly connected to the oil industry.[8] Internally in Bankers, these meetings were discussed with concerns; this was the first time a formal consultation process had been implemented in the area and actors within Bankers were worried that the meetings would stir up feelings of discontent among the residents. "*People will tell you everything that is wrong with their lives and say that it is all connected to the oil industry*", our team were told by company managers who considered the consultation process inappropriate to the complex context of Patos-Marinza. According to rumours within the company, these internal concerns were a product of the way the process had been initiated. Bankers had signed loan agreements with the international banks International Finance Corporation (IFC) and European Bank of Reconstruction and Development (EBRD), agreements that came with requirements to follow the banks' *Performance Standards for Environmental and Social Sustainability.*[9] This was something that, according to the rumours, not all senior managers had recognised at the time of signing. When the banks started to put demands on Bankers to comply with their sustainability standards, resistance within the company grew, partly out of the perception that outsiders were now telling the company what to do. This internal conflict was described on Bankers' web page in one simple sentence: "In May of 2009 we worked with the International Finance Corporation and European Bank for Reconstruction and Development to delineate an Environmental and Social Action Plan which is used to guide the development and implementation of our CSR program."[10] In my own experience of this process, it was longer and more difficult than corporate communication would ever disclose.

To structure the work around the new CSR activities and ensure that the company complied with IFC's and EBRD's requirements for social and environmental sustainability, Bankers hired new staff members of which many came from our consultancy team. IFC writes about this process in a review report from 2013: "Following IFC and EBRD advice, Bankers developed a Stakeholder Engagement Plan tied to its Social Management System" and "established a significant Community

[8] Bankers Petroleum (2011b).
[9] IFC (2012b); EBRD (2014).
[10] Bankers Petroleum (2016b).

> Relations team".[11] Since our Community Relations team was a new department in the company and a driving force for change towards compliance with the banks' sustainability standards, resistance from older actors became a common hindrance in the implementation of stakeholder engagement activities. The meetings we held with community members were filled with stories about impacts from Bankers' activities and included accounts about staff misconduct, corruption and unfair treatment. Those stories were not popular to communicate internally and amplified the internal resistance to the stakeholder engagement process. As the 'messengers', our own loyalties were often questioned, and we frequently had to defend ourselves against accusations such as: "*Who do you really work for – Bankers or the communities?*" On the other hand, the frequent meetings with communities did something to our team. Standing in between conflicting external and internal accounts of reality *did* impact our loyalties as we started to question who was giving us the right story.

I begin my tales about Patos-Marinza with this account, since it introduces many of the themes I will discuss in this dissertation: conflicts about environmental pollution and earth tremors; company-community dialogue meetings, as well as accounts about corruption and doubts about truth claims. All these aspects will be discussed in what follows. In addition, the above narrative highlights my role, thoughts and feelings as a CSR professional. Following Norman K. Denzin's appeal "to turn the autoethnographic project into a critical, performative practice, a practice that begins with the biography of the writer and moves outward to culture, discourse, history and ideology",[12] I will analyse my own role as a company representative and how I was part of reproducing the corporate hegemony[13] that I now as a researcher aim to understand. This is in line with Sarah Wall's description of the purpose of autoethnography: "to acknowledge the inextricable link between the personal and the cultural and to make room for non-traditional forms of inquiry and expression".[14] As is shown in the above narrative, my role in Bankers' was characterised by contradictory loyalties from the start, a dynamic that continued during my years in Patos-Marinza. On the one hand, I performed my role as a dedicated employee, carrying out Bankers' CSR program as detailed in policy documents

[11] IFC (2013).
[12] Denzin (2013/2016), p. 124.
[13] Laclau & Mouffe (1985/2014).
[14] Wall (2006), p. 146.

that privileged corporate interests and risk management. On the other hand, I saw myself as an internal change actor, working towards an ideal where oil operations could co-exist with minimal environmental impact and increased community well-being. The tension between this ideal and my corporate role is the starting point for this inquiry. As Denzin argues, autoethnography links "the personal to the political, the autobiographical to the cultural, the local to the historical" and is used as a source of insight in the quest to understand society.[15] In this dissertation, I use this approach to understand how sustainability standards and CSR practices, which I, in part, was responsible for implementing, contributed to the local construction of corporate hegemony in Patos-Marinza.

[15] Denzin (2013/2016), p. 125.

CHAPTER 1

Sustainability and the role of the corporation

Sustainability. A word that can make the pompous claim of describing the zeitgeist of our times. Sustainable development goals. Sustainable lifestyles. Sustainable packaging. Sustainable tourism. Sustainable business models. The word captures a society striving towards a better future, one that will solve the deep-seated problems defining how we live now. Often the term is paired with phenomena which are perceived as *not yet sustainable.* Lifestyles. Packaging. Business models. In other words, sustainability does not attempt to describe a society that aims to be maintained in its current form but a society that must change in order to survive. The word could thus be considered, in its expanded field of meaning, an oxymoron. It brings together the antithetical terms of maintenance and change; but what should be changed, in order to later be maintained, is open for countless interpretation. Twenty years ago, Zygmunt Bauman made the following description about fashionable words: "All vogue words tend to share a similar fate: the more experiences they pretend to make transparent, the more they themselves become opaque."[16] While globalisation was the word that Bauman scrutinised at that time, sustainability shares this fate today. Millions of other terms have been deployed to pin down its essence, to encapsulate what it contains and dismiss what it leaves out.[17] This text can in a wider sense be seen as part of that movement, however focusing specifically on how the word is used in the corporate world. Consequently, rather than to distil what the signifier sustainability *actually means* in the light of its growing field of signified phenomena, I will stay put in a specific corporate context where the word has been applied and translated into actions. That context is the Albanian oilfield Patos-Marinza and the main actor to have deployed this word was the Canadian oil company Bankers. What did sustainability do in this context and does that say something about its general meaning and function in the corporate world?

[16] Bauman (1998), p. 1.
[17] Kuhlman & Farrington (2010).

Corporations are today expected to be agents for societal change and sustainability, evident in discussions surrounding Agenda 2030 and today's obligatory sustainability reporting practices. At the same time, corporations are continuously criticised for unsustainable practices as contributors to extravagant consumption behaviours and extractive logics[18] that undermine environmental and social systems. This contradiction highlights the conflictual role of the corporation when it is increasingly involved in addressing environmental and social matters that have previously been conceptualised as outside the scope of corporate interest.[19] Within the academic field focusing on Corporate Social Responsibility (CSR), the political role of corporations has received increasing attention during the past decades.[20] Although it is still a marginal concern within management studies,[21] it has been discussed as a promising feature connected to the concepts of 'corporate citizenship'[22] and 'political CSR'[23], where hopes are expressed that corporations can engage with stakeholders in a form of 'deliberative democracy' and implement practices that 'fill the gap' of governmental vacuums and failures. The political role of the corporation is within this literature described as necessary and desirable, and CSR practices, specifically, are seen as promises for a conscious corporate sector and a sustainable society. In contrast, several management scholars with a critical approach have argued that sustainability standards and CSR activities, rather than promoting a necessary change of the economic system, function as hegemonic tools to maintain the status quo, preventing formal government interventions,[24] silencing radical critique from civil society,[25] and quelling community resistance and mobilisation.[26] Within this particular strand of literature, the corporate (and academic) discourse surrounding sustainability and CSR is not seen as beneficial for wider society but rather as a way for corporations (and management scholars) to sustain the very economic system that is causing social and environmental breakdown. As formulated by Subhabrata Bobby Banerjee "the emergent discourse on 'sustainability', which originally promoted sustainable develop-

[18] Sassen (2017) in Aneesh (2017).
[19] Friedman (1979).
[20] Matten & Crane (2005); Böhm, Spicer & Fleming (2008); Frynas & Stephen (2015).
[21] O'Doherty, Vachhani & De Cock (2019).
[22] Matten & Crane (2005).
[23] Scherer & Palazzo (2007).
[24] Fooks, Gilmore, Collin, Holden, & Lee (2013).
[25] Kourula & Delalieux (2016).
[26] Banerjee (2018).

ment as an alternative paradigm to the growth model, has like the modern Western environmental movement been hijacked by corporate interests."[27] Since sustainability standards and CSR practices continue to be developed and implemented in the business sector, there is a need for a detailed critique of the practical consequences they produce. In light of the prominence that sustainability has achieved on the global business agenda, the effects of practices promoted under this concept are likely to be of widely varying character. The societal impacts of corporate discourses around sustainability and CSR thus need to be scrutinised in relation to the specific contexts where they are implemented. This is precisely what I set out to do in this dissertation.

Land-based investments and sustainability standards

The oilfield in Patos-Marinza can be categorised as an extractive industry, and in a wider sense as a land-based development project. Major land-based development projects, such as dams, pipelines, commercial agriculture and extractive industries, are commonly motivated by broad regional and national economic interests but have a history of causing stress for affected local communities, owing to changes to existing land use patterns that result in environmental impacts, poverty, food insecurity and disempowerment.[28] These challenges of severe social and environmental impacts have led to frequent conflicts between local communities and investing corporations in land-based development projects. Examples of these corporate-community conflicts are abundant and include for example Shell's extractive operations in the Niger Delta,[29] the Finnish company Botnia's pulp-mill project in Uruguay[30] and the Australian company BHP's mining activities in Papua New Guinea.[31] The internet-based mapping tool *Environmental Justice Atlas* currently displays 3,285 conflicts between land-based projects and local communities worldwide, giving an indication of the global scope of these issues.[32] As Yengoh and Armah emphasise, "large-scale acquisition of land for a variety of investment purposes has raised deep concerns over the food security, livelihood and socio-economic

[27] Banerjee (2008).
[28] Satiroglu & Choi (2015); Cernea (2003); Yengoh & Armah (2015); Luning (2012).
[29] Matten & Crane (2005).
[30] Joutsenvirta & Vaara (2015).
[31] Gilberthorpe & Banks (2012).
[32] Environmental Justice Altas (2020).

development of communities in many regions."[33] Land-based investment areas are thus arenas where the inequalities of the global economic system become painfully apparent. As stated by the previous UN Special Rapporteur on Extreme Poverty and Human Rights, Magdalena Sepúlveda, "Unfortunately, economic development can have negative as well as positive impacts. Often, the poorest of the poor do not benefit from development, or even worse, it is undertaken at their expense"[34]. Irrespective of their controversial nature, land-based development projects are vital for the agenda of continued growth and modernisation. This is emphasised also by Michael M. Cernea, who was responsible for introducing sociological and anthropological approaches to the World Bank: "Demographic growth, urbanization and the inelasticity of land will continue to require changes in the current use-patterns of lands and waters."[35] Addressing the negative local impacts of such changes will no doubt remain a concern on the international sustainable development agenda, since the need for land–based development projects are still an ever-present part of the global economic and political landscape.

The controversial nature of many land-based development projects underline ideas around social and environmental sustainability as central to what could be considered a 'legitimate investment' but also puts the concept of sustainability in relation to complex issues regarding environmental and social impacts from development, local peoples' right to be heard and power struggles for natural resources and land. In response to the various conflicts and grievances worldwide, international finance institutions have developed detailed guidelines for how land-based projects should be planned and implemented in order to support their corporate clients to mitigate negative social and environmental impacts and enhance their clients' 'Social License to Operate'.[36] IFC, an institution within the World Bank Group focused on supporting private sector development in lower- and middle-income countries, describes how their sustainability standards "are directed towards clients, [...] and are designed to help avoid, mitigate, and manage risks and impacts as a way of doing business in a sustainable way."[37] IFC's sustainability standards can thus be seen as tools that translate the vague concepts of 'sustainability' and 'CSR' into

[33] Yengoh & Armah (2015), p. 9505.
[34] Amnesty International (2013).
[35] Cernea (2003), p. 3.
[36] IFC (2012a); IFC (2012c); EBRD (2008); EBRD (2014).
[37] IFC (2012b), p. i.

specific practices, requiring IFC's corporate clients to hire staff and contract consultants to implement the standards in a way that can be measured and assessed. However, while the international business community is continuing to produce tools and standards for how to objectively work with and measure sustainability and CSR,[38] the local context of many land-based development projects provides a harsh reality when industry dynamics, conflicting interests and power relations encounter each other in determinate spatial settings.[39]

Today, CSR or sustainability reporting borders on being an obligatory practice in land-based development, specifically, and the business world, in general. However, this practice has received critical attention from business scholars not only for being too simplistic but also for being contradictory to the fundamental idea of integrating social and environmental concerns into corporate performance.[40] Birgitta Schwartz and Karina Tilling argue that while sustainability standards are designed to support managers to implement sustainability measures, they also risk simplifying and unifying responses to complex and evolving issues.[41] Similarly, Tenbrunsel et al. claim that sustainability standards "might actually diminish the focus on substantive CSR because management may become principally concerned with symbolic activities that serve to minimally comply with requirements".[42] Maria Joutsenvirta and Eero Vaara point to controversial investment projects driven by multinational corporations as battlegrounds where the process of capitalist globalisation is legitimised and challenged, and the ideas of CSR and sustainability are put to the test.[43] They emphasise that:

> there is a need to focus scholarly attention on the ways in which the discussions around these cases reproduce and at times challenge widely held national and neoliberal assumptions, including prevailing (western) ideals about corporate social responsibility.[44]

Studies of sustainability standards and CSR practices in land-based development projects thus have the potential to highlight the contradictions and complexities that underlies thoughts around sustainability and respon-

[38] Schwartz & Tilling (2010).
[39] Luning (2012).
[40] Fleming & Jones (2013).
[41] Schwartz & Tilling (2010).
[42] Tenbrunsel et. al. cited in Aguinis and Galvas (2012), p. 940.
[43] Joutsenvirta & Vaara (2015).
[44] Joutsenvirta & Vaara (2015), p. 773.

sible business practices. What the large number of conflicts registered in the Environmental Justice Atlas indicate is that community resistance to land-based development projects is as common as the sustainability standards that accompany these projects. This doubtlessly raises questions about the local effects of these standards. As underlined by Banerjee, "that virtually all the mining corporations involved in community conflicts [...] have extensive CSR policies and stakeholder initiatives in place [...] casts serious doubts about the effectiveness of CSR".[45] Controversial land-based development projects driven by multinational corporations, such as in Patos-Marinza, can thus be seen as arenas where CSR practices and sustainability standards may strengthen corporate power but also as sites where these very practices are contested. As Banerjee emphasises: the study of "corporate-community conflicts can provide insights into the limits of CSR and highlight counter-mobilisation strategies of corporations".[46] Starting with corporate-community conflicts, rather than with agreements, thus has the potential to highlight what societal values are at stake when CSR and sustainability discourses are implemented in land-based project areas, as well as in the wider corporate sector. In the following sections I will briefly summarise some of the discussions around sustainability and CSR within management studies, before I return to Patos-Marinza and the research questions that this study aims to answer.

Discussions around corporate sustainability and CSR

The concept of CSR has been widely debated among business scholars during the past decades.[47] The notion has been broadly defined by Herman Aguinis as "context-specific organizational actions and policies that take into account stakeholders' expectations and the triple bottom line of economic, social, and environmental performance".[48] In the scholarly debate, CSR has been used as an umbrella term under which diverse perspectives on corporations and their role in society are discussed, ranging from instrumentalist and positivist research on the 'business case' for CSR[49] to interpretative and critical approaches based on hermeneutics and critical

[45] Banerjee (2018), p. 5
[46] Banerjee (2018), p. 5.
[47] Scherer (2018).
[48] Aguinis (2011), p. 855.
[49] Werther and Chandler (2005).

theory.[50] In order to provide a brief overview of the CSR literature most relevant to this study, I will summarise three major lines of research on CSR and their relation to the concept of sustainability: the business case for CSR; the ethical case for CSR; and CSR as a power tool.

The business case for CSR

Ever since Milton Friedman's famous claim that business should focus on activities aimed at making profit,[51] an abundant literature on the 'business case' for CSR has dominated management studies. This line of research accepts Friedman's underlying assumptions, namely that a free market-economy based on corporations aiming at profit maximisation is essentially beneficial to overall society. However, this literature is often formulated in opposition to Friedman's famous thesis, arguing that the market (and society) has changed in such a way that corporate concerns for social and environmental issues are understood as *necessary* for long term profit-making. This research thus starts from the viewpoint of 'the manager' and argues that, in a situation where increasing societal pressure is applied to companies to show that they care about social and environmental matters, CSR is a *must* for modern businesses. In an article about the evolution of the CSR concept from 1994, William C. Frederick describes the development of this line of research. He argues that before the 1970s, the concept of corporate social responsibility, or CSR_1 as he calls it, included philosophical debates about the role of business in society, trade-offs between social and economic goals and the moral underpinnings of CSR. Since then, he reasons, the concept of corporate social *responsiveness*, what he calls CSR_2, has gained the greatest traction, leaving philosophical questions regarding moral principles and the role of the corporation behind. Frederick writes:

> The many philosophic imponderables of the CSR_1 debate – why? Whether? for whose benefit? according to which moral principles? – are replaced by more answerable considerations of CSR_2 – how? by what means? with what effect? according to what operational guidelines?

In contrast to the philosophical approach of CSR,$_1$ Frederick emphasises that CSR_2 "is managerial in tone and approach" with a principal focus on

[50] Scherer (2018).
[51] Friedman (1979).

controlling corporate relations to society. Accordingly, the literature around the 'business case' for CSR argue that caring about social and environmental matters have become the 'business of business' as it is seen as beneficial to corporate legitimacy, risk management, and profit due to stakeholder pressure. As far as this strand of literature is concerned, the question whether one 'should or should not' becomes redundant; the question is rather *how* to implement CSR in a way that benefits the corporation (and sometimes society) the most. As an example of this reasoning, Werther and Chandler argue for 'strategic CSR' as 'global brand insurance' since affluent consumers now require companies to care about more than economic profit.[52] Their argumentation is thus not based on concerns about wider societal issues with which the concept of 'sustainability' is often connected, e.g. global warming and socio-economic inequalities. Instead, they argue for CSR strictly from a managerial point of view, meaning that CSR is not:

> a question of 'right' over 'wrong' in any absolute sense. Rather, it is a relative question of what constitutes good business practices now, with an eye for emerging societal demands that shape tomorrow's expectations. [...] It is about creating strategies that will make firms and their brands more successful in their turbulent environments.[53]

Ethical questions about right and wrong are thus disregarded as irrelevant by these authors. Instead they argue for CSR as a way to handle societal pressures and "turbulent [...] environments". In other words, CSR is simply seen as "good business practice". Correspondingly, Carroll argues that corporate executives are mostly interested in logical arguments for CSR that they can apply in their business thinking, such as reasoning linked to 'strategic advantage', 'risk management' or 'synergistic value creation'[54]. Environmental and social concerns are in this way reformulated into business risks and opportunities and the concept of sustainability is redefined to suit modern business thinking.

Even though the concept of 'Creating Shared Value' was coined by Porter and Kramer as an alternative to CSR, it fits nicely into the 'business case' discussion. These authors argue against CSR, which they claim is a "reaction to external pressure" and treated by business as a "necessary

[52] Werther & Chandler (2005).
[53] Werther & Chandler (2005).
[54] Carroll (2015).

expense".[55] Furthermore, they argue that "business is caught in a vicious circle" since "the more business has begun to embrace corporate responsibility, the more it has been blamed for society's failures".[56] As a counter reaction to what they perceive as an 'attack on capitalism', they argue that business should 'reinvent' their business strategies in line with the concept of 'Creating Shared Value' i.e. to make profit in a way that also responds to social or environmental needs. These authors thus take on the larger mission of 'saving capitalism' as a whole, not only the reputation or strategic advantage of the individual corporation. They argue:

> The capitalist system in under siege. In recent years business increasingly has been viewed as a major cause of social, environmental and economic problems. […] This diminished trust in business leads political leaders to set policies that undermine competiveness and sap economic growth. […] learning how to create shared value is or best chance to legitimize business again.[57]

In a way, the creating shared value regime can be seen as a modern neoliberal critique of CSR in line with the thinking of Friedman. Porter and Kramer argue that corporations should focus on those areas that create profit *and* correspond to social and environmental needs. They argue that this shared value approach will increase business legitimacy and strengthen public opinion around capitalism as a system that is "an unparalleled vehicle for meeting human needs, improving efficiency, creating jobs, and building wealth".[58] This echoes Friedman's argument that what is good for shareholders is good for everyone. While Friedman dismissed corporate philanthropy and CSR, maybe he would find this approach more appealing. However, proponents of the CSR concept, such as Crane et al. emphasise that the shared value approach by Porter and Kramer "bear striking similarity to existing concepts of CSR" and argue that their "argument holds up because they caricature the CSR literature" and "ignore several decades of work exploring the business case for CSR".[59] The 'creating shared value' approach can thus be seen as just another example of the 'business case' literature. However, in addition, Crane et al. argue that the shared value approach "ignores the tensions between social and economic

[55] Porter & Kramer (2011), p. 5.
[56] Porter & Kramer (2011), p. 4.
[57] Porter & Kramer (2011), p. 4.
[58] Porter & Kramer (2011), p. 4.
[59] Crane, Palazzo, Spence & Matten (2014), p. 134.

goals" and "does little to tackle any of the deep-rooted problems that are at the heart of capitalism's legitimacy crisis".[60] This critique could easily be extended to the 'business case' literature in general, which brings us to the second category of CSR research.

The ethical case for CSR

While the literature around the 'business case' for CSR is rooted in a managerial standpoint, the second line of research argues for the 'ethical case' for CSR. Here, CSR is not interpreted from the perspective of business interests but because businesses are seen as vital partners in realising the goal for a sustainable society. This line of research argues that businesses are the principal cause for a significant amount of social and environmental degradation, and thus need to start taking responsibility for the problems they have created. While critical of existing business practices, this strand of literature nonetheless posits that the business sector remains a key actor in searching for solutions to present day problems. As formulated by John Elkington: "In contrast to the anti-industry, anti-profit, and anti-growth orientation of much early environmentalism, it has become increasingly clear that business must play a central role in achieving the goals of sustainable development strategies."[61] Businesses are in this view seen as both part of the problem and the solution to the global challenges of inequality, poverty and climate change. Such sentiments are mirrored in international sustainability standards and can also be seen in the elevated role that the private sector has received in the work as partners towards Agenda 2030.[62] Within the 'ethical case' literature, "win-win-win strategies […] to simultaneously benefit the company, its consumers, and the environment"[63] are common, arguing that 'sustainability' can be addressed by corporations by a 'Triple Bottom Line' approach where people, planet and profit are given equal attention.[64] Elkington coined the Triple Bottom Line approach in 1997[65] as a way of operationalising the sustainable development agenda, expressed in the Brundtland Report, but in a language that "resonate[s] with business brains".[66] Elkington argues that he

[60] Crane, Palazzo, Spence & Matten (2014), p. 136 and 140.
[61] Elkington (1994), p. 91.
[62] UNDP Sverige (2019).
[63] Elkington (1994), p. 90.
[64] Kuhlman and Farrington (2010).
[65] Elkington (1997).
[66] Elkington (2004).

coined the concept Triple Bottom Line based on the feeling that "the social and economic dimensions of the agenda [...] would have to be addressed in a more integrated way if real environmental progress was to be made"[67]. According to Kuhlman and Farrington, the idea of sustainability as having three pillars stems from this 'managerial' idea of the Triple Bottom Line, now the dominant perspective on sustainability, as expressed for example in the United Nations Agenda for Sustainable Development.[68] According to these authors, the 'ethical case' for business involvement in sustainability issues has influenced how we view sustainability in a larger sense.

The Triple Bottom Line is one core concept that organises the literature around the 'ethical case' for CSR. However, other concepts are also central in this sub-field. Under the banner of 'corporate citizenship'[69] and 'political CSR',[70] business scholars have described a world in which state institutions are failing to deliver public goods and protect citizens rights, resulting in demands on companies to take on a set of responsibilities traditionally defined as belonging to the state domain.[71] This literature underlines a tension between state and corporate responsibilities when multinational corporations are operating within what scholars call a 'weak state' context[72]. Dirk Matten and Andrew Crane have emphasised that various stakeholders increasingly demand that multinational corporations (MNCs) take on the role of providing basic citizenship rights when corporations operate in contexts where these rights are missing.[73] They argue that:

> Globalization raises awareness of these "vacuums" and exposes western MNCs in particular to charges that they are "responsible" in some way for administering citizenship rights in such situations. This is because, in the absence of viable governmental protection, corporations become a kind of "default option" for administering citizenship rights.[74]

They give the example of Nigeria in which Shell was associated with the failure of the Nigerian state to protect the civil rights of the Ogoni people. Another recent example from Sweden is the case of Lundin Oil and the

[67] Elkington (2004), p. 1.
[68] Kuhlman & Farrington (2010), p. 3439.
[69] Matten & Crane (2005).
[70] Scherer & Palazzo (2007).
[71] Matten & Crane (2005); Scherer (2018).
[72] Garriga & Melé (2004); Rodriguez, Siegel, Hillman, & Eden (2006); Scherer (2018).
[73] Matten & Crane (2005).
[74] Matten & Crane (2005), p. 172.

investigation into two directors' alleged complicity in war crimes in southern Sudan between 1998 and 2003.[75] Matten and Crane highlight that such cases have led to demands that corporations should step in to protect civil rights when a government fails to do so. Similarly, Gavin Hilson[76] argues that when extractive industries operate in countries with high corruption and weak law enforcement, companies increasingly find themselves as a sort of alternative to the government, and corporate responsibility initiatives take the character of filling a 'governance gap'. This has spurred an intense debate about the political role of the corporation when investment activities are carried out in weak regulatory environments. Promoters of an extensive form of 'political CSR' claim that not only does it help to minimise corporate risks but that the private sector can be a driving force towards improved citizen rights and 'sustainable development'. These arguments are based on the idea of 'gap-filling', that companies will be an alternative to the government and self-regulate social and environmental impacts. Scherer et al. argue that:

> Globalizing society erodes established ideas about the division of labour between the political and economic spheres. Globalization calls for a fresh view concerning the political role of business in society and its creativity and contribution to social innovations and the public good.[77]

These authors emphasise that the question *if* corporations have a political role in society has been settled to the extent that today's question is rather *how* this political role (should) look. Hence, Scherer, Palazzo and Matten argue for a new conceptualisation of the theory of the firm that goes beyond Friedman's limited neoclassical definition[78] in taking public goods into account.

The critics of the 'ethical case' approach raise concerns about the additional power that it transfers to corporations. Minna Halme writes that: "by asking companies to take voluntary responsibilities beyond their business, we actually legitimize their increased power to decide about societal matters".[79] Following the reasoning of Halme, Peter Dobers emphasises

[75] Business and Human Rights Resource Centre (2018).
[76] Hilson (2012).
[77] Scherer, Palazzo & Matten (2014), p. 148.
[78] Friedman (1970).
[79] Halme (2010), p. 217-218.

that an important research task is to observe when companies are legitimised as decision-makers over the organisation of society.[80] When multinational corporations are operating in so called 'weak states', the process of implementing CSR programmes and international sustainability standards involves exactly such legitimisation of corporate power. In the 'corporate citizenship' literature, the dominating narrative emphasises that when state institutions are failing to take their role as guardians of citizen rights, the multinational corporation comes in as its substitute, providing jobs, infrastructure and business opportunities to local communities. The 'weak state' becomes the villain in this narrative, while multinational corporations are asked to perform role of the hero. This does not only reinforce the power of the corporation vis-à-vis the government and civil society, it also fails to acknowledge that the 'weak state' may be the very ground on which certain problematical business models are made possible in the first place.[81] This brings us to the third category of CSR literature, which sees corporate discourses and practices linked to CSR and sustainability as power tools.

CSR as a power tool

The third line of research sees CSR as a tool, the utility of which, for corporations, is to extend their power over society. This research points to how the work around sustainability has been co-opted by a corporate agenda (such as the Triple Bottom Line or Shared Value Approach) that promotes growth and profit making as equally or more important than social and environmental matters. Corporations are thus seen as using sustainability and CSR discourses to prevent a more fundamental change of the economic system and their position within it. As formulated by Colin Crouch:

> Of course, what firms need is a *reputation* for good behaviour rather than good behaviour itself. This can mean using claims and self-advertisement without actually changing behaviour. [...] it will always be cheaper to pursue reputation alone.[82]

Corporate discourses around sustainability and CSR can thus be seen as a form of window dressing, as a way for corporations to mask conflicts and enforce their ideological advantage rather than to reduce the social and

[80] Dobers (2010), p. 17.
[81] Kourula and Delalieux (2016).
[82] Crouch (2011), p. 142.

environmental impacts from their business models.[83] Accordingly, as formulated by the accounting scholar Crawford Spence, social and environmental reporting can be seen as "attempts to reduce antagonism toward business from various social segments, obtaining consent for its actions and thereby (re)producing its ideological hegemony".[84] Similarly, Gary Fooks et al. argue that CSR "creates an enabling milieu for socially harmful companies which externalise many of their costs to pass themselves off as socially responsible".[85] While some scholars dismiss sustainability reporting and CSR as superficial, other scholars go further and underline how corporations use CSR strategically. Management scholars have pointed to how both the CSR discourse and the stakeholder engagement activities it promotes, can be seen as systems of co-optation where environmental and social concerns are contained within the 'business case' for CSR. As an effect of this strategy, corporate antagonists are neutralised through corporate dialogues and alliances.[86] This critical approach to CSR thus underlines that activities promoted under the CSR umbrella can be understood as systems of 'neutralisation', as practices of 'compromise' with the goal to maintain the power of corporations in contexts where they are criticised for environmental and social impacts. As emphasised by the business scholars Peter Fleming and Mark T. Jones:

> we need to go further than simply dismiss CSR as a piece of harmless propaganda. Matters are more serious since it is also a concrete corporate practice interconnected with marketization, corporate coercion and commodification. In other words, it has material effects.[87]

Following this appeal by Fleming and Jones, an important task for management scholars is to study the societal effects of corporate sustainability and CSR, especially with a critical approach that acknowledges the larger power structures of which sustainability and CSR practices are a part. In other words, there is a need to critically explore the functions of sustainability and CSR, which the 'business case' literature promotes, such as 'handling turbulent environments' or 'saving the capitalist system'. The aim of such research would thus be to understand more about how corporate sustain-

[83] Spence (2007); Kallio (2007); Kourula & Delalieux (2016); Fleming & Jones (2013).
[84] Spence (2007), p. 856.
[85] Fooks, Gilmore, Collin, Holden & Lee (2013), p. 284.
[86] Burchell & Cook (2013); Fooks, Gilmore, Collin, Holden & Lee (2013.)
[87] Fleming & Jones (2013), p. xiv.

ability, and CSR operate as hegemonic practices, especially in 'turbulent' contexts where companies face extensive criticism and corporate power is challenged.

The political role of the corporation is a core issue in this line of CSR research. However, rather than seeing corporate involvement in societal issues as necessary and desirable, it is viewed as deeply problematic and undemocratic. This puts this line of research in stark opposition to the 'ethical case' literature, as it is often critical of some of the underlying assumptions in concepts such as 'political CSR' and 'corporate citizenship'. Fleming and Jones highlight the ideological effects that the debate about 'political CSR' and 'corporate citizenship' entail. They argue that the reasoning behind these concepts fails to acknowledge the business prospects that may arise from *exploiting* the vacuums left by 'weak states' and how weak regulations may be an *opportunity* for businesses to extend their power. Fleming and Jones argue that: "because MNCs by definition operate in multiple host countries, they have the opportunity to enhance their structural bargaining power against workers and states, thus reduc[ing] claims by these stakeholders on their income streams."[88] From this viewpoint, the lack of regulation and legal enforcement in relation to environmental issues, labour standards or taxation is an opportunity for multinational corporations to avoid costs rather than 'vacuums' that need to be filled by corporate engagement. Fleming and Jones thereby question the interpretation that globalisation is an 'inevitable' process that MNCs have to 'handle', instead arguing that the 'weak state' is a phenomenon that MNCs have been part of creating as active agents. They emphasise that the:

> so-called 'vacuum' created by an absent state often remains unfilled, sometimes as a result of intentional activities undertaken by MNCs themselves as key agents in shaping the neo-liberal discourse which has dominated the globalization process and of which they are the primary beneficiaries.[89]

This view is shared by scholars whose research show that CSR activities have been used by corporations to influence public policy and prevent regulations that could otherwise have been beneficial to public welfare. Fooks et al. point out that their research of the tobacco industry show that companies are mainly interested in CSR "due to its potential to promote

[88] Fleming & Jones (2013), p. 42.
[89] Fleming & Jones (2013), p. 44.

policy outcomes that work against public welfare"[90] and emphasise that this is especially true for CSR activities in countries with lower awareness of the dangers of tobacco. Similarly, Alamgir and Banerjee show how global standards for factory safety enhance the legitimacy of MNCs in the garment industry but do not address the underlying issues of exploitative pricing and procurement.[91] CSR practices and sustainability standards can thus be viewed as convenient tools for multinational corporations to handle competing societal pressures as well as serving to prevent further regulation. In this sense, corporate sustainability and CSR can be interpreted as contributing to an elegant narrative in which an actor (the corporation), who thrives in the context of the 'weak state', is portrayed as the hero.

Theorising the political role of the corporation

As indicated in the above discussions about the 'ethical' and 'critical' perspective on CSR, the political role of corporations have been theorised from two competing perspectives in the CSR literature. Glen Whelan calls these a 'positive' and 'negative' view on CSR. Scholars within the 'ethical case' literature, who embark from Habermas' political theory of deliberative democracy, embrace the 'positive' view and underline CSR and 'consensus solutions' between stakeholders as something desirable that can enhance public welfare. In contrast, critical scholars inspired by, among others, the Gramscian notions of hegemony, a Foucauldian understanding of discourse and power, as well as Laclau and Mouffe's discourse theory, highlight the 'negative' side and thereby see CSR processes as inseparable from capitalist hegemonic regimes and practices of co-optation,[92] which serve as ways for companies to work against desirable public welfare reforms and community protests. In the following two sections I will elaborate on these two strands of thought and how both have informed the theoretical framing of my study.

Deliberative democracy and CSR

Many business scholars have engaged with Habermas' framework of deliberative democracy to understand the political role of businesses in society

[90] Fooks, Gilmore, Collin, Holden & Lee (2013), p. 284.
[91] Alamgir & Banerjee (2019).
[92] Whelan (2013).

and the way corporations shape regulations and discourses in dialogue with civil society and state actors. Scherer, Palazzo and Matten write that:

> In order to analyse these interactions between companies and civil society, various approaches from political theory have been applied. In particular, the theory of deliberative democracy has become an important theoretical frame of reference over the past few years.[93]

Habermas' framework delineates a conceptualisation of democracy that differs from traditional liberal democracy. While liberal democracy focuses on individual rights and voting systems, deliberative democracy emphasises a process-oriented approach where decisions are taken based on communication between groups and organisations.[94] According to this view, the legitimacy of decision-making is dependent on processes of free and open deliberation in which consensus can be reached between all actors involved. Habermas emphasises that if actors focus on the goal of reaching mutual understanding and consensus, they can avoid self-interested strategic decisions and instead reach intersubjective agreements that take into account their own positions as well as others'. Habermas acknowledges that power asymmetries and self-interested motivations are obstacles in such a process but nonetheless argues that actors should strive towards securing an 'ideal speech situation' where fair processes can be ensured, and corruption hindered. This ideal includes a neutralisation of power imbalances through inclusion of all concerned actors, prevention of intimidation and the creation of conditions that give all actors the possibility to make their voices heard.[95]

Within business studies, the concept of 'political CSR' is used to capture the central ideas of Habermas and their application in discussions about the political role of the corporation. Habermas' ideas have been used to analyse empirical situations where corporations are collaborating with civil society and government agencies to create national or international policy and thus contributing to new national and global governance models. Based on Habermas' 'ideal speech situation', Scherer and Palazzo claim that the "legitimacy of a given [business] decision can be based only of a communicative process of sensemaking and consensus building among the

[93] Scherer, Palazzo and Matten (2014).
[94] Scherer & Palazzo (2007).
[95] Dawkins (2015), pp. 6-7.

actors involved".[96] Furthermore, they argue that if a corporation acts in a context of cultural pluralism and of the fragmentation of values and interests (such as the multinational corporation in the 'weak state' context discussed previously) the only way to pacify conflicting demands is via such communicative processes. Scherer and Palazzo emphasise that: "Through ideal discourse it should be possible to decide on the justification and reasonableness of social claims and interests and to commence an ethically justified [business] strategy".[97] These ideas thus strive towards finding consensus for a corporate strategy, picturing a deliberative process between companies and civil society where all interests are taken into consideration and mutually beneficial solutions can be found.

Agonistic pluralism and CSR

While advocates of deliberative democracy perceive consensus as a desirable and possible outcome, agonistic pluralists embrace struggle and conflict as a necessary and constitutive part of pluralistic democratic societies. As prominent advocates of agonistic pluralism, Laclau and Mouffe argue that "any form of consensus is the result of a hegemonic articulation" and that conflict on the other hand is the "very condition of possibility" for the democratic project.[98] Hence, consensus solutions are viewed by agonistic pluralists as hegemonic operations that tend to silence weaker groups and can end up increasing injustice and acts of oppression. Dissensus is therefore viewed as a necessary condition for the formation of political alternatives to the existing state of things.[99] Laclau and Mouffe criticise Habermas idea of deliberative democracy and "that a final resolution of conflicts is eventually possible" and emphasise that consensus, "far from providing the necessary horizon of the democratic project [...] puts it at risk".[100] In line with their view that reality has to be simplified in order to be understood, a consensus agreement is a simplification of reality, a specific way of understanding 'the social' rather than a compromise that takes into consideration all interests and views. They underline that any consensus solution is always predicated on exclusion of unacknowledged meanings. This highlights the danger with deliberative democracy and stakeholder engagement especially when these processes are

[96] Scherer & Palazzo (2007), p. 1103.
[97] Scherer & Palazzo (2007), p. 1103.
[98] Laclau & Mouffe (1985/ 2014), p. xviii.
[99] Dawkins (2015).
[100] Laclau & Mouffe (1985/ 2014), p. xviii.

focused on achieving a final goal of consensus. The danger is that these processes reproduce power relations already established in the local setting. This is a point underlined by Helmut Wilke and Gerhard Wilke in their critique of Scherer's and Palazzo's consensus driven view of CSR. They emphasise that the concept of 'deliberative democracy' becomes problematic when it becomes a panacea for all the ills in complex globalised society. They argue that the deliberative model of democracy is based on an idea of common goals and values when "the point of complex democracy is that there are no common goals, values and goodwill, but instead highly contested and competing goals, distinctive and divisive values".[101] Cederic Dawkins, another critic of the deliberative CSR model, argues that consensus fits badly with the competitive, profit focused values of the capital markets. He stresses that even though deliberative democracy takes into account power asymmetries among companies and stakeholders, the focus on consensus makes the model inappropriate for company – stakeholder relations. He argues that it is:

> to be expected that the value systems of capital markets (focused primarily on profit) and those of various stakeholders (focused on other interests) will clash. Therefore, an objective of consensual stakeholder relations in a system that is based on competition [...] does not fit well with this model.[102]

Dawkins argument is thus that globalised capitalism and deliberative governance models do not satisfactorily fit together, since the interests of multinational corporations versus other stakeholders are fundamentally conflictual. Fleming and Jones agree stating that: "We find the notion that a private, hierarchical, authoritarian institution such as the MNC would have an interest in furthering democracy to be deeply problematic". Burchell and Cook agree, underlining that:

> Mouffe's notion of agonistic pluralism helps to contextualise this ongoing battle surrounding the discourse of SD [sustainable development] and CSR, suggesting a process of continual hegemonic confrontation over their precise meaning and application and emphasising the innate contestability at their core.[103]

[101] Wilke & Wilke (2007).
[102] Dawkins (2015), p. 8.
[103] Burchell and Cook (2013), p. 751.

Laclau's and Mouffe's framework thus highlights how conflicts between corporations and communities are based on contesting understandings of reality, including fundamental conceptualisations of what 'corporate responsibility' and 'sustainable development' are. Acknowledging these contesting understandings also means recognising the hegemonic exclusion of interpretations that a consensual agreement entails. The concept of hegemony must therefore be at the core of any understanding of the agonistic view on CSR and its criticism of deliberative CSR models. As hegemony is central to my study of sustainability and CSR practices in Patos-Marinza, I will further elaborate on the thoughts of Gramsci, Laclau and Mouffe in Chapter Two when I develop my theoretical framework. Below, however, I will briefly discuss how the concept of hegemony has been used within management studies and how it frames my research aim.

MNCs through the lens of hegemony

The concept of hegemony has been applied by several critical management scholars looking into discourses and power in relation to controversial development projects and multinational corporations.[104] Steffen Böhm et al. argue for the use of this "neo-Gramscian" approach to analyse multinational corporations in order to understand how their legitimacy is upheld by a "ruling order that blends both force and consent".[105] Böhm et al. emphasise that a hegemonic regime can be understood both in terms of processes that keep it in place but also in terms of processes of resistance, so called 'counter-hegemonic' articulations. Similarly, Levy[106] highlights how the concept of hegemonic regimes not only describes the maintenance of dominant systems during longer periods of time but also emphasises change and the potential of agents to mobilise resistance. Accordingly, a neo-Gramscian approach has been used by those who study the multinational corporation as a "contested terrain"[107] examining struggles around restructuring decisions,[108] global production networks,[109] CSR activities[110] as well as national and international policy debates.[111]

[104] Banerjee, Carter & Clegg (2009); Spence (2007); Levy & Egan (2003); Vaara & Tienari (2008).
[105] Böhm, Spicer & Fleming (2008), p. 173.
[106] Levy (2008).
[107] Contu, Palpacuer & Balas (2013).
[108] Contu, Palpacuer & Balas (2013).
[109] Levy (2008).
[110] Kourula & Delalieux (2016).
[111] Nyberg, Wright & Kirk (2018); Glynos, Klimecki & Willmott (2015).

While several scholars have addressed the power and discourses of multinational corporations on national and international levels,[112] less has been written about struggles at what Alessia Contu et al. call the "production site",[113] meaning a geographical area where industrial operations are carried out, including potential residents and other stakeholders who are not necessary part of the industry. The focus on production sites provides an opportunity to examine sustainability struggles in a specific setting where the corporation acts as the main organiser of the local environment and social relations. Based on a theory of hegemony, the local power of multinational corporations can be seen as relying on, as formulated by Levy, "consensual processes that accommodate subordinate groups to some degree, through a measure of political and material compromise and by the dissemination of ideologies that convey a mutuality of interests".[114] From this perspective, power is dependent on constant compromises, on giving subordinate groups a certain level of influence in order to keep the overall power structure stable. Consensus based CSR solutions are in this perspective seen as an effective strategy to maintain corporate power. This view is based on Gramsci's conceptualisation of hegemony as a social state where "the development and expansion of the particular group are conceived of, and presented, as being the motor force of a universal expansion, of a development of all the 'national' energies".[115] Accordingly, through the concept of hegemony, foreign investments by multinational corporations can be scrutinised as activities that, with the help of sustainability and CSR, are promoted as beneficial to all of society even though benefits and negative impacts are unequally distributed between groups. As Dawkins describes: "Hegemony occurs when one socially dominant group is successful in promulgating its reality, such that others accept it as the only sensible perspective".[116] Hegemony is thus linked to the discursivity of reality and to the idea of a dominant worldview that forms our perception of what reality and truth is. This adheres to the development of the concept of hegemony by Laclau and Mouffe who understand hegemony as a conceptual tool for deconstructing power relations and argue that "scrutinising the so-called 'globalised world' through the category of hegemony [...] can help us to

[112] Spence (2007); Levy (2008); Joutsenvirta & Vaara (2015); Fooks, Gilmore, Collin, Holden & Lee (2013).
[113] Contu, Palpacuer & Balas (2013).
[114] Levy (2008), pp. 951-952.
[115] Gramsci (1929-1933/1999), p. 406.
[116] Dawkins (2015), p. 8.

understand that the present conjuncture, far from being the only natural or possible societal order, is the expression of a certain configuration of power relations."[117] Hegemony as a concept is thus useful for unpacking the discursive configurations in a specific context and to understand what social realities are promoted and excluded as a result of that specific configuration.

Research purpose and questions

The purpose of this dissertation is to contribute to a deeper understanding of the relationship between corporate power and sustainability discourses. According to Political Discourse Theory, 'discourse' is to be understood in a wider sense than just "talk and text", encompassing actions and any artefact with a semiotic element. I will examine how hegemonic and counter-hegemonic discourses and articulations, pertaining to sustainability and CSR, were played out at the local level, in the context of Bankers' extractive operations and implementation of international sustainability standards in Patos-Marinza. By employing the concept of hegemony to analyse conflicts within the Albanian oil industry, I want to make visible the micro-level processes in which corporate power were reinforced and challenged in a local setting and to better understand what role the implementation of sustainability standards and CSR practices played in this dynamic. Thus, I ask:

- What role did international sustainability standards and CSR practices play in the conflicts between Bankers and the communities of Patos-Marinza?

In line with my autoethnographic approach I will further ask:

- How can I understand my own role as a CSR professional within this dynamic?

And finally, these questions will help me to answer my general research question:

- In what way can corporate discourses around sustainability and CSR be understood as hegemonic articulations?

[117] Laclau & Mouffe (2014), p. xvi, in Laclau & Mouffe (1985/ 2014).

As I have described above, in the business world, sustainability and CSR are used as sometimes complementary and sometimes synonymous concepts. In the empirical chapters, I use these words as they appear in the specific context I am studying, though in the final chapters I will discuss their meaning and impacts on a wider scale. In Patos-Marinza, 'sustainability' was introduced into the context by means of the implementation of sustainability standards; international standards that guided the development of the company's social and environmental management program.[118] The corporate activities to which this gave rise were sometimes reported as 'environmental and social management' and sometimes, in a more aggregated fashion, as 'CSR'. Based on this context, CSR could thus be seen as the practical activities to which the discourse surrounding sustainability in the business sector gives rise. However, as discourse is understood as both material and verbal, the concepts and practices connected both to sustainability and CSR can be seen as part of one discursive configuration.[119] The pedantic reader may therefore be frustrated with the contradictions in how I use of these words. They overlap, interpenetrate, and encapsulate each other. Nevertheless, I will not present a final closure of their meaning because this openness is key to their strength and appeal in the corporate world and beyond.

The critical reader may further object to my generalising use of 'corporate' in my third research question, asking how it is possible to make such wide knowledge claims from the study of *one* specific context. In addition, it may also be said that Patos-Marinza can be classified as a 'worst case' scenario for sustainable business practices, on point of fact that the oil industry is unsustainable to its very core. However, my contribution should not be understood as intended to say something about *all* corporate contexts but rather as the development of a framework which can be used as a thought model to examine corporate sustainability claims and hegemonic articulations in other settings. As I described above, while several scholars have emphasised CSR and sustainability as hegemonic tools, there is a need for studies that show what sustainability and CSR 'do' in local settings. CSR can be expected to work in a manifold of ways in different contexts, and so my intention here is not to generalise but to paint a picture of the power techniques employed in Patos-Marinza in relation to the sustainability standards that Bankers' implemented. These descriptions may thereafter

[118] IFC (2009a); EBRD (2009).
[119] Spence (2007), p. 864.

work as a guide to identify hegemonic mechanisms in similar settings elsewhere, where sustainability standards and CSR policies are implementted as a 'solution' to conflicts between companies and other actors. In other words, the contribution I seek to make within the research fields of sustainability and CSR, and specifically as part of the critical line of CSR research, is a conceptual framework that may function to highlight similar dynamics in other settings. In this sense, a 'worst case' scenario may facilitate the creation of such a framework that may have been harder to delineate in other corporate contexts.

An overview of chapters

I will answer my research questions through a retrospective study of Bankers' operations in Patos-Marinza between 2009 and 2016. During this period, Bankers' had a Canadian senior management and loan agreements with the international banks IFC and EBRD. For four years (between 2010 and 2015) I worked with Bankers as a consultant and member of staff in Bankers' Community Relations department, which, as part of my auto-ethnographic approach, has contributed to why this timeframe has been selected. In my analysis of this context I focus on three areas of company-community conflicts, characterised by strong specific community demands and corporate responses formally guided by IFC's sustainability standards. These company-community conflicts have been chosen for they have the potential of making visible how resistance was mobilised by the communities of Patos-Marinza as well as the continuous construction of corporate power linked to Bankers' CSR activities. The dissertation will be structured in the following way:

Chapter 2 describes the theoretical background to the empirical story about Patos-Marinza, starting with a discussion about Gramsci's conceptualisation of hegemony and how it was later developed (in a significant way) by Laclau and Mouffe.[120] In this chapter I will briefly outline Political Discourse Theory, how I apply this framework in my analysis and what it means for my discussion about CSR and sustainability.

Chapter 3 discusses methodological considerations, including my auto-ethnographic approach and positionality in relation to other subject positions in Patos-Marinza. I also describe how the empirical material has been

[120] Laclau & Mouffe (1985/2014).

generated, how I carried out the analysis of the material, and finally I discuss the ethical considerations for the research process as a whole.

Chapter 4 provides a closer introduction to Patos-Marinza and two discourses that competed to define Bankers' operations in the area: a corporate hegemonic discourse describing corporate activities as an 'investment', on the one hand, and a counter-hegemonic discourse describing company activities as an 'invasion', on the other. Following this chapter, Chapter Five to Seven are structured according to three specific areas of community grievances.

Chapter 5 describes complaints about Bankers' land acquisition, which, according to the company, was based on voluntary market-based transactions and stakeholder consultation but led to conflicts between local residents and was haunted by stories of clandestine practices and 'middlemen'. This chapter highlights how market-based solutions, promoted in line with international sustainability standards, divided community actors and brought some residents into the warmth of a corporate alliance.

Chapter 6 focuses on the continuous debate about poor air quality in the area, where the company stated that air quality was ensured according to industry standards while community members expressed fears of detrimental health impacts due to poor air quality. In this chapter I discuss Bankers' grievance mechanism and examine how specific grievance cases were isolated and satisfied in the name of sustainability and CSR, thereby hampering community mobilisation by breaking potential chains of equivalence between demands.

Chapter 7 portrays a conflict about recurring seismic events, instigating intense debates about the origin of 'natural earthquakes' (the company's position) or 'tremors' caused by oil-field activities (the community's position). In this chapter I examine how corporate-community dialogue and joint fact-finding processes neutralised the corporate position as the 'objective' perspective by focusing on technology and experts. In doing so, larger underlying political questions surrounding the very existence of the oilfield were obscured.

Chapter 8 summarises my analysis of Patos-Marinza and goes on to discuss the various ways in which Bankers' maintained its hegemony by responding to community grievances in accordance with its CSR policy and IFC's sustainability standards. In addition, I discuss my role as a CSR professional in this dynamic and my part within Bankers' hegemonic regime. Finally, I discuss how these findings can support the examination of corporate hegemony and sustainability discourses in other contexts based on the three hegemonic mechanisms of transformism, corporatisation and depoliticisation.

Chapter 9 briefly elaborates on how resistance in Patos-Marinza can be understood, and the internal constraints hindering further mobilisation. Based on this analysis, alternative roads to encourage community mobilisation and new hegemonic visions are discussed based on the concepts of radical democracy and pluralistic agonism. Furthermore, I discuss what I learnt from applying Political Discourse Theory to the empirical context of Patos-Marinza and what this study may add to this theoretical field. Finally, I reflect on my autoethnographic approach, what it can bring to the research fields of sustainability and CSR and how future research can elaborate on the methodological insights I gained from this dissertation.

CHAPTER 2

Hegemony and Political Discourse Theory

My main theoretical inspiration in this dissertation comes from two sources: Gramsci's concept of hegemony, as developed in his *Prison Notebooks,* which he wrote while incarcerated as a political militant in an Italian prison between 1929 and 1933, and Laclau and Mouffe's development of Gramsci's original insights, from their seminal book *Hegemony and Socialist Strategy* (1985) and further developed in subsequent individual works.[121] Based on these three thinkers, hegemony can be understood as broadly an interminable process that takes on the form of a never-ending power struggle and is linked to the ontological view of our lived reality as a continuous battle for the organisation of societal structure and truth. While I take my point of departure in Gramsci's thoughts about the role of force and consent in the construction of hegemony, it is ultimately Laclau and Mouffe's theoretical framework that has a determinant role in my analysis. Political Discourse Theory has emerged as a significant theoretical perspective within the fields of management and organisation, and prominent scholars within critical management studies have highlighted this theory as a promising lens through which to study both power and emancipatory struggles.[122] In this dissertation I want to show with what Political Discourse Theory can contribute, in the research fields of CSR and sustainability, and in the discussion about conflicts between multinational corporations and other societal actors.

Gramsci and hegemony

In the previous chapter I briefly mentioned how a neo-Gramscian approach to multinational corporations analyses the use of force and consent in the creation and maintenance of a power system. Below I will further elaborate on Gramsci's thinking how I will apply aspects of it in this study.

[121] Laclau (2005); Mouffe (2013).
[122] Willmott (2005); Contu, Palpacuer & Balas (2013).

Gramsci was born in the province of Cagliari in Sardinia, in a family of Albanian origins on his father's side. He became a leader of the Italian Communist Party but, by the late 1920s, was placed in a Fascist prison cell.[123] It was during his time in prison that he wrote his renowned *Prison Notebooks*, in which the notion of hegemony is developed to analyse the rise and consolidation of bourgeois power in western societies. His aim was to learn from the successes of the bourgeoisie in order to articulate a hegemonic project for the working class, i.e. a project led by the working class to gain state power in the west.[124] Hegemony, understood in Gramscian terms, means leadership of one group over others; hegemony is a project of leadership. For Gramsci, the bourgeoisie gained power in western societies by means of creating consent surrounding their own leadership over other classes. The hegemonic project can thus be understood as a project aimed at gaining legitimacy among a number of allied groups who would support the hegemon to attain power. Gramsci knew that when in a position of power (and command over the state), the hegemon also has access to means of dominance, i.e. to force. However, Gramsci emphasised, the hegemon has to continue to produce consent among its allies in order to remain in power. Power, for Gramsci, is maintained by force and consent, by hegemony (leadership) of allied groups and domination over antagonistic others. Gramsci wrote:

> A class is dominant in two ways, namely it is "leading" and "dominant". It leads the allied classes, it dominates the opposing classes. Therefore, a class can (and must) "lead" even before assuming power; when in power it becomes dominant, but it also continues to "lead".[125]

Through this analysis, Gramsci created a general theory about the dual nature of power in history and the use of force and consent when one social group becomes dominant.[126] In a hegemonic struggle, Gramsci describes how between ideologies, one social group eventually wins leadership:

> bringing about not only a unison of economic and political aims, but also intellectual and moral unity, posing all the questions around which the struggle rages not on a corporate but on a "universal" plane, and

[123] Buttigieg (1992), pp. 65-94.
[124] Thomas (2009/2010).
[125] Gramsci (1929-1930/ 1992), pp. 136-137.
[126] Anderson (1976).

> thus creating the hegemony of a fundamental social group over a series of subordinate groups.[127]

The rule of one group is thus secured by incorporating the demands of other groups into what is depicted as a 'universal' common vision beneficial for all but which ultimately serves to establish one group's domination over the others. In Gramsci's analysis of the bourgeois class and their attempts to gain and maintain power in western societies, he highlights how they did so by incorporating and assimilating potential political opponents into their own project. He argues that: "Force can be employed against enemies, but not against a part of one's own side which one wishes rapidly to assimilate, and whose 'good will' and enthusiasm one needs."[128] What Gramsci means here is that the revolutionary new way in which the bourgeoisie achieved domination over state laws, alongside their monopoly of violence, was through framing their project as beneficial to all.

Political Discourse Theory and radical contingency

Following Antonio Gramsci, Ernesto Laclau and Chantal Mouffe's Political Discourse Theory can arguably be called one of the most important developments in the concept of hegemony.[129] In their seminal work *Hegemony and socialist strategy*, Laclau and Mouffe argue that "the very wealth and plurality of contemporary social struggles has given rise to a theoretical crisis",[130] since those struggles (e.g. feminism, environmentalism, anti-globalisation movements) cannot be adequately explained by classical Marxist theory. In response to this "crisis", they launched a new strategy for the left, one that recognises the plurality of present-day emancipatory struggles and is not locked into the classical Marxist ideas of the centrality of the working class and the necessary transformation of society by means of a 'social revolution'. They argued that the concept of hegemony, as it was developed from Lenin to Gramsci, contains something that dissolves the basic categories central to Marxist theories, for instance class relations, the topographical categories of the economic base and superstructure, along with the 'necessary' laws of History. For Laclau and Mouffe, the concept of hegemony introduces "a *logic of the social* which is incompatible with those

[127] Gramsci (1929-1933/1999), pp. 405-406.
[128] Gramsci (1929-1933/1999).
[129] Laclau & Mouffe (1985/2014).
[130] Laclau & Mouffe (1985/2014), p. xxii.

categories."[131] They proceed to explain Political Discourse Theory as an alternative framework for understanding the structuration and transformation of society as a discursive totality.

Political Discourse Theory builds on the structural linguistics of Ferdinand de Saussure and poststructuralist theory. It emphasises discourse as the ontological basis for how society is experienced and understood. Accordingly, Laclau and Mouffe describe social reality as 'overdetermined' – meaning that there are more interpretations of the world than can be captured through one totalising conceptualisation.[132] 'Science' is for example only a word and can never fully represent all the thousands of practices and meanings it claims to incorporate. Due to this surplus of meaning, various discourses compete to define reality and exclude other interpretations of the world. What science is – is under constant negotiation. However, in order to understand anything, to create meaning, we need to fix reality into a whole. This means simplifying reality in order to make sense of it. For example, and returning to the example surrounding science: certain practices are designated as science owing to a set of *similar* characteristics they are said to share, and to the exclusion of others. The simplification of things into classes and subclasses is an unavoidable part of human communication. As Laclau argues, "without that fictitious fixing of meaning there would be no meaning at all."[133] However, any ultimate fixing of meaning is also impossible; there are always things that evade our conceptual apprehension, thus the fixing of meaning is both a *necessary* precondition for sense and yet remains ultimately *impossible* at the same time. By extension, and as Laclau and Mouffe argue, 'society' is also both a necessary and impossible discursive object. It is *necessary*, since in order to have social meaning, a social whole fixing the terms of sense must be presupposed, i.e. in trying to make sense of our surroundings, a certain sense of 'closure' is required. At the same time, it is *impossible*, since this fixation, this closure, cannot be given and thus this thing we call society, which we always take for granted, is continually shifting its discursive limits; society is what Laclau and Mouffe call 'radically contingent'. Under a permanent condition of contingency, this process of defining reality remains at the core of every struggle for power.[134] And even if a certain

[131] Laclau & Mouffe (1985/2014), p. xxiii.
[132] Laclau & Mouffe (1985/2014), p. 97.
[133] Laclau quoted in Spence (2007), p. 858.
[134] Laclau & Mouffe (1985/2014).

simplification of reality, in order to make sense of the world, appears successful, no act of simplification is ever final, since the hegemonic struggle is without end. Concepts change meaning over time – as is the case with the idea of 'science', for example – and subjects who see the world differently will always have the possibility of challenging our established conceptualisation of reality. The fluidity and contingency of the social world, and how we understand it, is in Political Discourse Theory explained by the surplus of meaning of each 'sign'. This surplus of meaning provides the basis for new articulations and the transformation of already circulating discourses, all of which changes the way we understand society.

This view of reality as a struggle for the fixation of meaning is the basis for understanding Laclau and Mouffe's theoretical framework; it applies not only to linguistics but also to how society is structured. Laclau and Mouffe emphasise that "a discursive structure is not merely a 'cognitive' or 'contemplative' entity; it is an articulatory practice which constitutes and organises social relations".[135] This means that all aspects of the social world are discursive, i.e. what we do and say, how we perceive and use material objects as well as our own identities, or 'subject positions' are dependent on societal webs of meaning. Thereby, as formulated by Grant et al., Political Discourse Theory makes "no difference between the linguistic, behavioural and material aspects of social practice because they all contribute [...] to shaping the socio-material order".[136] This means that we can never step out of the discursive, never reach an 'essential' or 'true' version of the world. Instead we are limited to our historical and discursive contexts that (in)form our view of reality. As Laclau and Mouffe explain:

> The fact that every object is constituted as an object of discourse has *nothing to do* with whether there is a world external to thought, or with the realism/idealism opposition [...]. An earthquake or the falling of a brick is an event that certainly exists, in the sense that it occurs here and now, independently of my will. But whether their specificity as objects is constructed in terms of 'natural phenomena' or 'expressions of the wrath of God' [or as the consequences of oil extraction], depends upon the structuring of a discursive field. What is denied is not that such objects exist externally to thought, but rather the different asser-

[135] Laclau & Mouffe (1985/2014), p. 82.
[136] Grant, Iedema & Oswick (2009), p. 223.

> tion that they could constitute themselves as objects outside any discursive condition of emergence.[137]

Consequently, Laclau and Mouffe do not deny that a material world exists. What they do stress is that humans can never reach a pure understanding of 'reality' and how it is essentially constituted. Instead they emphasise that we always understand reality through the discourses, the structures of meaning of which we are a part.

Articulations and relations between signs

In line with the structuralist thinking of Saussure, Laclau and Mouffe agree that we can only understand the meaning of a sign in relation to other signs. However, while Saussure and other structuralists saw language and the meaning of signs as synchronously fixed, Laclau and Mouffe, aligning themselves with the post-structuralism of Jacques Derrida and Jacques Lacan, see the meaning of signs and the structure of language as subject to constant change. Laclau and Mouffe thus emphasise that the discursive structures of which we are a part are subject to change, while meanings can only be partially fixed. Specific discursive structures are stabilised and changed as the result of what Laclau and Mouffe call 'articulations' and 'dis-articulations'.[138] Laclau and Mouffe define an articulation as "any practice establishing a relation among elements such that their identity is modified as a result of the articulatory practice" and discourse as the "structured totality resulting from the articulatory practice".[139] This means that an articulation can be anything from a speech, a text or an action that in turn changes the way the relation between signs is understood. As formulated by Gunnarsson Payne, an articulation is thus a "linguistic or non-linguistic event or action that puts one discursive 'sign' in relation to other 'signs', linking them together and thereby temporarily fixing the meaning of these discursive elements".[140] An articulation can for example be a company communicating that an investment is based on "western technology" and "western know-how" and thereby establishing a relation between 'the East' and 'the West' where 'the East' is framed as subordinate. During an articulatory process, a sign such as 'the West' is defined or re-

[137] Laclau & Mouffe (1985/2014), p. 94.
[138] Gerber (2012).
[139] Laclau & Mouffe (1985/2014), p. 91.
[140] Gunnarsson Payne (2017), p. 257, my translation.

defined through speech or actions, which also changes the definition of 'the East'. If 'the West' is defined as advanced, 'the East', as its opposite, becomes defined as underdeveloped. This articulation can take the form of speeches, newspaper articles and YouTube videos. But it can also take the form of paying 'expats' from 'the West' more than 'locals' from 'the East' or creating a company structure based on 'western' institutionalised models.

Laclau argues that discursive signs can be connected based on two opposing types of relation: "a relation of *combination* if they are constituted through differentiation from each other, and a relation of *substitution* if they can replace each other within the same signifying context".[141] In a relation of combination, the terms receive their meaning through a 'logic of difference', i.e. as oppositions. As in the example above, if 'the West' is defined as advanced, 'the East' as its opposite is defined as underdeveloped. In a relation of substitution, on the other hand, terms receive their meaning through a 'logic of equivalence', that is, they are linked together by means of similarities in meaning, indicating a commonality lying beyond them. An investment can at various times be articulated as based on western technology, skilled expat workers, certified health and safety systems, and corporate social responsibility. The 'structured totality' of these continuous articulations by the corporation, linking various terms together through 'chains of equivalence',[142] is the discourse in which western capitalist investments are framed as beneficial to the subordinate East. In this discourse, the concept of 'west' is linked through a logic of equivalence to signs such as 'skilled' and 'advanced'.

The continuous articulation, dis-articulation and re-articulation of signs and discourses means that meaning and power is never fully consolidated but always contested. Laclau and Mouffe emphasise that relations of power are contingent but, through processes of 'hegemonic articulations', one set of norms can become temporarily dominant and seen as objective.[143] The temporary fixity of meaning depends on 'nodal points'; these are the core signs that provide "the cement that creates the stability for these discourses".[144] A pertinent example here is Crawford Spence's discussion surrounding the notion of the 'business case' as a nodal point in the discourse about sustainability and CSR. Spence argues that articulations around the

[141] Laclau (1997), p. 309.
[142] Laclau (1997).
[143] Laclau & Mouffe (1985/2014).
[144] Carpentier (2005), p. 200.

'business case' for CSR forms a discourse that marginalises more radical notions of 'sustainable development' and in effect leads to less ambitious notions and practices of CSR.[145] The articulations around the 'business case' are thus examples of how a discourse within a certain area is stabilised and come to guide social action.

'Society' and 'the political'

The concepts of antagonism and hegemony are key to understanding Laclau and Mouffe's ontology, according to which reality is seen as radically contingent i.e. a continuous struggle for the fixation of meaning. The idea of hegemony, then, becomes coterminous with the category of 'society', which, as a discursive order, is constructed through a series of hegemonic practices in a context of contingency. This means that society is not a 'natural' or 'objective' order but formed through hegemonic articulations that exclude other possibilities. As Mouffe formulates it, this means that:

> every order is the temporary and precarious articulation of contingent practices. Things could always be otherwise and every order is predicated on the exclusion of possibilities. Any order is always the expression of a particular configuration of power relations.[146]

When a specific order is viewed as 'natural', it means that the hegemonic articulations, the practices of power that created it, have been covered over and made invisible. This dynamic of hegemonic articulations, which at the same time creates society and removes its tracks, can thus create a view of society as 'objective'. As Mouffe emphasises: "It is in this sense that every order is political"[147], i.e. every order is political because it has been created by a particular hegemonic formation but made to look like an 'objective' order where the tracks of its creation has been hidden.

Since every order, every society, is created from a condition of radical contingency, it means that counter-hegemonic articulations can challenge it and try to install a new hegemonic order. This is highlighted through Laclau and Mouffe's concept of 'the political', which Mouffe describes as "the antagonistic dimension [...] inherent to all human societies".[148] The political can thus be understood as the possibilities for an alternative order

[145] Spence (2007).
[146] Mouffe (2013), p. 2.
[147] Mouffe (2013), p. 131.
[148] Mouffe (2013), p. 2.

that have been excluded in the present power configuration. The political haunts all societies, all social orders, and threatens to disclose their lack and cracks, opening up for other visions of a different society. This antagonistic dimension of society thus always threatens to reveal the social order as fundamentally lacking, disclosing the possibilities of another social order that has been excluded but can never be eradicated.

Fluid subject positions and antagonistic frontiers

Laclau and Mouffe emphasise the role of flexible and contradictory 'subject positions' of social agents and their relation to hegemonic articulations. Their theory is formed as a reaction to certain essentialist tendencies in Marxist theory where, for example, the working class is seen as a "unified and homogenous agent" with a "rational identity". Within the Marxist worldview, the hegemonic task is solely to form class alliances in the quest for a socialist society.[149] Laclau and Mouffe criticise earlier Marxist theorists for assuming this essentialist view on identity and link the fragmentation of the working class to the increasing heterogeneous character of social agents in contemporary society. Instead, they mean, subject positions are fluid and "fragmentation exist[s] *within* the social agents themselves" meaning "that these therefore lack an ultimate rational identity".[150] The fluid character of social actors and their subject positions is thus a core feature of Laclau and Mouffe's theoretical framework that extends articulatory practices to account for the very construction of political identities that confront one another in various conflicts. This means that subjects never have 'true' identities or group affiliations. Following on from the notion of the subject as fluid comes the conclusion that all social relations are fluid. Laclau and Mouffe explain: "As every subject position is a discursive position, it partakes of the open character of every discourse".[151] Any antagonistic relation is thus always fluid and groups are never stable. The subject positions of the actors themselves are discursive and are at stake in the very struggle for hegemony.

Through hegemonic articulations, subject positions and antagonistic frontiers can temporarily stabilise into what Gramsci called 'historical blocs'.[152] Laclau and Mouffe explain:

[149] Laclau & Mouffe (1985/2014), pp. 74-75.
[150] Laclau & Mouffe (1985/2014), p. 74.
[151] Laclau & Mouffe (1985/2014), p. 101.
[152] Laclau & Mouffe (1985/2014), p. 122.

> on the one hand, the open and incomplete character of every social identity permits its articulation to different historico-discursive formations – that is, to 'blocs' in the sense of Sorel and Gramsci; on the other hand, the very identity of the articulatory force is constituted in the general field of discursivity – this eliminates any reference to a transcendental or originative subject.[153]

The discursive ontology of subject positions thus means that they can be formed through various articulations but also be temporarily stabilised into 'blocs' and on various sides of a given antagonistic frontier. As will be presented in my analysis of Patos-Marinza, this means that the subject positions of actors are not fixed but open to re-articulation. While someone living in the local community can become a company ally, a previous loyal employee can change into a fierce company antagonist. The relative openness of the subject positions and collective subjectivities makes the hegemonic battle a struggle about the actors themselves. Actors can move from one alliance to another, but alliances can also change and new groups can form as new articulations transform the social structure.

Community demands and chains of equivalence

In *On Populist Reason* Laclau argues that instead of seeing groups as preconstituted, the smallest unit of analysis should be understood as the 'demand'. Accordingly, the group should be analysed as the result of an articulation between various demands.[154] Laclau depicts a situation in which residents in a local community have issues with housing and end up requesting to the local authorities that their situation be improved. If nothing happens then this request may develop into a demand for change. Once the authorities have ignored these demands then the local community may recognise that demands from other groups are also not being met by the authorities. In this heightened state of unmet demands, chains of equivalence can start to form between groups. Here, Laclau emphasises that:

> If the situation remains unchanged for some time, there is an accumulation of unfulfilled demands and an increasing inability of the institutional system to absorb them in a *differential* way (each in isol-

[153] Laclau & Mouffe (1985/2014), p. 100.
[154] Laclau (2005), p. 73.

> ation for the others), and an *equivalential* relation is established between them.[155]

Laclau emphasises that if this goes on there will be a widening gap, an antagonistic relation, between the institutional system and 'the people'; or, as he formulates it, a "dichotomisation of the local political spectrum through the emergence of an equivalential chain of unsatisfied demands".[156] This dichotomisation of the local context through the emergence of an antagonistic frontier and an equivalential chain comprised of unsatisfied demands, poses a threat to dominant groups. The threat is that one group will act hegemonically over other groups by formulating their demands in more general terms and thus creating a foundation for alliances to form that can oppose dominant institutions. Laclau depicts the creation of an antagonistic frontier and a chain of equivalence between unmet demands as the first two steps in the formation of a 'people'. The last step is the emergence of a higher level of political mobilisation through the formation of "a popular identity which is something qualitatively more that the simple summation of the equivalential links".[157] The formation of a popular identity needs what Laclau calls an 'empty signifier', that is the process whereby the demands of one group are split from their particularity and assume a representational status for all the demands constituting a chain of equivalence. This is what Gramsci called a 'universal' project. For example, an alliance of groups demanding 'food', 'work' and 'infrastructure' can gather under the empty signifier of 'justice' and unite in a common identity of 'the people' that challenges the current institutional order.

Laclau emphasises the Gramscian dialectic between 'corporate' and 'hegemonic' classes as important to understand the limits of one group to act hegemonically over other groups. Gramsci describes a 'corporate' class as a social segment of the population which:

> poses only those questions that interest its actual physical members, its immediate 'corporate' interests (corporate in the special sense of the immediate and egoistic interests of a particular restricted social group).[158]

[155] Laclau (2005), p. 73.
[156] Laclau (2005), p. 74.
[157] Laclau (2005), p. 77.
[158] Gramsci (1929-1930/ 1992), p. 147.

A corporate group in the Gramscian sense thus formulates a project only for their own members, thereby limiting the group's possibility to act hegemonically, i.e. to incorporate other groups within a larger alliance. Laclau takes the example of a labour union which:

> can act as a rallying point for a variety of other social demands, but the fact that it has to defend the interest of the workers within a very precise institutional framework can act as a fetter to its hegemonic ambitions.[159]

A group has a higher chance of becoming hegemonic the more it can articulate demands in general terms and, in so doing, appeal to other groups. Gramsci discusses the Jacobins as an example of when a 'corporate class' becomes a 'hegemonic class'. He writes that the Jacobins became hegemonic during the French revolution because they did not only represent the immediate interests of the French bourgeoisie but:

> they also perceive[d] the interests of tomorrow and not just of those particular physical individuals, but of the other social strata of the third estate which tomorrow will become bourgeois, because they are convinced of *égilaté* and *fraternité*.[160]

Égilaté (equality) and *fraternité* (brotherhood) can be seen as the empty signifiers which brought together an alliance of classes under the hegemonic Jacobins, thereby fostering a sense of a 'people' that could overthrow the system. If an empty signifier is mobilised, then owing to the overdetermined character of the signifier in question, various groups can form new alliances. In the case of the Jacobins, 'equality' and 'brotherhood' can be described as overdetermined because various groups could fill them with different meanings and thus unite under concepts otherwise open for diverse interpretations.

The notion of a 'corporative' class is also vital for understanding not only the ability to create counter-system mobilisations but also "the reaction to antagonistic mobilisations from those in power",[161] which is my main interest with respect to Bankers' reactions to acts of resistance in Patos-Marinza communities. Laclau writes about "those in power" that:

[159] Laclau (2006), p. 113.
[160] Gramsci (1929-1930/ 1992), p. 147.
[161] Laclau (2006), p. 113.

> their general politics can be summarised in one formula: to de-mobilise the underdog. The anti-political move par excellence consists in obtaining, as much as possible, a situation in which all interests become corporative, preventing the formation of a 'people'.[162]

What Laclau is getting at here is how those in power have an interest in isolating and separating demands, that is, in fact, trying to prevent the very formulation of demands in the first place. Those in power can thus use various techniques, such as the isolation of demands in a way that separates them from other demands or by the satisfaction of demands that renders them impotent to mobilise further. By preventing chains of equivalence to form between groups, the antagonistic frontier soon starts to become dispersed and blurred, with those in power becoming, as a consequence, less threatened. Another way to prevent the mobilisation of a counter-hegemonic alliance is to construct competing chains of equivalence in a way that disperses the antagonistic frontier and brings actors to the side of those already in power. Gramsci calls this process *transformism.* He describes it in the following way:

> the formation of a ruling class [...] with the absorption of the active elements [...] from the allied as well from the enemy classes. Political leadership becomes an aspect of domination, in that the absorption of the elites of the enemy classes results in their decapitation and renders them impotent.[163]

The "absorption of the active elements" is thus a formula to include opponents in the alliance of the powerful with the intention of making antagonistic groups "impotent". Laclau describes this as a situation when:

> the dichotomic frontier, without disappearing, is blurred as a result of the oppressive regime itself becoming hegemonic – that is, trying to interrupt the equivalential chain of the popular camp by an alternative equivalent chain.[164]

The implication here is that the same demands can be the object of competing hegemonic projects. The struggle for hegemony thus decides which equivalential chain will be stronger. To take an example closer to my em-

[162] Laclau (2006), p. 113.
[163] Gramsci (1929-1930/ 1992), p. 137.
[164] Laclau (2005), p. 131.

pirical context, the demand for 'employment' could be linked to a protest movement that is opposing Bankers' activities, which can be depicted as causing layoffs and leaving people unemployed. But 'employment' could also be linked to the side of the corporate alliance advocating for an expansion of Bankers' activities, by means of the argument that such expansion will create jobs. Such hegemonic articulation would thus incorporate potential employees into the equivalential chain of the corporate alliance.

The affective dimension – fantasmatic narratives and enjoyment

Above, I have briefly given the basic outline of *how*, according to Laclau, the formation of a 'people' takes place; from isolated heterogeneous demands, through chains of equivalence and empty signifiers, to a 'universal' global demand. However, as Laclau notes, this analysis is missing one explanatory dimension. What it cannot describe is *why* certain popular movements gain momentum while others fail; it does not explain why people become attached, or as he calls it 'invests' in, some societal projects and not in others. Laclau writes:

> The different signifying operations to which I have referred so far can explain the *forms* the investment takes, but not the *force* in which the investment consists. It is clear, however, that if an entity becomes an object of investment – as being in love, or in hatred – the investment belongs necessarily to the order of affect.[165]

To explain the 'force' behind social inertia or change Laclau thus introduces the psychoanalytical concept of 'affect' as a vital explanatory dimension. This insight is based on the work of the French Psychoanalyst, Jacques Lacan, whose thoughts have received a growing interest within organisational studies during the past two decades.[166] Scholars have been arguing that the Lacanian approach is an overlooked resource for organisational theory as it provides an alternative lens on the crucial organisational concepts of subjectivity, power and resistance.[167] Lacanian insights are today increasingly used to explore how subjectivities are constructed and emerge in different discursive configurations and work contexts, high-

[165] Laclau (2005), p. 110.
[166] Contu, Palpacuer & Balas (2010); Cederström & Hoedemaekers (2010); Fotaki, Long & Schwartz (2012).
[167] Cederström & Hoedemaekers (2010); Fotaki, Long & Schwartz (2012).

lighting the fragmented nature of subjects rather than an assumed stable 'essential' unity.[168] As formulated by Sheena Vacchani:

> Lacan's subject is not an intuitively apprehended "individual". But may be understood as a structural position within a configuration held in place by important social signifiers' [...]. Lacan, in this sense, offers a framework by which to understand the subject as it relates to a theory of consciousness, language and meaning.[169]

The affective dimension of social and political theory has further been emphasised by Jason Glynos and David Howarth in their book *Logics of Critical Explanation in Social and Political theory* from 2007. This work has become a guiding text for many studies that apply Political Discourse Theory to understand empirical phenomena, through what they call a 'logics approach'.[170] One of the key features of this approach is the notion of *fantasmatic narratives* (or *fantasmatic logics*) which according to the authors "provide the means to understand *why* specific practices and regimes 'grip' subjects"[171] and thus relate to what Laclau calls the affective explanatory dimension. According to Glynos and Howarth, the use of the concept of fantasmatic narratives in empirical research can contribute to a deeper understanding of the 'inertia' of social practices, i.e. why some regimes are kept intact over time, but can also be used to explain change, and its speed, when it happens.[172] Fantasmatic narratives have the function that they 'cover over' the lack that is always present in subject positions and the social totality itself. When 'the political' dimension appears through dislocations of 'the social'[173] the fantasmatic operates as a way for the subject to reinstitute a feeling of closure and fullness. As formulated by Glynos and Howarth:

> The operation of fantasmatic logics can thus reinforce the social dimension of practices by covering over the fundamental lack in reality and keeping at bay what we have labelled 'the real' [the political dimension]. In this respect, logics of fantasy have a key role to play in 'filling

[168] Contu, Palpacuer & Balas (2010); Vacchani (2012).
[169] Vacchani (2012), p. 1242.
[170] Glynos, Klimecki & Willmott (2015).
[171] Glynos & Howarth (2007), p. 145.
[172] Glynos & Howarth (2007), p. 145.
[173] Glynos & Howarth (2007), p. 111.

> up' or 'completing' the void in the subject and the structure of social relations by bringing about closure.[174]

Glynos and Howarth thus emphasise that fantasmatic narratives are a way for subjects to cope with the incompleteness of meaning, to experience and to join together incompatible elements of the social. By doing this, fantasmatic narratives can support the maintenance of a social regime by creating an outlet for the subject to handle the contradictions that the regime produces. They take the example of workers who perform their tasks flawlessly yet speak about their workplace in a distanced and cynical way. In organisational studies this has been described as workers maintaining a 'cynical distance' to their organisation,[175] and several studies have shown how such 'transgressions' uphold a particular organisational regime rather than challenge it.[176] Stavrakakis emphasises that transgressions thus can work to reinforce a regime or a particular ideal rather than contesting it. He argues that this is because transgressions of an ideal can serve as a source of "fantasmatically structured enjoyment" for the subjects.[177] He writes:

> the space of the officially sanctioned ideals, is revealed as incomplete, and – paradoxically – it receives support from a clandestine supplement of self-transgression [...]; the lack in the Other [the symbolic order] demands a fantasy support, ultimately an indirect anchoring in the (partial) jouissance [enjoyment] of the body.[178]

The subjects in a particular work situation can thus handle the complex contradictions of the organisation by a fantasmatic narrative that allows them to continue to work for organisational goals while at the same time telling themselves that they have autonomy or are even working against the organisation. In my analysis of Patos-Marinza, I will apply these theoretical insights to understand my own reasoning and transgressions as a CSR professional but also to understand subject positions involved in the various forms of resistance articulated in Patos-Marinza communities. Jason and Glynos mean that fantasmatic narratives can be empirically identified by asking "whether or not they resist public official disclosure" but also by the often contradictory features that fantasmatically structured enjoyment

[174] Glynos & Howarth (2007), p. 146.
[175] Fleming & Spicer (2003).
[176] Burawoy (1979).
[177] Stavrakakis (2010), p. 68.
[178] Stavrakakis (2010), p. 68.

possess, "exhibiting a kind of extreme oscillation between incompatible positions".[179] In my analysis of Patos-Marinza it is thus in the missing pieces of, and contradictions within, accounts that I will investigate the fantasmatic or affective dimension of political mobilisations.

Applying the concept of hegemony in Patos-Marinza

While Gramsci used his concept of hegemony to understand the rise and consolidation of power by the bourgeoisie in the western states of his time,[180] I will use hegemony to analyse the continuous construction of corporate power in Patos-Marinza. This translation of a concept and theory from one time and context to another can bring new insights. At the same time, specific conceptual modifications are required; for example, my level of analysis is not the state, but the geographical area of Patos-Marinza. Instead of analysing how one social group can gain or maintain state power, my aim is to understand how a corporation (Bankers) could maintain power over a geographical area where grievances and spontaneous protests were common occurrences. Gramsci distinguished between two types of leadership, one aimed at *gaining* power through the formation of an alliance; the second aimed at *maintaining* power once dominance is achieved.[181] It is the second sense of leadership I want to focus on in this book; that is, the maintenance of corporate power in Patos-Marinza through processes of force and consent. Now, one may object to this aim, thinking that this does not strike one as a very interesting project since Bankers had a concession agreement with the Albanian government and thus the legal right to control Patos-Marinza. That concession agreement can thus be seen as the main force behind the Bankers' dominance. This is in fact the answer that a senior representative of the local government gave in an interview with me. When the representative heard that my thesis was about company-community relations, they suggested that I should write my dissertation about "why Albania does not develop" instead. I said that in some ways my project is about that topic since I wonder why people in the area are poor and the money from oil industry goes abroad. The representative answered that this is "because the concession agreement that the central government made with the company was done without thoughts

[179] Glynos & Howarth (2007), p. 148.
[180] Anderson (1976).
[181] Thomas (2009/2010), p. 163.

about the local people".[182] This politician is right; the concession agreement and the state's monopoly to enforce it with violence (police force) is of course an important part of understanding corporate dominance in Patos-Marinza. But this reliance of an underlying force cannot explain the total grip of Bankers' hegemony in Patos-Marinza. As emphasised by Yannis Stavrakakis, force cannot be the only reason why a hegemonic structure is maintained:

> Moving beyond the banal level of raw coercion, which – although not unimportant – cannot form the basis of sustainable hegemony, everyone seeking to understand how certain power structures institute themselves as objects of long-term identification and how people get attached to them is sooner or later led to a variety of phenomena [...] debated under the rubric of 'voluntary servitude'. The central question here is simple: Why are people so willing and often enthusiastic – or at least relieved – to submit themselves to conditions of subordination, to the forces of hierarchical order?[183]

Similar to what Stavrakakis emphasises here, my experience from Patos-Marinza indicates that Bankers' hegemony did not need enforcing through the state police most of the days but was generally constructed in other ways, closer to the Gramscian notion of consent. It is these daily local practices that I want to underline, in particular the CSR practices that resulted from Bankers' implementation of IFC's sustainability standards. By showing how corporate hegemony was continuously constructed in Patos-Marinza, I aim to transform corporate power from a taken for granted phenomenon (that is, from an omnipotent concession agreement) to concrete daily practices that were continuously reinforced and challenged.

[182] Interview, local government representative, October–November 2017.
[183] Stavrakakis (2010), pp. 63-64.

CHAPTER 3

Moving from practice to autoethnography

This is a method chapter, and as is customary, I will herein describe how this final text has come about. As I mentioned in the prologue, I see this project as a process that started several years before I became a PhD student, as fragments of thoughts that I wrote down in my diary while I was still emerged in the constant conflicts to which working life in Patos-Marinza exposed me. Let me start by giving you some examples of these thoughts:[184]

> Diary note 2013-09-20
>
> Stupid meeting […]. It started with senior management telling us to arrange meetings with the local community and ended with them saying to do nothing since they had to start building without a permit.
>
> Diary note 2014-04-02
>
> Our wells are getting very close to Belina village and residences that are nice and newly built. There is a need for a new plan for the oilfield with buffer zones between residences and wells.
>
> Diary note 2015-04-11
>
> I had hoped that the day would be calm but it started directly with meetings in Marinza with people who wanted jobs, compensation for land etc. Then Belina and Kallm residents blocked the road to the bridge and I had to promise them a meeting with senior management to open it again. Now I worry that this was a bad idea.

In the examples from my diary above, I can see how I perceived my subject position as torn between my loyalties to the communities of Patos-Marinza and Bankers' senior management. During the course of the years I worked in Patos-Marinza, and in the following years as a PhD student, these thoughts where reformulated and expanded into this text. Needless to say,

[184] Diary entries are translated from Swedish.

my subject position in relation to Patos-Marinza has changed in various ways during these years. An important aspect of Political Discourse Theory is the notion that nothing exists outside the discursive, meaning that there is no 'objective' location from which the researcher can observe the world. Research is consequently always located within certain discourses and the process and product of research becomes a part of the struggle for hegemony within the context it studies.[185] When I moved from oil industry to academia, new discourses became available to me that helped me to look at my old experiences in a new light. This does not mean that I was transformed into an objective researcher, only that my subject position became linked in another way to the struggles for hegemony in Patos-Marinza. In the following chapter I will try to give you a sense of how this process took place and how it finally ended up in the order of words that you now have in front of you.

Emancipatory knowledge goals

To start with, I want to briefly discuss the emancipatory knowledge interests to which I adhere. Mats Alvesson and Jorgen Sandberg[186] describe Jürgen Habermas' three basic forms of knowledge interests: *the technical* – focused on functionalist cause-and effect relations through which society and nature can be controlled; *the practical-hermeneutic* – focused on a deeper understanding of the human experience and culture; and *the emancipatory* – represented by critical theory approaches, focused on revealing power relations as a way to liberate subjects from repressive relations.[187] My project is aligned with the emancipatory knowledge interest, which Alvesson and Sandberg describe as "critical examinations of institutions, ideologies, interests and identities" in order to encourage "critical insight, rethinking and liberation from, or resistance to, unnecessary forms of domination".[188] Peter Svensson has summarised this knowledge goal in an article in *Dala-Demokraten* as "motverkansuppgiften" which can be translated as the task of counteraction. Svensson writes that: "Society is created of people who think, speak and act. Thoughts and language allow action but can also limit people's possibilities to change their lives and society for the better. The task of critical social science is to target [...] the effects of

[185] Gerber, Gunnaryson Payne & Lundgren (2012).
[186] Habermas (1972) in Alvesson & Sandberg (2013).
[187] Alvesson & Sandberg (2013).
[188] Alvesson & Sandberg (2013), p. 21.

thoughts and language [and to] offset oppressing and negative tendencies in society"[189]. To assume the task of counteraction is thus to question dominant norms and power structures in society. Interpretation therefore becomes an inevitable political and a tool for emancipation. Oliver Marchart describes this as "the very task of, among other post-foundational theories, deconstruction and hegemony theory"[190]. Viewed from Political Discourse Theory, the emancipatory project can be defined as an attempt to reveal the contingency of a hegemonic social system that frames itself as 'closed' and a reactivation of 'the political' in a system framing itself as objective. My aim is to carry out the task of counteraction by using my own experiences from Patos-Marinza as a methodological approach to criticise a social regime from within, as well as my own role in the reproduction of the same regime.

Autoethnography and work-life experiences

While the term autoethnography is relatively new in management studies, the use of the researcher's own work-life experiences has long been part of organisational ethnographies. In the beginning of the twentieth century several scholars entered workplaces incognito to understand the working lives of the lower and middle classes with an emancipatory knowledge goal of improving working conditions and societal conditions.[191] Czarniawska defines 'participant observation' as a situation "when an employee becomes a researcher or a researcher becomes an employee", emphasising that such studies can only be conducted "with exceptional luck of obtaining access",[192] referring to examples such as Michael Burawoy as a machine-tool operator, and John Van Maanen and Jennifer Hunt as police trainees. A more recent example of a researcher who uses her own work-life experience as empirical material is Karen Ho[193] who studied Wall Street bankers and their daily production of 'shareholder value'. Even though none of these works apply the term autoethnography, they show that first person practitioner knowledge and work-life experiences have an important part to play in organisational studies. The application of work-life experiences in organisational studies is thus not a new phenomenon but the use of the term autoethno-

[189] Svensson (2017), my translation.
[190] Marchart (2007), pp. 134-135.
[191] Zickar & Carter (2010).
[192] Czarniawska (2014), p. 7.
[193] Ho (2009).

graphy provides enhanced opportunities to highlight 'practitioner knowledge' as a methodological strength rather than an unwanted bias.

Even though autoethnographic approaches are gaining momentum they are still a novelty in many academic settings[194]. In organisation and management studies, autobiographical material has mainly been used by scholars scrutinising their own role as academics and the academic institutions of which they are a part [195] while there is still a need for more studies that use this approach in the study of organisations outside academia.[196] As a PhD student adopting an autoethnographic approach, I have experienced this novelty through critiques of my methodology as both unscientific and unethical. In response to these criticisms, I maintain that autoethnography presents an opportunity to inquire into the hidden sides of organisations, using previous work-life experiences as a form of 'participant observation'.[197] Organisations are often framed as a positive phenomenon, fundamental to coordinate human action and increase efficiency in our efforts to reach common goals. However, the growth of critical management studies (CMS) indicate that an increasing number of scholars are concerned with the negative aspects of organisational action such as domination, exploitation and unethical behaviour.[198] This critical approach to organisation and management also requires innovative methodological approaches. While the hegemonic regime in social science still privileges logico-scientific thinking[199] and positivist methods for data collection and interpretation,[200] autoethnography function as a counter-hegemonic articulation with its emphasis on new forms of inquiry, narratives and inspiration from fictional writing.[201] In the current debates about organisational ethics and corporate social responsibility,[202] autoethnographic inquiries brings the promise of opening the 'black-box' of organisations and increasing the understanding of political struggles behind corporate practices. As I hope to show in the following chapters, autoethnography also provides a possibility for the researcher to analyse her previous (or current) work-life experiences and how it is linked to the articulation of hegemonic regimes.

[194] Wall (2006); Holman Jones, Adams & Ellis (2013/2016); Doloriert & Sambrook (2011).
[195] Brewis (2005); Prasad (2013); Thanem & Knights (2012); Ulus (2019).
[196] Vickers (2019).
[197] Czarniawska (2014), p. 7.
[198] Alvesson, Bridgman & Willmott (2009); Cederström & Hoedemaekers (2010).
[199] Gabriel (2013).
[200] Alvesson & Kärreman (2011).
[201] Ellis, Adams & Bochner (2011).
[202] Aguinis & Galvas (2012).

Satoshi Toyosaki and Sandra L. Pensoneau-Conway describe autoethnography as "a praxis of social justice", adding that: "In approaching social (in)justice, we underscore the minuteness of our performative moments of making and remaking social injustice in our micro-social everyday contexts".[203] Autoethnography thus underlines a new aspect of the emancipatory knowledge interest – a reflection of our own participation in the creation and recreation of larger power structures of which we all are a part.

Autobiographical narratives

The autobiographical narratives I use in this book were the first texts I wrote when I began my PhD in September 2016. The intent was to capture my thoughts as a professional before being socialised into the academic realm. The autobiographical narratives are comprised of recollections, with the help of photos, documents and diary notes, and are representations of my perspective on the context in Albania at the time. As I lived through these events, I did not take any structured field notes, nor did I consider of the possibility to use them in a research project. The "*quotes*" in italics are thus not direct quotes, but representations of dialogues that have remained, as part of my wider construction of memories from Patos-Marinza. These narratives are similar to what John Van Maanen calls 'impressionistic tales', described as "a dramatic recall" with the intention of drawing "an audience into an unfamiliar story and allow[ing] it, as far as possible, to see, hear and feel as the fieldworker saw, heard and felt"[204]. Autoethnography is in this sense intimately linked to narrative thinking,[205] which Yiannis Gabriel states "does not seek to establish fixed relations between causes and effects but contents itself with establishing the links between people's actions and their outcomes by locating them in believable plots".[206] He separates logico-scientific and narrative thinking and emphasises that these two types of thinking are linked to different views of truth and knowledge and generally adhere to different methodologies. Gabriel underlines the "narrative contract" as key to the relationship between the author and the reader of a story. The narrative contract is "an implicit understanding that the storyteller will deliver a narrative that is at least sincere and meaningful" and in return, the audience allows the author "poetic

[203] Toyosaki & Pensoneau-Conway (2013), p. 561.
[204] Van Maanen (1988/2011), p. 103.
[205] Ellis, Adams & Bochner (2011).
[206] Gabriel (2013), p. 106.

license to deviate from verifiable 'facts' and to embellish".[207] Similarly, Carolyn Ellis, Tony E. Adams and Arthur P. Bochner argue that autoethnographers "value narrative truth based on what a story of experience does – how it is used, understood and responded to"[208] by readers and participants. Autoethnography is thus based on the recognition that truth is variable and changeable as "people who have experienced the 'same' event often tell different stories about what happened".[209]

Ellis, Adams and Bochner describe how autoethnographers use aspects of autobiography and ethnography when producing their texts. Just as authors of autobiographies, researchers writing autoethnographies aim to produce aesthetic and engaging texts using storytelling to bring readers into the plot, thereby affording the reader the opportunity of getting closer to the researcher's own experience. Just as ethnographers, authors of autoethnographies aim to produce 'thick' descriptions of personal and interpersonal experiences to facilitate the understanding of cultures by insiders and outsiders.[210] I call my narratives 'autobiographical' when presented in their original form, written during my first months of PhD studies. They function as notes from 'participant observations'[211] of a specific time and place I experienced in the past. My principal aim with harnessing these first-person reflections is to make the context of Patos-Marinza come alive for you as a reader. Gazi Islam highlights that the line between the researcher and informant becomes blurred in autoethnography and involves a process where the researcher needs to engage in a process of distancing from the self.[212] In the analysis, I view these autobiographical narratives as articulations of a corporate representative (me), and how, as a practitioner, I was part of reproducing and/or challenging corporate hegemony in Patos-Marinza trough the implementation of IFC's sustainability standards. That analysis is my autoethnographic endeavour in which my autobiographical narratives, and the conversations and actions they describe, are viewed as articulations of and between certain discourses.

[207] Gabriel (2013), p. 118.
[208] Ellis, Adams & Bochner (2011), no page number.
[209] Ellis, Adams & Bochner (2011), no page number.
[210] Ellis, Adams & Bochner (2011).
[211] Czarniawska (2014).
[212] Islam (2015), p. 240.

Documents, news reports and social media content

In addition to my autobiographical narratives, I have used various documents, web pages, YouTube videos, Facebook posts and news reports as empirical material to construct the story of Patos-Marinza from a corporate and community perspective. There is an abundance of documentation available for the company-community conflicts in Patos-Marinza, since they were discussed in both local and national media, through Bankers' corporate communication channels, as well as in reports produced by IFC and EBRD, NGOs and on community Facebook pages. The use of documents and interviews to complement the autobiographical narratives relates well to the aim and process of an autoethnography that Ellis, Adams and Bochner describe as making the "characteristics of a culture familiar to outsiders and insiders" and "might require comparing and contrasting personal experiences against existing research, interviewing cultural members, and/or examining relevant cultural artifacts".[213]

In addition to autobiographical narratives and interviews with staff members (which I will discuss in the next section), my empirical material to capture the hegemonic/corporate perspective on Patos-Marinza conflicts includes:

- Relevant pages from Bankers' website, such as those describing the company history, CSR work, corporate structure and operations and documents (e.g. corporate annual reports and news updates available on Bankers' web page). My purpose with using this material was to capture content on the web page that represented the years between 2009 and 2016. Since, by the end of 2016, Bankers changed ownership, it was important to save these web pages early in my research process, before changes occurred in the company;
- Corporate communication videos available on Youtube describing Bankers' general operations, environmental remediation work and community relations programs, as well as a longer video describing Bankers' history as part of the company's 10th anniversary celebration in 2014;
- Reports about Bankers' sustainability performance available on the web pages of IFC and EBRD, produced by the same organisations;

[213] Ellis, Adams & Bocher (2011), no page number.

- Reports from the Compliance Advisor/ Ombudsman of IFC (CAO), who became involved in Patos-Marinza after an official complaint was filed by a group of community representatives. These reports, available on the CAO web page, outline the assessment process carried out by CAO representatives as well as records from the dialogue groups that subsequently took place involving company and community members;
- An interview with Bankers' CEO by an investor network during the annual World Oil and Gas Week 2015, available on Youtube;
- Corporate public information documents and community relations reports, which were generously sent to me by Bankers after a formal email request. These documents were based on surveys and meetings with residents in the oilfield and include a *Social Baseline* and a *Social Impact Assessment* for Patos-Marinza from 2010–2011, reports about Bankers' grievance mechanism, annual reports about Bankers' community investment programme, public disclosure material that was part of Bankers stakeholder engagement activities and a summary of a Community Survey carried out in five Patos-Marinza villages during 2015.[214] Since I was part of producing these documents, in my role as a consultant and Community Relations Coordinator, their content was already familiar to me. Nonetheless, with a new found distance on proceedings, they provided me with an opportunity to analyse how activities were officially motivated and described by the company at the time.

In addition to interviews and group discussions with community members (further discussed below), my empirical material to capture the counter-hegemonic/community perspective on the Patos-Marinza conflicts includes:

- Bankers' community relations reports (as listed above), which, although they were written by company representatives (including me in my previous role), outline the community counter-hegemonic perspective in their descriptions of the community grievances and concerns that were brought up in corporate-stakeholder meetings;
- Reports from the CAO outlining the arguments of community representatives present in dialogue groups set up by the CAO;

[214] See list of all documents in the section: *Empirical material – Reports and webpages.*

- A report about Bankers and Patos-Marinza from the international NGO Bankwatch, describing impressions from their visit to Patos-Marinza in 2014 and their conversations with community members. Civil society organisations were rare in Patos-Marinza during 2009 and 2016, and to my knowledge there are no other NGO reports about the area available from this time;
- Posts from three Facebook groups created by anonymous actors from Patos-Marinza villages, including photos from community protests, caricatures of Canadian oil workers and posts criticising the company for social and environmental impacts as well as corruption;
- Videos available on Youtube from four news agencies offering different perspectives on the Patos-Marinza conflicts during the period, 2009–2016. As the politics behind Albanian media is complicated and inconsistent, [215] I chose these based on their content (giving different perspectives) rather than based on formal (or informal) political affiliations, which would have been hard for me to delineate. These videos show interviews with community members, corporate representatives and governmental officials during periods of protests in Patos-Marinza.[216]

In my experience, a characteristic trait of the company-community conflicts in Patos-Marinza between 2009 and 2016 was that state institutions intervened very rarely or only when they were formally required by legal procedures. Politicians were sometimes present in protests covered by media outlets to promise improvements or to place demands on Bankers but were then absent in company-community dialogue groups or other social initiatives initiated by Bankers. Consequently, I have not accessed any state reports addressing the social situation in Patos-Marinza. The state reports I have used are of a more technical nature and include those from the state-owned oil company Albpetrol describing the technical details of the oilfield and those from the transparency initiative EITI describing oil industry tax payments. In my analysis, the perspective and role of state institutions on these conflicts is therefore addressed mainly as an absence.

[215] Zguri (2017).

[216] If you want to see the events of Patos-Marinza 'in action' I recommend you follow the links to these news videos which are provided in the section: *Empirical material – YouTube videos.*

Interviews with employees, corporate partners and local government

CSR is often studied from the perspective of senior managers, focusing on policies and guidelines, official systems and sustainability reports. This study seeks to get behind the formal CSR systems and policies, which have guided my methods for generation of empirical material. Writing autobiographical narratives is one such method where my memories from my time as a CSR professional are used as testimonies from 'within'. As I will describe in this section, another method is the focus on interviewing Albanian middle-level managers, lower level staff and collaboration organisations in the oilfield, rather than Canadian senior management. These actors were closest to the 'ground' and thus familiar not only with formal systems but also with how they were carried out in practice. In addition, local communities have an important part to play in this ground level investigation, and my interviews with local residents will be further described in the next section.

Barbara Czarniawska has highlighted the agony of doing fieldwork,[217] which is something to which I could especially relate when returning to Patos-Marinza in October–November 2017 to make the first round of interviews. Having worked in Patos-Marinza for many years previously, my worries and stress were related to returning in a new role to a place I once called home. Czarniawska writes that: "Entrance into a new field begins with extensive positioning, especially on part of the researcher".[218] Even though the field was not new to me I had to reposition myself – once a company representative, now a researcher. I started this process by emailing the Bankers' managers and staff for interviews, describing my project and including an introductory letter.[219] While some did not reply, most answered with a positive note saying that they were waiting for my arrival. When I arrived in Fier in October–November 2017, Bankers' office seemed as open to me as if I was an employee, and I could freely walk around the corridors to greet old friends and have a coffee in the cafeteria. Thus, despite my worries, the first phase of my fieldwork went well; interviewees, including my former colleagues and local corporate partners, expressed that they were pleased to participate and emphasised that a study about Patos-Marinza would be of value to actors living and working there.

[217] Czarniawska (2014).
[218] Czarniawska (2014), p. 78.
[219] See introductory letter to participants in Annex 1.

Instead of encountering resistance and suspicion (as I had expected), interviewees received me with curiosity and generosity, sharing their opinions on the situation. During this time, the company was in a period of transition; at the end of 2016, it had been sold to Chinese investors. My feeling was that these changing circumstances had brought with it an additional openness from staff; the Canadian management was about to leave while the Chinese management was slowly taking over. Staff and middle management described the period as uncertain, and my feeling was that this lack of direction made staff even more willing to share their views on the company with me.

In this first round of interviews, I selected persons that I had met in my previous role as a company representative, from former colleagues to acquaintances in partner organisations and government authorities with whom I had met on a few occasions. Based on my previous knowledge of the interviewees, they were chosen in order to provide contrasting perspectives on the context and narratives of events that challenged or complemented my own. In total, thirteen in-depth interviews were carried out. These interviews included: Bankers' management and ground level staff; previous Bankers' or contractors' employees; representatives from the local government and from Bankers' partner organisations. Eleven interviews were undertaken during my first field visit in October–November 2017, while the remaining two took place during my second field visit in September 2018. All of the interviewees are Albanian citizens. The interview language was primarily English but with my conversational proficiency in Albanian, two were conducted in Albanian on account that the interviewees were more comfortable with speaking in their native language. The interviews varied from half an hour to two hours, with most lasting around one hour. Eleven out of thirteen interviews were recorded; all were partially or fully transcribed.[220] In the two interviews conducted with government representatives, detailed notes were taken, since the interviewees were uncomfortable with being recorded.

As a previous insider in this research context, I define my role as an *active interviewer* while my respondents are *narrators of experiential knowledge.*[221] James A. Holstein and Jaber F. Gubrium emphasise that this approach corresponds to a constructivist view of knowledge as a "diverse, multifaceted, and emerging resource and that access to it is actively selec-

[220] See details under *Empirical material – Interviews with corporate representatives and partners.*
[221] Holstein & Gubrium (1995).

tive and constructive".[222] Accordingly, I see the interview situation not as a moment where 'truth' is revealed and where, as an interviewer, I should minimise my impact. Instead, I understand it as a situation where particular stories about the past are co-constructed by the interviewees and me through our particular roles in the present moment. Holstein and Gubrium write that "the active interviewer does far more than dispassionate questioning: [...] she *activates narrative production*".[223] As an active interviewer, I used my own experiences to form a dialogue about the confusing situations we had shared in the past, and encouraged interviewees to tell their own stories about Patos-Marinza. This interview format resembles what Czarniawska calls a "narrative interview", according to which "interviewees are encouraged to control their own performances, rather than responding to the interviewer's cues".[224] The interview guide,[225] although formulated in terms of specific questions, was thus used as a guideline for certain areas to be discussed, rather than as a constraining document. In addition, new questions were added for each interview, depending on the themes and narratives that emerged in each situation.

As with any social interaction, the dynamic of the interview situation is not something that can be controlled. It varies in accordance with the actors involved and the interplay between them. As a previous insider, but now outsider, asking questions about the interviewees' specific work situations, I could expect various reactions. Eda Ulus and Yannis Gabriel writes:

> When a stranger or outsider crosses into organizational terrain and begins asking questions, those answering may feel duty bound to present their working life in a positive manner. Yet, research situations may spawn very different emotional relations [...]. In a discussion of workplace emotions, respondents may discover an opportunity to confess or disclose troubling work matters that they would not disclose to 'insiders', treating the interview exchange, consciously or unconsciously, as a therapeutic space.[226]

In the interview situations between my former colleagues and I, I experienced both these responses. Some seemed to hold up a façade, answering officially and diplomatically to my questions, treating me as the outsider I

[222] Holstein & Gubrium (1995), p. 30.
[223] Holstein & Gubrium (1995), p. 39, emphasis in original.
[224] Czarniawska (2014), p. 35.
[225] See interview guide in Annex 2.
[226] Ulus & Gabriel (2018), p. 230.

had become. As I sometimes had previous knowledge about their opinions and thoughts from our conversations in the past, I found these performances frustrating and somewhat hurtful, since it appeared that they did not trust me. Others, on the other hand, spoke more freely than I would have ever expected, sharing their perspective in a highly personal manner, sometimes asking me to turn off the recorder when a particularly sensitive story was told. At those moments I felt myself bursting with renewed confidence in my insider status, feeling that I was accessing a reality upon which few outsiders would be able to touch. Ulus and Gabriel write that:

> Our own emotions, in seeking to overcome what may be deep cultural or social divides, are a valuable source for understanding some of the limits of research interviews.[227]

The feelings I experienced during interviews were a reflection of the clashes between my previous knowledge and what I was told in the interviews, between being an insider and an outsider, between my past role as a relatively integrated foreigner and my current status as a brief visitor who had left Albania for another life in Sweden. Oscillating between these various subject positions was sometimes highly uncomfortable but also vital to my research journey, making me think deeply about 'truths', alliances, hegemonic narratives and fantasmatic enjoyment.

I ended each interview by asking what the interviewees thought about my study and what they would like to read about in the final book. The interviewees emphasised different aspects that they considered important. One Bankers' representative, Rezart, underlined the need to understand the perceptions of local communities:

> Actually, personally I will not choose technical books, I would choose books that will help me understand the specifics of people in that area [Patos-Marinza], the specifics of, I would say, their perceptions. Because I might not be here for long, but they will be there, their kids will be there, their families will be there, they will not move from there.[228]

In another interview, a local government representative emphasised that the book should address the distribution of wealth from Patos-Marinza:

[227] Ulus & Gabriel (2018), p. 236.

[228] Interview, Bankers representative, October–November 2017.

> the oil of Marinza is not only for Marinza residents, but it is a resource for all Albanian people. It belongs to all people and it is the duty of politicians to spread this richness for the country. But Marinza people are the first people who feel the noise, the earthquakes and everything else so they should, out of all of the Albanian people, be treated first.[229]

Another Bankers' representative, Jonida, stated that I should make sure to show the context from different viewpoints and to give a balanced picture of events:

> you have lived in Albania, but you have been part of expats, and lived as a local, and worked very closely with locals, compared to other expats as well, and you have seen both sides of the medal, what Canadians and westerners think, and what Albanians think and you, who are in the middle, are the best person to judge about that.[230]

After the completion of the first round of interviews, I left Albania with this murmur of voices in my head, each telling me their own version of what was important to say about Patos-Marinza. I did not feel like I was in the "middle" and able to "judge". I felt guilty, as if I was exploiting those actors who continued to struggle in a setting I had decided to leave.

Group interviews and family visits in Patos-Marinza villages

While it was emotional and exciting to interview my old colleagues and acquaintances in Bankers and Bankers' local partners, starting the interviews with local communities felt even more sensitive. In Patos-Marinza there are five villages that surround the central oilfield. It was in these villages that I had spent a considerable part of my working days as a corporate representative. Among other things, our community relations team carried out surveys and focus groups as part of the social baseline and social impact assessment. We held interviews as part of the development of the social management programme, met with people who filed complaints through Bankers' grievance mechanism and organised regular stakeholder meetings linked to our monitoring and evaluation process. During these years, some of the meetings with residents were intense and conflictual but, for the most part, they ended on a friendly note. These meetings were in actual fact the best part of my job. It linked to my fantasmatic narrative of

[229] Interview, local government representative, October–November 2017.
[230] Interview, Bankers representative, October–November 2017.

wanting to 'make a difference' to peoples' lives by mitigating harms that the oil industry produced. On the other hand, I could never quite understand how residents could be so patient with our team while at the same time they were furious with Bankers and had continuous grievances that we, as company representatives, were unable to solve. When I returned to Patos-Marinza in my new role as a researcher, to an area where most problems had stayed the same, the endless discussions with angry residents and our teams' inability to do something about most of their grievances was a living part of my legacy. As an illustration of how this legacy interacted in my new encounters with residents, let me give you an example from one field day when my translator and I walked through one of the villages in the quest for people to interview.

> The second person we met in the village was a man digging a ditch in his front yard. We spoke to him through the fence that separated his property from the sidewalk where we were standing. The man recognized me and said that we had met many times in the past. [The translator] explained to the man that I wanted to know more about the issues of the residents and how they got along with Bankers. The man replied to the translator: "*I have met Sara so many times and she has been writing and writing in her notebook but nothing has changed*". Then he asked me directly: "*How many years have you been with Bankers Sara?*" "*Four years*" I answered [excluding the year as a consultant]. "*Yes*", he said, "*in four years you could have done something, but nothing has been done. So, it does not matter if I speak to you or not*". The man continued to explain that some time ago the residents had organised a protest about a new oil lease and blocked a local road. But then the company had given 300 euros to some of the leaders in the protests in order for them to stop and so they did. He said that the company had offered him money as well but he had refused to take it since he did not feel comfortable to take money when the others were protesting. [...] I asked if these things happened also during my time with the company and the man said: "*Yes, these things have always been happening*".[231]

While comments like the one above, addressing issues of corporate corruption and my past inabilities to help residents, were common, most people were still willing to speak to us. Owing to how I only have a conversational

[231] Notes from my field diary (5th of September 2018).

proficiency of Albanian, I worked together with a local coordinator/translator in order to organise the community interviews in a manner suitable to the context and to ensure that residents clearly understood that I now entered their villages in a new role. For the role of translator, I engaged a person with good knowledge both of the area and the oil industry, due to their previous experience in the security sector. As in most small communities, family and friend relationships in the area are highly important and complex. It was thus vital for me to avoid hiring someone with a bad reputation or bad relationships with the local residents. Even if the person selected had been working in the security sector – a position with the possibility of conflict with communities – I based my decision on my previous knowledge of them as having a good reputation and for being a 'people person'.

We conducted interviews in three of the oilfield villages; Marinza, Belina and Zharrza. These were chosen because they have the largest number of households in direct vicinity to oil wells. Moreover, their residents have filed the largest number of grievances to Bankers in the past. We organised the interviews in three different ways: as pre-arranged group interviews; as spontaneous family visits; and as short chats on the local streets when we walked around the villages (such as the one from the field note above). The process of preparing for group interviews was similar to the one I had used when visiting new villages in my past role; the commune and, thereafter, village representatives were informed about the process. Before I arrived in Patos-Marinza, the translator prepared for the group interviews by meeting with village representatives on more than one occasion, explaining the purpose of the research project and asking them to gather people who would be willing to speak to us. The group interviews were organised at local cafés and attendance varied from four in one village to eight in the other two. The café locations meant that the interviewing environment could not be controlled. People walked in and out during the conversation; some people joined in while others left. Sometimes people at other tables overheard the discussions and wanted to air their thoughts. While this certainly made the transcription of interviews more difficult, since several conversations took place at the same time, it allowed for free discussions and made the participants more comfortable. The interviewing context was thus similar to a 'normal' café discussion. The café environment allowed the participants, the translator and I to discuss a context of which we had all been part for many years, sharing memories and jokes as well as arguments and disagreements.

To include women's voices in the group interviews was a challenge we did not manage to overcome. Women did not turn up for the meetings voluntarily and when we invited women who were present in the venues, they sat down at the table but rarely spoke. I realised that another type of meeting was necessary in order to include women's voices in the study. My experience, from supervising survey teams in the area, was that a spontaneous home visit is a good method to initiate conversations with women. Many women in the area are working with household tasks during the day but are also usually free for a chat if the opportunity arises. We therefore visited a total of 10 households in the three villages, and spoke to women who had time and were interested to speak with us. Men also attended these interviews, if they were at home, as well as children and relatives who were visiting. These family visits provided a calmer interview situation than the cafés, and I sensed that people felt even more comfortable to speak their mind in their own home. In addition, we also had eight short chats with residents we met on the village streets as we walked between houses. While these were brief, they gave us a quick sense of the relationship that people had with Bankers and sometimes brought up stories of encounters between Bankers' staff and residents.

Our selection of participants in these village conversations can be described as random and spontaneous. This random selection I deem suitable for the purpose of understanding the counter-hegemonic narratives available in the villages. In the group interviews, and during some family visits, people could discuss their relationship with Bankers together. This generated a variety of discussion points on which people agreed and disagreed. Since participants had been previously briefed about the purpose of the interview, they usually started speaking without being prompted, raising all manner of issues they had with Bankers. As with the individual interviews, I encouraged this free conversation and only used the interview guide to ensure that certain areas were covered. However, since my study focuses on the period between 2009 and 2016 I was mainly interested in participants' perception about Bankers under Canadian management. In order to encourage the participants to speak about the past I repeatedly asked about how it was "during my time as an employee" or "during the Canadian time" compared to "now". The participants also used references to the past themselves, for example when explaining that "during the Canadians" it was like that and "now" it is like this. Sometimes I used my own recollection of events as 'memory joggers' for participants, asking them about their view about a particular incident or encounter. My previous knowledge of past events were also vital for understanding what the participants were discussing; sometimes I could understand discussions better than the translator due to my previous role as an insider and participant in the same events. This knowledge also helped me to ask follow-up questions to go deeper into issues I had only heard briefly before or to challenge participants when they told me things about which I had contrasting information. Due to a change in my role, I could now ask more openly about contentious issues, such as bribes, the local government, residents' encounters with Bankers' staff and why people did not protest more often. However, my past role and knowledge also brought with it difficulties. For example, participants sometimes assumed that I knew "everything", and therefore felt as though they had no need to explain. Expressions such as "but you already know this" or "you should tell us instead" were common, which meant that I had to reiterate the purpose of my visit and my new role as a researcher. People also sometimes thought that I was still working for the company and started to give accounts of their present grievances. Moreover, people sometimes grew suspicious of my new role, questioning if I was in their village for another purpose. As people came and left the group interviews and family visits it was thus important to explain my research aim and process over and over again, to counter some of the distrust and misunderstandings present in the room.

With my conversational proficiency in Albanian I could understand much of the interview conversations without a translator but used the translator's English accounts as a backup to ensure that we understood the conversations in the same way. When I transcribed the interviews I thus had both Albanian and English accounts on tape, with often the Albanian accounts being more detailed. The quotes I use in the empirical chapters are therefore my own direct translations from the Albanian accounts, using the translator's English summaries to validate my interpretations. The quotes are sometimes edited slightly, so that their meaning is properly conveyed to you as a reader. Listening through the recorded interviews and reliving the interview situations was an important part of my analysis; it brought me back to Patos-Marinza, made me hear things from the interviews I had not recognised at the time and highlighted aspects of the context that I had not previously considered important.

Analytical approach and methods

I started my PhD process with the conflicts in Patos-Marinza nagging in the back of my mind, and I searched for a theoretical frame that could help me to better understand them. Political Discourse Theory offered such a frame as it understands society based on antagonism and conceptualises power as something related to objectivity and truth. This view of society was highly applicable to my experiences from Patos-Marinza, allowing me to view these conflicts in a new light. As I explained in the previous chapter, Political Discourse Theory delineates a political ontology of reality in which 'society' is only a consequence of hegemonic articulations, which hide 'the political' under a cover of objectivity. 'Society' is accordingly described as an 'impossible object'. The outside to whatever constitutes the inside always threatens to reveal inconsistencies and show that another reality is possible. This means that every society is viewed as a constant battle between forces that wants to redefine reality and organise society in a different way. My experience from Patos-Marinza was that 'truth' was relative and continuously debated, and that events could always be interpreted in several ways. Political Discourse Theory therefore, provided me with new insights into this struggle for truth that I previously noticed, but without a theoretical frame to analyse more deeply.

Political Discourse Theory is different from other forms of discourse analysis in that it is not only verbal accounts and texts that are analysed discursively but all aspects of social relations. The first consequence of taking this approach is that I view *verbalisations*, such as an interview or a policy document and *actions*, such as a well construction or an air-monitoring programme, as discursive practices in the oilfield. They are speeches, text and actions that are produced by and contribute to the continuous production of specific discourses. Likewise, I view *artefacts* such as an oil well, an office, a residence and a drainage ditch as materialisations of various discourses.[232] Secondly, Political Discourse Theory views subject relations as relatively fluid and as possible to rearticulate in various discourses. This means that I view identities and groups as lacking any ultimate fixity and thus I refrain from looking at the conflicts in Patos-Marinza as taking place between fixed groups with predetermined identities. While I repeatedly refer to 'the company' versus 'the community' I assume that these are 'alliances', that actors belonging to them can change over time, and that this is a key aspect in understanding hegemony as an ongoing and interminable struggle.

I divided the analysis of my empirical material into two stages; the first focusing on the overall discourses in Patos-Marinza and the second focus-

[232] Lindqvist (2012).

ing on specific demands from local communities and how Bankers responded to these. In the first stage, which I present in Chapter Four, I identified two competing discourses that struggled to define Bankers' activities in Patos-Marinza. This analysis was carried out by structuring the texts, actions and artefacts in my empirical material as *supporting* or *opposing* Bankers' activities. The outcome was the creation of two analytical word clouds to better understand how various concepts were linked as discursive formations. In this analysis I used analytical concepts from Laclau and Mouffe, such as 'logics of equivalence', 'logics of difference', 'nodal points', and 'empty' signifiers. This analysis resulted in the identification of two nodal points - the 'investment' and the 'invasion' – that hold together two competing discursive formations in Patos-Marinza and give meaning to other signifiers in each discursive structure. In addition, I identified two groups of alliances representing each side of this debate, and an antagonistic frontier that divided the context into two opposing camps. This first part of the analysis thus aimed to give an artificially coherent and static picture of the dynamic and competing discourses and hegemonic relations in Patos-Marinza. You may object to this fictional dichotomous structuring of the social by asking: *Was not reality messier and more complicated than this static picture depicts? Why must the discursive struggle be fixed in these, not so surprising, opposing sides? Were there not more narratives available in the context?* To this I will answer that this fictional structuring was important for my own thought process, for trying to describe what the hegemonic narrative in Patos-Marinza consisted of and what the most challenging critique of this narrative looked like. In the process of experimenting with different signifiers as nodal points in the hegemonic and counter-hegemonic formations, I could better see how other signifiers and related social processes changed their meaning. The concept of the 'investment' was structuring a narrative so natural to me that it was only in light of the same activities being described as an 'invasion' that the political logics of hegemony revealed themselves. The 'invasion' was thus the most challenging concept against Bankers' hegemonic version I could find in my empirical material; an important first step in the process of analysing what was holding back that counter-hegemonic version of reality. While this way of structuring the social into two opposing narratives hides many of the nuances and complexities in the social, it also allowed me to analyse how hegemonic and counter-hegemonic formations were strengthened and challenged through various articulations, including how sustainability standards came into play within this dynamic.

In the second part of my analysis, which I present in Chapters Five to Seven, hegemony as a never-ending process becomes visible. The constant re-articulation of discourses and subject positions comes into focus by looking in detail into conflicts that are linked to the overall discursive structures described in Chapter Four but where arguments and positions are articulated in specific ways. This analysis shows how corporate hegemony was continuously constructed as a reaction to community resistance, i.e. what in Chapter Four appears dichotomously fixed is in Chapters Five to Seven continuously challenged, rearticulated and enforced. I have structured this analysis according to three demands (i.e. counter-hegemonic articulations) from local communities and the responses from Bankers guided by IFC's sustainability standards. This selection highlights specific aspects of Bankers' hegemonic articulations and the role of IFC's sustainability standards in the construction of corporate hegemony. I started this second part of my analysis by categorising my empirical material into eight conflicts based on particular community-led demands. Out of these I selected the three conflicts that illustrate the different ways in which Bankers' responses could be understood as hegemonic articulations. I then proceeded to categorise relevant parts of my empirical material into these three conflicts and then further, within each conflict, into the two competing discourses I identified previously. This second part of the analysis connects to Laclau's analysis of popular movements by examining how 'chains of equivalence' were formed between community members and how corporate efforts sought to isolate demands, breaking these chains through 'hegemonic articulations.' 'Logics of equivalence' and 'logics of difference' are key concepts in this analysis as well as Gramsci's notions of 'corporative interests' and 'transformism'. As part of this analysis I also highlight how not only verbal or written expressions but also actions and materialisations such as dialogue groups and money transfers are used as articulations in the hegemonic struggles of Patos-Marinza.

Writing and the representation of others

While first surprised by the sense of confidence and freedom with which many of my former colleagues and local residents spoke to me in the interviews, I realised that this was based on my previous role as a company employee and the relationships I had built in the past. After having spent several years in the context I am presently studying, I have established certain loyalties and bonds to the actors in the area, all of which go beyond the relationship of a researcher and her interviewees. This study is made in their name, portraying their reality and claiming to say something about their lives. While I left the hardships of Patos-Marinza behind and placed myself in a comfortable chair in a Swedish university, they had to continue to struggle in this reality, making jokes as the most constructive way to stay sane. By having the privilege to share this context for some years, I feel that it is my responsibility to tell their story, as vividly and engaged as I can, acknowledging the fact that I have been privileged with *money and a room of my own,* which Virginia Woolf highlights as a prerequisite for any writer.[233] My feelings towards Patos-Marinza are in line with how D Soyini Madison describes the emancipatory knowledge goals of critical ethnography, which, according to her, starts from a sense of responsibility, duty and commitment to address conditions and processes of injustice within a particular context. She writes: "The conditions of existence within a particular context are not as they could be for specific subjects; as a result, the researcher feels a moral obligation to make a contribution toward changing those conditions toward greater freedom and equity".[234] While I have few hopes that a Swedish dissertation could change anything in a context so far away, it is still my ambition, however modest its effects.

Ellis, Adam and Bochner write that "when we conduct and write research, we implicate others in our work".[235] In traditional ethnographies, the location and some of the actors are easily identifiable, even though the author has done her best to change any names and any revealing circumstances. The possibility for readers to identify actors in the study therefore means that results may have implications on the actors' lives. In autoethnographies, such 'relational ethics' become even more complicated, since the author involves herself as well as acquaintances, friends or even family in the research process.[236] As this study reveals both the place (Patos-Marinza) and the name of the company (Bankers), I have made continuous efforts to keep particular identities anonymous. The gender and names of interviewees and in my autobiographical sections are all fictional, and stories and quotes have sometimes been slightly amended to ensure that identities are protected. In my introduction to the interviewees, I explained my new role as a researcher without having any current affiliation to Bankers.[237] The interviewees were also informed that their names, positions or personal

[233] Woolf (1928/2012).
[234] Madison (2005), p. 5.
[235] Ellis, Adams & Bochner (2011), no page number.
[236] Ellis, Adams & Bochner (2011), no page number.
[237] See introductory letter in Annex 1.

details would not be disclosed in my final text. This means that I am careful not to include any interview extract that could reveal the identity of the interviewee to readers, mindful that the text may be read by people who are or were themselves part of the events in Patos-Marinza.

Madison writes beautifully about the ethical issues regarding the representation of Others: "with all the good intentions, excellent craftsmanship, and even with the reliability and eloquence of a particular story, representing Others is always going to be a complicated and contentious undertaking".[238] Likewise, Ester Barinaga emphasises that academic texts often contribute to the creation of groups, by describing them as homogenous and unified to readers, even though the described actors may not recognise the group themselves. She emphasises that by the creation of fictive groups "writing, even academic writing, is to commit violence on the described".[239] My experiences from Patos-Marinza show that the groups described in this thesis, such as 'employees' or 'communities', are heterogeneous and thus the very categorisations I deploy are problematic. A senior manager and a local resident may have closer views on the role of the company than two neighbours or two colleagues. This also underlines the need not to simplify and to let a variety of voices in the context be heard. This is what I have tried to do in this text.

In the last stages of finalising this text, I added fictional vignettes to the empirical chapters. One vignette places you as a reader alongside my colleague and I on an imaginative working day (Chapter 4), and the following three vignettes place you as a reader in the position of an imaginative resident in Patos-Marinza (Chapter 5, 6 and 7). These are other attempts to bring you as a reader into the context I experienced, trying to convey some of the feelings and frustrations I felt when I listened to the concerns of residents in the area both as a company employee and as a researcher. Of course, as a former corporate representative and now PhD student, I do not know how it is to live in Patos-Marinza. Nevertheless, I believe we all have to try to make such fictional journeys in order to speak about sustainability in a democratic sense; placing ourselves in the shoes of 'the other' and imagine what conception of sustainability would be meaningful in that position. The inclusion of these texts is my contribution to the movement within management studies to 'write differently'; an effort to move away from the 'scientific' language that dominates and restricts academic texts

[238] Madison (2005), p. 3-4.
[239] Barinaga (2015), p. 161, my translation.

and to embrace writing that, as formulated by Sarah Gilmore et al., "is concerned with broadening, widening and deepening knowledge and understanding by giving our ideas space in which they can flourish, create new meanings, help us learn and become human".[240]

To write is to reduce reality,[241] to exclude aspects that complicate the picture, to select and order our messy life into black and white signs. Political Discourse Theory emphasises that we all need to simplify reality in order to understand, that the competing meanings of each word and each context means that simplification is obligatory and unavoidable in order for us to make sense of our surroundings.[242] When I wrote this story about Patos-Marinza, the things I left out were reacting in different ways. Some were screaming for my attention. Some were waving their goodbyes with a smile. Others were hiding in dark places. The things I left out all have their reasons for wanting to be, or not, included. Some have integrity and enjoy their privacy. Others demand a central place in the sunrays of my description. The things I left out are themselves reasons why my research project can be understood as a discursive articulation. It is a simplification and thus a contribution to the hegemonic struggle in Patos-Marinza, an endeavour to describe a social context that can be viewed in many other ways. The things I left out are other stories about Patos-Marinza. Stories which haunt this text from the outside, stories that did not fit in this book.

[240] Gilmore, Harding, Helin & Pullen (2019), p. 4.
[241] Alvesson & Sköldberg (1994).
[242] Winter Jørgensen & Phillips (1999/2000).

CHAPTER 4

"A great investment for all Albanian people"

Let us now wander back into Patos-Marinza, where my exploration of the ins and outs of corporate hegemony takes place. I will start by bringing you as a reader with me on a fictional yet typical working day, and share some of the sights, smells and sensations that characterised my professional role between 2010 and 2015.[243]

When we arrive at the gates of Bankers' main office in Fier city, we have to press the button on the gate monitor so that the person working in the reception can let us in. The area outside the gate is already filled with people, mostly men, who have errands with Bankers; a few with invoices to be paid, others with land papers that should be updated, some with old grievances that our community department has failed to resolve. A few of the men address us as we approach the gate and start repeating their complaints that they have told me many times before. You experience the situation as tense (maybe you already regret that you came with me?). I tell them, in my usual way, that they have to speak to our grievance officer. The gate opens and closes behind us while they continue to negotiate with the reception to let them in. We enter the modern air-conditioned office, and head straight down to the cafeteria to make the day's first cup of espresso. In a few minutes the bus with the rest of the office staff will arrive and the newly wiped floors will be filled with high heels and polished shoes. Another day at the office has started.

The list of registered grievances is growing so my colleague, you and I take one of the white Toyota pickups, which are parked in the backyard of the office, and wave to the guard as he opens the iron gates to the office premises. From Bankers' office, we drive a few hundred metres north on the main road towards Tirana and then turn right at the gas station, into a narrow but busy road. We pass the school Flatrat e Dijes, attended by most middle-class

[243] Fictional narrative, written in August 2020 with support of a Youtube video (Nick Carlsson, 2013) as a memory jogger.

children in Fier, and the new prison building, which people say (with a hint of the usual irony in their voice) will be filled with Albanian prisoners from the EU. Vast agricultural fields expand on both sides of the road but you notice that few modern agricultural equipment is visible. Instead we see a few women and men with bent backs in the middle of the fields as they work their lands by hand. The traffic is comprised of a mix of brand new Mercedes, minivans, horse carriages filled with agricultural produce, old Mercedes and a tractor. "There is nothing better than a German car to handle Albanian potholes", my colleague explains with a laugh. In the village of Sheqishta we turn left and soon the first oil deposits appear just behind the residences along the road. My colleague and I explain to you that several of the residents have complained about the smell from vent gases that are released from the black deposits, which store the oil until trucks come and pick it up. But we also emphasise that this is a relatively calm area. "Most likely the residents in the houses closest to the wells have been paid a decent amount in land rental from Bankers. That money would make any smell bearable", I say (with that hint of irony again).

As we continue on the narrow road, we enter the village of Belina and more oil deposits and pipelines become visible from the road. This is closer to the centre of the oilfield and as we turn right to enter the road to Bankers' Central Treatment Facility, the smell from vent gases is so intense that we have to close the windows. We explain to you that residents living in Belina are used to this smell, they are surrounded by the oil industry and, unless they are lucky to sign a land contract, many have no possibility to move somewhere else. You notice that on this road, the traffic includes oil trucks that create large clouds of dust as they pass us on the road. Grievances concerning these trucks are also frequent; dust covers the crops growing along the road and potholes become larger due to their weight, sometimes making it difficult even for German cars to pass. We are on our way to Marinza, another village located directly in the main oilfield. The family we will visit have complained about the noise coming from the oilrigs at night. My colleague and I already know there is little we can do about the noise. Company monitors have told us that the noise is within industry standards. No mitigation measures are necessary. The family is poor, their old house desperately needs repair, the husband and son are without work and two children are in need of schoolbooks and clothes for the new school year. We come to their home to listen to them once more; we write down their requests and fill another sheet of grievance information. When we sit down in their small living room we are served Raki made from grape and sweets from a small glass bowl. They tell us about their hardship while their children watch us with curious eyes. You are horrified by the poverty displayed just next to thousands of barrels of oil. When we are about to leave, the older son puts a watermelon from their produce in the trunk of our truck, "as a thank you and a sign of respect", the husband says, "for listening to our concerns". The watermelons are all ripe now, so the prices on the market have fallen, with profits after transport being close to zero. When we come back to the main office we go down to the cafeteria and share the slices of watermelon with another cup of espresso. The family is now another number in our growing grievance database. You feel tired (I will let you go home now). The watermelon tastes delicious after a hot day in the field.

In the following four chapters I will tell you about my former employer Bankers, a Canadian oil company that struggled to uphold its hegemonic position as a narrator and organiser of Patos-Marinza, the area in south-central Albania in which the company operated between 2004 and 2016. The discourse describing company activities as an 'investment' was Bankers' hegemonic story. This discourse gave meaning to company activities and incorporated various groups in the Albanian society into a corporate alliance. Landowners gained money from land rentals, young men were employed, businesses received orders and the local government collected taxes. The story about the 'investment' was a story aiming at closure, of incorporating 'all' as beneficiaries of the oil industry and thus trying to reduce grievances and requests from society by satisfying them. However, a set of unmet demands from the communities of Patos-Marinza was endangering this all-encompassing vision, interrupting the corporate narrative, threatening to create an antagonistic frontier between the company and local residents. A counter-hegemonic discourse describing company activities as an 'invasion' was articulated, protests were held, roads blocked and oil deposits vandalised. In the following chapters I will tell you the story of a company that tried to uphold its hegemonic position in the face of demands that continuously reminded it of its impossibility of ever becoming complete, of its failure to satisfy all.

An interview with Bankers' CEO

I will now leave the stage to the former CEO of Bankers, Donald, who will introduce the company to you. After all, who would be a better person to describe the company's success in Albania? The following extracts are from an interview with Donald in December 2015, published on YouTube by the

Oil and Gas Council.[244] A young woman, Charlotte, representing an online news portal for investor advice,[245] conducts the interview. The video shows Charlotte and Donald standing on opposite sides of a small coffee table; both are dressed in black suits and behind them is a screen filled with a small logo of the "World Oil and Gas Week". The "World Oil and Gas Week", which took place in London during 2015, is an event where oil and gas companies and potential investors meet and speak about various investment opportunities around the globe.[246] It is a local place in the global economy, just as Patos-Marinza is a local place connected to the same investment flows. In one place capital is gathered from investors, in another it is mobilised for production. In a bright and pleasant voice, Charlotte starts the interview with a summary of the company and an introduction to its CEO, Donald:

> Charlotte – Bankers Petroleum is a Toronto and AIM[247] listed oil producer with assets in Albania and currently focused on developing Patos-Marinza, the largest onshore oilfield in Europe. Well, I am joined by the Chief Executive of the company, Donald. Hello Donald.
>
> Donald – Ah, it's good to see you Charlotte.
>
> Charlotte – So tell me, tell us a bit more about this Patos-Marinza field, what do you have there?
>
> Donald – Yes, so the Patos-Marinza field is the largest hydrocarbon deposit in continental Europe, its actually 80 years old, so we are, we are the second concessionaire after Albania went democratic in the early 90s, we actually had a chance to take it over, so we have been 10 years in Albania. But it's a, it's a very interesting field, it's a heavy oil field, ah, lots of individual sands [geological layers], so we drill horizontal wells across all the sands, and we have an opportunity to grow the field. In fact, when we started it was around 600 barrels [of oil] a day, its almost 20.000 barrels [of oil] a day now.[248]

Donald presents Patos-Marinza as eighty years old and the largest oilfield on continental Europe, thereby underlining its importance. He also emphasises the fast growth of Bankers' production to highlight the company's

[244] The oil and gas council is a global network for oil and gas executives.
[245] Proactiveinvestors (2009).
[246] Oil & Gas Council (2015).
[247] Bankers' Shares were traded on the Toronto Stock Exchange (TSX) and the AIM Market in London, England under the stock symbol BNK.
[248] Oil & Gas Council (2015, December 6).

success during the ten years it has been operating in Albania. In addition, Donald notes that Patos-Marinza consists of heavy oil. Heavy oil is thicker and less valuable per barrel than light oil and requires a higher number of wells per square metre. It also needs other extraction techniques than light oil, for example water injection into the ground to make the heavy oil flow better.[249] Horizontal wells, which Donald mentions, is a technique where you first drill vertically into the ground and then deviate the well bore in a curve at a certain depth to enter the oil reservoir with a near horizontal angle.[250] These extraction techniques and the production of wells is something I will come back to; they are at the core of understanding the relations between company and community. So far, the interview has focused on the past; but investors want to know about the future, about the potential for making money. Charlotte continues the interview in her pleasant voice:

> Charlotte – Okay, tell us a bit more about the overall growth strategy of the company, because it's in three parts, isn't it?
>
> Donald – Mmm, so we have three things we focus on [...], so we drill a lot of wells, if you look last year we drilled 160 wells, we probably drill 60 this year, they're about a million [dollars] a piece. They're very quick though, so we drill them in about ten and a half days, put them on production in 18 days, so our job is to manufacture inexpensive horizontal wells in Albania. The second thing is to also focus on [cost] margin, so we have taken about 8 dollars of operating costs [per barrel of oil] out of the business over the last three years, focusing on not flaring gas and burning it for consumption, getting out of the diesel business, finding ways where we were trucking [oil], to remove trucking and putting it [oil] in pipelines instead, so, there has been a tremendous effort to transform our costs. And the third thing, which is new to us, eh, is something called enhanced oil recovery, we have started to, where it makes sense, inject a fluid in the ground [...].[251]

Donald sums up Bankers' strategy as based on three components: drilling horizontal wells at a fast pace, reducing costs in operations, and using water injection to enhance oil extraction. This is what investors want to hear: the potential to increase extraction and thus revenues, measures to reduce costs and thereby increase profits. But in his answer, there is no

[249] Proactiveinvestors (2009).
[250] See pictures of technique in Bankers Petroleum (2010), p. 12.
[251] Oil & Gas Council (2015, December 6).

indication of this being an oilfield where people live. To "drill a lot of wells" means to produce noise and air pollution in the vicinity to residences, to "remove trucking and putting it in pipelines instead" means to reduce dust from trucks on agricultural crops but also a complicated procedure of renting agricultural land for the construction of pipelines. To "inject a fluid in the ground" may signify enhanced oil production for investors but is an unknown technique to residents living in the area, and thereby further heightens potential fears about its consequences. These various materialisations of the oilfield and the way they are described are linked to corporate hegemony and community resistance. They are articulations of a hegemonic discourse in which Patos-Marinza is described and materialised as an oilfield with the consequence that alternatives visions of the area, linked to, for example, agriculture or residential uses, are marginalised. Charlotte takes no notice of this marginalisation but continues to ask about the company's relationship with Albanian authorities, indicating that this relationship may be a concern for investors.

> Charlotte – […] so you have been in Albania over ten years now I suppose, and there you are the largest foreign direct investor and one of the largest private employers in the country, I imagine your relationship with the Albanian authority is pretty good?
>
> Donald – I think we try to manage the relationship quite a bit obviously. We're, I think, 6% of the GDP, so we have a very important relationship in the country, so we not only work quite closely with the government of Albania around how do they think about fiscal take, how do they think about the regulatory environment, essentially we bring west to the east, so if you think about it, we bring, western technology, western know how, western, business practices into an emerging market in Albania, so they see us as, I think, a real opportunity to develop the country and develop this asset, very much the way we developed in western Canada, which for us has created a unique relationship with them.[252]

The postcolonial thinker Dipesh Chakrabarty, states that the history of countries "tend to become variations on a master narrative", which is the narrative corresponding to "the history of Europe".[253] Similarly, Donald's answer puts the company in a superior position in relation to the Albanian

[252] Oil & Gas Council (2015, December 6).
[253] Chakrabarty (1992), p. 1.

government emphasising that the company brings 'western' technology, know-how and business practices in to the 'emerging market' of Albania. This places Albania as the 'east', a country that is now given the opportunity to develop "the way we developed in western Canada".[254] This reasoning is a typical example of a discourse in which large parts of the world are portrayed as lagging behind Europe and North America (in this case Canada) but can be moved along a universalised path of greater development with the help of foreign investments,[255] such as Bankers' investment in Albania. Bankers' investment is thus something that will bring a 'western' future to Albania, as the only imaginable progress from the country's 'underdeveloped' present. Through the logic of equivalence, what it means to be 'Western' in this discourse is linked with concepts of 'modernity', 'technology' and 'skills'. 'Eastern' becomes its opposite via a logic of difference. But Charlotte is not a postcolonial scholar with the goal to criticise Donald for how he portrays the world. She instead concludes the interview by asking once more about the company's future:

> Charlotte – Then again, I'd like to know where you see the company in five years time […]?
>
> Donald – […] we want to find a solution for trying to heat some water to inject in the ground to produce this enormous resource at the southern end of the field, which we can't spend time on now, because everything we have is really developed on cold flow [water injections]. So that's the beauty of this thing, it's a wonderful sandbox to play in, so we have a development that has plenty of opportunities for the next several years but this opportunity to heat that oil and produce for many, many generations to come.
>
> Charlotte – Well Donald, thank you very much.
>
> Donald – Ah, my pleasure Charlotte.[256]

Donald describes Patos-Marinza as a "wonderful sandbox to play in"[257] for extractive companies, due to the opportunities for further oil extraction using heated water injections. The fact that this 'sandbox' is home to around 10,000 residents is never mentioned. The absence of local residents in the interview, points to a large divide between investor choices pro-

[254] Oil & Gas Council (2015, December 6).
[255] Banerjee & Linstead (2001).
[256] Oil & Gas Council (2015, December 6).
[257] Oil & Gas Council (2015, December 6).

moted in London and oil industry impacts in Patos-Marinza. Patos-Marinza portrayed in one part of the world does not correspond to the place experienced in another. Some actors view it as a place for potential high returns on investments; other actors view it as a home.

These opposing perspectives on Patos-Marinza highlight two different narratives of Bankers' activities that will run in parallel throughout this dissertation. One is the narrative of Bankers' operations as an 'investment'; the other is the narrative of Bankers' operations as an 'invasion'. The understanding of Bankers' activities as an 'investment' is a hegemonic discourse; a discourse that portrays Bankers' activities as beneficial to the Albanian population at large while it diminishes the power struggles and negative impacts from oil extraction. In contrast, the understanding of Bankers' activities as an 'invasion' can be seen as a counter-hegemonic discourse; a discourse that questions the legitimacy of Bankers' activities and highlights the losses imposed on particular groups in Albanian society. Let us continue by examining more closely these two discursive structures.

Bankers' investment in Patos-Marinza

In order to understand the context in which Bankers activities are framed, we have to start from the beginning. Patos-Marinza can be seen as an example of the "hot spots" of environmental pollution[258] created during communist rule in Albania, which was otherwise characterised by 'accidental' environmental protection due to low economic development.[259] While other countries in Eastern Europe modified their production technologies in the 1950s and 1960s, the pollution of industrial areas in Albania were aggravated during the rule of the Hoxha regime.[260] A Bankers' representative, Gramos, who worked in Patos-Marinza during the communist period recalls the conditions when he first came to the field in the 1970s:

> I saw every road covered in an oily mud, the wells and the surrounding areas full of leaked oil, the workers who were servicing the wells without health and safety measures and in very bad working conditions [...]. When I started working, I put on rubber boots and I kept them on for six months due to the oily mud that was covering the field. And then, another problem arrived with springtime; the mud became dust that filled the air as vehicles moved around. The vehicles at that time

[258] UNEP (2000), p. 10.
[259] Green (2003), p. 65.
[260] Green (2003), p. 66.

> were open and the people who travelled in them became covered with dust, as if they had been immersed in powder.[261]

Stories such as these, about the degraded and filthy oilfield during the communist period, were common among older oil workers like Gramos, who admired the new technologies that were later introduced by Bankers. Klodian, a representative from Bankers' partner organisation, living in another part of Albania, explained that issues with pollution in Patos-Marinza were well known during the communist period:

> Also during the Communist Regime they had some problems there [Patos-Marinza] especially for pollution and the quality of air. They used the old technology with lots of negative impacts to the environment.[262]

When communism fell in 1991, the Albanian Democratic Party came into power and privatised the hydrocarbon sector as part of the efforts to introduce a market economy in the previously closed communist system.[263] Anglo Albanian Petroleum (AAP), a partnership between the UK company Premier Oil, IFC, the Austrian company OMV and the Albanian state company Albpetrol, signed the first concession agreement for the field in 1994. However, the modernisation of the oilfield went slowly and in 2000, an environmental assessment by UNEP reported that families in Patos-Marinza were exposed to severe health risks due to the oilfield's poor management:

> Severe soil and groundwater contamination comes from several sources. […] Oil wells […] are perforating the clay layer and very probably allowing hydrocarbons to contaminate the drinking water supply. The field's pumps are very poorly maintained and leak significant quantities of oil into the surrounding environment. Oil is transported from the pumps to pre-treatment facilities in the field via pipelines. The pipelines are also poorly maintained and lose significant amounts of oil.[264]

This pollution, which is attributed to the previous regime, and which Gramos and the UNEP report describe, is an important part of Bankers'

[261] Interview, Bankers representative, October–November 2017.
[262] Interview, representative, Bankers' partner organisation, October–November 2017.
[263] UNEP (2000), p. 12.
[264] UNEP (2000), p. 24.

story. It opens up the space for Bankers to speak of "improving" what is otherwise described as an environmentally degraded brownfield. In 2004, after AAP abandoned their concession, Bankers signed a new concession agreement with the Albanian government, giving the company 100% control over the assets in Patos-Marinza.[265] On their web page, Bankers describe how the company in the following years revitalised the oilfield with the help of investments in modern technology and remediation of the extensive historic pollution.[266] In 2009, Bankers signed a US$110 million loan agreement with IFC and EBRD to fund investment and working capital needs for Albanian assets and to support the clean-up of environmental pollution caused by previous mismanagement. The President and CEO of Bankers at the time, stated in the company's press release that:

> this $110 million debt financing is more than just a credit facility; it's a strategic investment with two influential global organizations who have significant presence and initiatives in Albania. Their financial support at this time of tight credit markets is vital to carrying out a large development project at the Patos Marinza oil field and we particularly appreciate their expertise, and efforts to involve other stakeholders, in tackling the environmental clean-up challenges ahead of us.[267]

In the same press release, representatives for IFC and EBRD expressed their satisfaction with the agreement. IFC's Global Head for extractive industries explained that:

> While IFC provides financing to help improve recovery rates and accelerate domestic oil production, we also help the company to contribute to environmental remediation initiatives aimed at improving living conditions in the surrounding area.[268]

EBRD's Operations Leader for the project joined these voices and declared that:

> With this project, the EBRD is providing much-needed long-term funding to support private investments in the Albanian oil sector. By investing to modernize in Bankers Petroleum's operations, the Bank is

[265] Bankers Petroleum (2016a), Bankers was then named Saxon but changed name to Bankers in 2006.

[266] Bankers Petroleum (2016a).

[267] Bankers Petroleum (2009, May 11th).

[268] Bankers Petroleum (2009, May 11th).

> helping to revamp the oil industry in Albania, by fostering further privatization and helping set high standards of environmental management.[269]

All parties thus emphasised how the environmental clean-up was an important aspect in their decision to invest in Bankers. Such emphasis ensured that other potentially new negative impacts emanating from the revitalisation of the oilfield were marginalised in the discussion. Instead, actors describe a win-win situation in which the oilfield would be modernised and expanded while the local environment and living conditions would improve.

This revitalisation, which introduced new technology to the oilfield, such as horizontal drilling, made Bankers one of the largest employers and taxpayers in the country. In 2015 the company reported to have 1700 direct and indirect local employees, and to have made a cumulative tax contribution of US$575 million to the Albanian Government.[270] In one interview, a local government representative described this success story, stating that:

> The Canadian company is a great investment for all Albanian people, the technology, the people employed, the improvement of environment, of taking the oil from the earth.[271]

In this statement, Bankers' project is articulated in terms of its 'universal' character; "all Albanian people" means that the corporative project of the particular group (Bankers) is articulated as beneficial to every Albanian citizen. By means of this investment the company became one of the main contributors to economic development and employment in the Fier region. One of Bankers' representatives, Jonida, explained this impact on the wider area from the Canadian investment:

> They gave a western flavour to the whole area, not only Patos-Marinza or the villages around but the whole Fieri area. Like, you know, a western company is working in Albania, and this made Albania look like a normal country. [...] They created an opportunity to Albanian people, that live in the Fieri area, to stay at home and be a part of something that many people from Albania left home in order to become part of. So, we have more than half of our population who left

[269] Bankers Petroleum (2009, May 11th).
[270] Bankers Petroleum, (2016d).
[271] Interview, local government representative, October–November 2017.

> the country to be part of something like that. For Albanians it's a dream to be part of advanced societies. And to have like a sort of flavour, a taste that you are living in your home and you are still working for something which pays you decently and treats you as a human being; this is quite a privilege, I would say.[272]

As was the case with the interview with Bankers' CEO, Jonida expresses a relation of equivalence between 'the west' and a variety of value-laden signifiers, such as 'advanced societies' and 'decent' working conditions. Through this articulation, Bankers help Albania "to look like a normal country", an articulation of the company as the hero.

In 2014, Bankers celebrated this success story on its tenth anniversary in Patos-Marinza. In a Bankers' produced video,[273] called *Patos-Marinza Oilfield – awakening the sleeping giant*, the story of the company's ten years of success was published for YouTube audiences.[274] In the film, various pictures of Bankers' modern equipment in Patos-Marinza are shown while a voice-over explains:

> With the use of horizontal drilling, Bankers broke every record of production in this field. It produced a historic maximum, 18,000 bopd [barrels of oil per day], setting a new record. The price of the shares reached a historic value of 10 dollars per share. But the real achievement of this oilfield, the one which brought its renaissance was its doubling of proven and possible reserves [measures of how much oil is available for future extraction].[275]

The video changes to a frame showing Bankers' General Director in a shirt and tie sitting in a leather armchair in his office. He states proudly:

> The biggest discovery made in Albania in the past 30 years, is Patos-Marinza oilfield. Bankers' investment made this discovery possible and doubled its extractable reserves.[276]

Bankers' success is celebrated in the film, both in terms of the clean-up of the historic pollution and the introduction of new technology that increased extractable reserves and the rate of production. The local com-

[272] Interview, Bankers representative, October–November 2017.
[273] Participant observations (2014).
[274] Albania Oilfield (2014, January 24), quotation of English subtitles.
[275] Albania Oilfield (2014, January 24), quotation of English subtitles.
[276] Albania Oilfield (2014, January 24), quotation of English subtitles.

munities are also framed as beneficiaries and partners in this success story. While showing scenic views of green agricultural fields in Patos-Marinza the voice-over describes local communities as the "most important partner of Bankers in this giant project",[277] continuing:

> The company operates with the belief and intention of being a good neighbour and responds to all needs of the community in a [community] investment plan, which has seen growth and concrete results from year to year.

The film shifts once more, showing Bankers' CEO sitting in front of a painting in his office dressed in a black suit, blue shirt and a shiny grey tie. He states seriously:

> We want to be the partner of choice in the country. A very powerful legacy is the way we develop and work with the communities. So, in everything we do, from dust mitigation to building and working with schools we act as community partners, not just from the environmental point of view but also from a broader stakeholder manager point of view, so that everyone looks as Bankers as the right partner in the country.[278]

These statements, whether expressed in interviews, films or in written documents, help to comprise the discourse of Bankers' successful 'investment' in Patos-Marinza. The promoters of this discourse include Bankers' management, local government representatives and IFC and EBRD. This is thus an alliance of actors, a hegemonic bloc, which articulates and stabilises this discourse around the nodal point of the 'investment', linking it together with other signs, such as 'clean-up', 'technology', 'community investments' and 'employment'.

In the video interview with Bankers' CEO, the company's 'investment' in Albania is portrayed as an opportunity for the Albanian government to 'develop' the country. The foreign 'investment' is thus framed as what Gramsci calls a 'universal' project, something to which the entirety of Albania will have access, with no specification of who will win and who will lose from expanding the oilfield. The physical and economic expansion of the corporation and its dominance over Patos-Marinza oilfield is thus described as beneficial to all groups via a presumed economic development

[277] Albania Oilfield (2014), in Albanian with English subtitles.
[278] Albania Oilfield (2014, January 24), quotation of English subtitles.

of Albania's economy. This discourse also frames the subject position of the local residents in a particular way. Residents are viewed as beneficiaries of, and potential allies to, the corporation. The Bankers representative, Gramos, explains:

> Those who work with Bankers but are residents in Marinza, Zharrza, Patos or other locations, are very happy and express high regard for the company management. But those who are not working in Bankers but are residents in Marinza, they are asking to be part of Bankers, and this means that they like Bankers. But when they are unable to be employed by the company and, as for all the things that one cannot achieve, they start to complain.[279]

According to Gramos, local residents are thus desperate to be part of Bankers' alliance. Any complaints raised by villagers are disregarded because of Bankers' lack of possibilities to provide everyone with good employment prospects. This potential incorporation of community members into the corporate alliance resonates with how Gramsci described the expansion of bourgeoisie power in western societies. Gramsci wrote:

> In former times, the dominant classes were essentially conservative in the sense that they did not seek to enable other classes to pass organically into theirs; in other words, they did not try to seek to enlarge, either "technically" or ideologically, the scope of their class – they conceived of themselves as an exclusive caste.[280]

Gramsci argued that bourgeois power was different to how dominant classes conceptualised their power previously. While feudal lords or slave owners saw themselves as fundamentally different from their subordinates, the bourgeois class articulated a project in which everyone could potentially be included. The potential for subordinates to become part of the ruling class was thus a way in which the struggle between classes could be de-politicised. As formulated by Peter D. Thomas, a contemporary interpreter of Gramsci's thinking, the attempts by the bourgeoisie to preserve their power was accomplished:

> through the prevention of the emergence of competing (organized and institutionalized) perspectives. The de-politicization of politics – that

[279] Interview, Bankers representative, October–November 2017.
[280] Gramsci (1930-1932/2007), p. 234.

> is, the conversion of formerly expressed political debates into purely bureaucratic and technical questions.[281]

Similarly, through the narrative of the ‘investment’, where people in subordinate positions (‘locals’) have the imagined possibility of employment and income benefits, Bankers’ activities in Patos-Marinza could be framed as a ‘universal’ project, beneficial to all. Following Gramsci’s thoughts around hegemony as both force and consent, one could argue that while the formal concession agreement ensured Bankers’ dominance in Patos-Marinza based on force (state police), the narrative of ‘investment’, which speaks of bringing ‘development’ and ‘employment’ to the area, ensured that Bankers’ hegemony was based also on consent, incorporating ‘groups’ – such as the Albanian government, IFC and EBRD, local staff, contractors and community members – into an alliance. When we view the hegemonic discourse in Patos-Marinza as a narrative, it is a story about a degraded oilfield in a post-communist country, which has been revitalised and cleaned by means of foreign investments. Through foreign investment, the country is given an opportunity to develop, fostering further private investments, creating jobs, and improving living conditions as a consequence. This is a storyline we recognise and have heard before: a global hegemonic order predicated on a ‘western’ model of development.[282] To understand this model as a particular discursive formation, an alternative narrative is needed.

Bankers’ invasion of Patos-Marinza

Even though we have passed the 25th anniversary since the collapse of the Albanian communist regime in 1991, Patos-Marinza continues to be a battleground for the introduction of market economics into the region. Here, conflicts with local communities constitute the other side of Bankers’ story. Patos-Marinza is an area where many residents live in poverty due to widespread unemployment and low levels of agricultural development. In 2014, a network of environmental and human rights groups in Central and Eastern Europe focused on monitoring public finance institutions such as IFC and EBRD, called the Bankwatch Network, conducted a fact-finding mission in Patos-Marinza. In the report from their visit, the following summary was made:

[281] Thomas (2009/2010), pp. 150-151.
[282] Chakrabarty (1992), p. 1.

> Pollution goes hand in hand with extractive industries, and the Patos-Marinza area has been exploited for decades, so the team was prepared for the unpleasant smell in the air, sludge pits, rusty scrap heaps, dusty roads and heavy lorry traffic. What the team was unprepared for was the level of poverty and abject squalor of the local villages. Poverty of this scale in communities living in the shadows of extractive industries is not typical, at least not based on our observations over more than a decade and half across Eastern Europe. This is even more unexpected given the financial support for Bankers from two well-known public financial institutions with explicit mandates related to development: in the case of the IFC, the alleviation of poverty; and the promotion of environmentally-sound, sustainable development, in the case of the EBRD.[283]

The rapporteurs were surprised with the level of poverty found in an area rich in oil resources. This sense of surprise was, in part, because Bankers project was supported by IFC and EBRD. Bankers' activities are framed in connection with notions of 'dust', 'smell', 'exploitation' and 'poverty', while local communities are described not as 'beneficiaries' but as "living in the shadows of extractive industries".[284] Here we have the articulation of an alternative, counter-hegemonic discourse in which Bankers' activities are seen as harmful rather than beneficial.

Connected to this discourse were rumours of clandestine practices during the concession agreement process between Bankers and the Albanian government. In a special programme transmitted in December 2015 by the public TV-Channel, Ora News, the Albanian state was described as a "banana republic" and Bankers was depicted as having gained access to the concession agreement through clandestine and illegal means. A reason for such suspicion was an especially short period between the founding of the company and it securing the concession agreement. The programme also drew attention to the fact that Bankers was registered in the Cayman Islands; a renowned location for tax evasion practices.[285] A former Bankers representative, Gezim, told me to turn off my recorder, and proceeded to recount a similar story:

> Do you know how Bankers came to Albania? AAP left Patos-Marinza because the joint venture with Albpetrol did not work. At the same time Saxon [previous name of Bankers] came into the country in

[283] Bankwatch Network (2014), p. 4.
[284] Bankwatch Network (2014), p. 4.
[285] Ora News Emisione (2015, December 2), my translation.

> record time. It was [Robert] who was part of AAP and who later, when AAP withdrew, went back to Canada to look for investors, they paid something to the prime minister and in two months, from May to July 4th 2004, the concession was signed with Saxon, the same concession valid today with Bankers. The concession was made without any tender and in record time. [...] We say [in Albania] that "if an army goes into a garden and the general takes an apple from the tree the last soldier will take the plants with the root." Corruption starts from the top.[286]

In another interview, a former representative for one of Bankers' contractors, Ervis, explained:

> We are a poor country, poor state, okay, a lot of corruption, and as you know in the third world these things happen, and we are talking about huge money like that investment, nobody can say no, so they gave it to somebody who didn't deserve it. Albanian people deserved the oil-field.[287]

Several interviewees thus mentioned the public view of Bankers' activities as illegitimate and based on corrupt practices, in collaboration with the Albanian government rather than a form of cooperation that would benefit the Albanian people.

Interviewees also spoke about how Bankers' takeover was understood to be connected to the loss of employment. Klodian, a representative of Bankers' partner organisation, explained that, when compared to the current situation, during communism employment in the oil industry included most of the local households:

> So, in the social aspect it has been very good for the people there [during communism], because 90% of the employees have been from the place there.[288]

Ervis, quoted above, connected Bankers' poor reputation in local communities to the corporate takeover of oil wells belonging to the state owned company Albpetrol, and shared with me a story about when Bankers and its contractors started working in the area:

[286] Interview, former representative, Bankers, October–November 2017.

[287] Interview, former representative, Bankers' contractor, October–November 2017.

[288] Interview, representative, Bankers' partner organisation, October–November 2017.

> So, if we go back to 2005, really they [local communities] hate, call it like this, the Canadians, because most of the [...] communities around were employed for Albpetrol. So when you know someone is coming, with money, you know it is the start of the countdown. [...] The real sparks with the community came at that point, if I remember it right, it was when we took the first wells, and [...], as I remember, Albpetrol just sent home around 500 people, or a bunch of people they sent home. [...] So, there it started, so we [Bankers and Bankers' contractors] started invading. And when you start invading and take from 25 [wells] to another 25 [wells], another 50 [wells] so, you [community members] know that its a question of time.[289]

The process of taking over oil wells from the state-owned company Albpetrol was thus, in this interview, articulated as an 'invasion' rather than an 'investment'. While Bankers, IFC and EBRD describe this takeover as a 'clean-up' operation and as an 'opportunity to develop', Ervis describes how residents saw the same activities as a threat. He explains how people connected Bankers' takeover with the loss of jobs in Albpetrol. Thus, Bankers' 'invasion' is articulated in connection to widespread 'unemployment' among local residents, and not lucrative employment opportunities.

The discourse organised around the nodal point of the 'invasion' thus works as a counter-hegemonic force in Patos-Marinza. Even though it stops short of envisioning an alternative path for the area, it depicts Bankers as a threatening 'other' and makes possible the articulation of a chain of equivalence between community members voicing different grievances against the oil industry. One example of community mobilisation is a video posted on YouTube by the TV-channel, Vizion Plus Albania, in September 2013. It shows a protest by local youth outside the offices of Bankers. In the video, young men with painted faces and naked upper bodies soaked in what appears to be crude oil, march outside Bankers' main office in Fier, holding a large sign proclaiming: "Bankers! Stop! Oil wealth not disaster!" In the video a journalist interviews one of the men, who, in a formal voice, declares:

> We have gathered in front of the company's office, to break the silence that citizens have kept for several years, and to start an era of resistance against the abuses of this company. During these years, the land in Fier trembles and shakes due to Bankers' bad management of the oil. Zharrza and Fier are shaking, but the government should be the ones

[289] Interview, former representative, Bankers' contractor, October–November 2017.

> shaking and Bankers should be trembling. This is only the start of our resistance.[290]

Bankers' activities are here articulated in relation to 'abuses' and 'bad management'. They are opposed by threats of counter actions and acts of resistance; for example when the young man proclaims that "the government should be shaking and Bankers [...] trembling"[291] as part of a community-led series of protests.

During interviews, community members clearly articulated this counter-hegemonic discourse. They would raise issues about air pollution, earth tremors, unemployment, dust and noise. These specific concerns were often discussed separately, one by one. But they would also be linked together by articulations framing the company as an 'invader' who 'exploits' the area for money while the people remain poor and suffer the consequences. For example, when discussing air quality issues, Ermal, a resident in Patos-Marinza, spoke of Bankers' activities in terms of 'damage', 'war' and 'genocide':

> Before they conquered countries with force in order to steal resources. Now they take the land peacefully but what about the people that live here [in Patos-Marinza]? Is it not genocide here? You have a community that is living in a place that is not suitable to live in [due to the gas emissions], what do you call that? Genocide? There are international laws protecting civilians in war times, but this [situation] is the same even though it is peace, the damage on the people is the same.[292]

Ermal connects the specific operations of Bankers with foreign invasions, emphasising that, even if the 'occupation' is peacefully conducted, the local population suffers. In a group interview, the local resident Berti argued that the corporation is free to operate as they please in the area:

> The company, Sara, works as it wants in the community; they know that we are poor, that we do not have any income, that we do not mobilise and do not rise to protest, so they can do whatever they want.[293]

Berti speaks of a situation entirely conducive to corporate exploitation, a context in which people are too poor to protest and in which company

[290] VizionPlusAlbania (2013, September 13), my translation.
[291] VizionPlusAlbania (2013, September 13), my translation.
[292] Family visit, Patos-Marinza, September 2018.
[293] Group interview, Patos-Marinza, September 2018.

activities can be undertaken unregulated. In the same interview, a group of men (Artan, Ergys and Edison) describe the company bosses as thieves, earning outrageous amounts of money while regular people suffer:

> Artan – We do not know for example who the main owner of the company is, the most powerful Canadian for example, the highest boss, we have never met the highest boss to explain our complaints.
>
> Sara – And why do you think that the bosses never came here [to the village]?
>
> Ergys – Because the thieves do not want to be exposed.
>
> Edison – They take billions while people here are suffering for a piece of bread. We have to go and sign our names in the pharmacy to get medicine [to sign the name means get a loan at the pharmacy if you cannot pay] while they go on vacation.[294]

These are narratives I heard many times while working in Patos-Marinza. During my time as a Bankers' employee, protests and negative media reports about Bankers were common[295] and several Facebook pages were active in seeking to stop the company's operations.[296] Issues discussed in the media and on Facebook pages related to environmental pollution, to community health risks, to a lack of employment opportunities and economic disparities between local people and foreign investors and expats. One such example was the graffiti plastered on several walls in the city of Fier. The words "Bankers leave" were displayed accompanied with a crossed out human face, and with the text "Risk" written underneath.[297] Such writings were indicative of a growing opposition demanding that Bankers leave the area, since the company's activities were perceived as a threat to the lives of local residents. A further example is a media report from 2013, posted on YouTube by the TV channel Vizion Plus Albania, documenting one of many community protests.[298] The video shows a road in the middle of Patos-Marinza near the village Kallm I Madh. A large group of men are seen gathering on the road, blocking the road with their bodies. Another shot shows a line of heavy oil trucks and pick-up vehicles being prevented from either entering or leaving the oilfield. The oilfield is

[294] Group interview, Patos-Marinza, September 2018.
[295] See for example VizionPlusAlbania (2013, September 13). Kanali Shtate (2013, November 22).
[296] www.facebook.com/nopetroleum, www.facebook.com/VetVetDyHere.
[297] My photo, 2015, my translation.
[298] VizionPlusAlbania (2013, December 9), my translation.

completely blocked, with men from Kallm I Madh village showing their outrage. A voice-over explains that the men are gathered to protest against the destruction of their local road by the heavy oil traffic as well as the seismic tremors they perceive to have been caused by the oil industry. A journalist asks an older man in a black leather jacket and cap about the men's grievances. He explains: "We want the road to be paved, first of all; second, the seismic events; third, the environmental pollution".[299] This video thus articulates that the destruction of local roads, the creation of earth tremors and environmental pollution are damages that Bankers' activities are responsible for.

Similar grievances were expressed in Facebook groups created by local residents. In one Facebook post, a map of Albania is displayed as a container with a layer of oil in the bottom and an oil pump extracting the oil on top. The picture states "Endure Albania! The end is near!"[300] It understands the country's oil resources as a burden that must be tolerated until all oil has been fully extracted. One of the 3000 followers of this Facebook page have commented on the post saying: "The end is coming to people not to the oil. People do not be fooled by those corrupt politicians but take the fight in your own hands!".[301] On another Facebook page, red lines cross out Bankers' logo. On the top of the logo it reads: "genocide of the Albanians".[302] These community protests and Facebook posts refer to Bankers' operations as damaging to the local population. Ideas such as 'endurance', 'fight', 'corruption' and 'genocide' are used to frame Bankers' activities as a siege or an 'invasion' rather than as a legitimate 'investment'. This counter-hegemonic discourse clearly states that not everyone is a winner from Bankers' activities; some people are suffering and want its operations to cease. It breaks the narrative of an 'investment' beneficial to all and thereby threatens Bankers' hegemonic position.

But while local communities expressed their strong dissatisfaction from the moment I entered Patos-Marinza in 2010 until I left in the end of 2015, Bankers continued to expand its operations. As mentioned in Chapter Three, civil society organisations in the area were few and state institutions kept a formal and passive role. Patos-Marinza could thus be described as a governance 'vacuum' where conflicts between the company and local resi-

[299] VizionPlusAlbania (2013, December 9), my translation.
[300] @vetvetdyhere (2015a, September 10), my translation.
[301] @vetvetdyhere (2015a, September 10), my translation.
[302] @nopetroleum (2015, April 28), my translation.

dents were left for antagonistic actors to solve. So, in this 'weak state' context, and in light of community protests, what measures did the company take to maintain its position and continue to expand oilfield operations?

The role of IFC's sustainability standards

Regardless of the 'weak state' situation and the lack of civil society in Patos-Marinza, the local protests against Bankers' oil operations nonetheless reached the international community by way of the Compliance Advisor/Ombudsman (CAO), an independent recourse mechanism financed by the IFC, where people affected by IFC financed projects can send their grievances and ask for support. In March 2013, CAO received a formal complaint from an environmental leader representing the community of Zharrza in Patos-Marinza oilfield.[303] In the *CAO Case Progress Report* from 2016 it is summarised that "[t]he complaint raises concerns about the impact on local communities of the extraction techniques used by Bankers at the Patos-Marinza oilfield, and questions Bankers' compliance with IFC's sustainability standards."[304] Just as in the Bankwatch report, mentioned above, the IFC standards were used as a reference point for the CAO complainant, a formulated sustainability policy to which Bankers' practices could easily be compared. A similar reference to the IFC standards was made by Bankers' representative Rezart in an interview, arguing that the concept of 'invasion', picked up by disgruntled local residents, originated from the implementation of IFC's standards in the area:

> Sara – But do you think this approach, the IFC approach, do you think it changed the communities' view of the foreign company?
>
> Rezart – Of course!
>
> Sara – In what way?
>
> Rezart – I would say something, [laughing] now they were considering foreigners like 'invaders' [...] they [the communities] thought that they had a lot of rights, and influence on the business, which, I cannot say that they should not be part of our decision-making process, but they should not influence. While the communities, the perception that they got from the way how IFC implemented their standards, they thought that they had the right to influence our business. And because we

[303] CAO (2013a).
[304] CAO (2016).

> [Bankers] were being stronger, and not following what they [the communities] were asking, then they totally changed perception about us.[305]

According to Rezart, IFC's standards introduced a new discourse into the area in which local residents perceived they had the right to influence the business. When Bankers did not comply with the community's demands, the residents started to describe Bankers' operations as an 'invasion', at least this is how Rezart saw things. This view is similar to the process I describe in my autobiographical narrative at the beginning of this chapter, where the introduction of the IFC standards were met by scepticism from Bankers' management:

Internally in Bankers, these meetings [consultation meetings with local communities] were discussed with concerns; this was the first time a formal consultation process had been implemented in the area and actors within Bankers were worried that they would stir up feelings of discontent among the residents.[306]

The internal perception was thus that the consultation process was dangerous for the company – a way of putting ideas in the heads of residents they would otherwise not have. From this perspective, the practices advocated in IFC's sustainability standards were not viewed as a tool for the consolidation of the company's power in the area, but rather as a threat to corporate hegemony. The threat was precisely the emergence of an alternative discourse that might alter residents' views on the company.

However, while some internal actors within Bankers saw IFC's sustainability standards as a threat to corporate hegemony, their implementation also provided Bankers with an opportunity to underline its hegemonic narrative of an investment that benefited everyone. In that way the 'alternative' point of reference promoted by the IFC standards is still a discursive formation that takes for granted certain assumptions of the corporate hegemonic narrative, for example that the area is articulated as an 'oilfield' and the company activities as an 'investment'. On this particular point, the reader may disagree, thinking: *But Bankers is investing in Albania! That is not a discourse it is the reality!* In fact, this particular thought provides a clue to understanding the hegemonic status of the discourse framing Bankers' operations as an 'investment' – deemed 'objectively' the right way to conceptualise what Bankers was doing in Albania. With their loan

[305] Interview, Bankers representative, October–November 2017.
[306] Autobiographical narrative, written in 2016.

agreement, IFC and EBRD joined Bankers in an international alliance for an 'investment' that would 'modernise' and 'clean up' the oilfield. The obligatory implementation of sustainability standards, which came attached with these loan agreements, brought with it a promise to strengthen corporate-community relations, using internationally recognised processes such as stakeholder engagement, grievance management and social impact assessments to mitigate impacts, "as a way of doing business in a sustainable way".[307] While this may sound promising for advocates of corporate social responsibility, it will sound the alarm for agonistic pluralists who embrace conflict as a necessary ingredient in all modes of social relation. Sustainability standards promise that investments can be carried out just as before while potential negative impacts on the environment and the local community will be mitigated. IFC's standards thus provided a slight amendment to Bankers' hegemonic narrative, a strategy in which the company can be seen to be criticising itself in order to avoid reputational damage. Cederström and Marinetto identify this as a core characteristic of CSR: "a strategy that makes the corporation appear on the same side as critics".[308] From this perspective, the sustainability standards are a hegemonic intervention, a promise of a win-win situation in which the company can gain profits while the environment is cleaned up and the community develops economically. A counter-hegemonic vision for Patos-Marinza can with this promise be even harder to articulate – the area *is* an oilfield and *everyone* benefits from its expansion.

The sustainability standards can thus be viewed as both a promise and a threat, depending on which interests are taken into consideration. Some corporate managers, who saw the sustainability standards as an introduction of a counter-hegemonic discourse in the area, a way of stirring up community discontent, may have perceived them as a threat. Other corporate managers, as well as advocates for consensual CSR, may instead regard them as an opportunity for building international and local alliances by promising benefits for all, where corporations project themselves as potential allies in the quest for a sustainable society. Environmental activists may, on the other hand, see the introduction of sustainability standards as a threat to proper and necessary change away from the oil industry, which the realisation of a sustainable society requires. Here, pluralistic agonists would agree, understanding that the introduction of

[307] IFC (2012b), p. i.

[308] Cederstöm & Marinetto (2013), p. 426.

sustainability standards, entailing consensus solutions and 'benefits to all', can strengthen the hand of corporate hegemony.

While this discussion highlights the ideological effects of sustainability standards, these standards also have local practical implications when implemented by corporations. In understanding how Bankers could control Patos-Marinza and continue oilfield operations, it is important to understand the practical implications regarding how the sustainability standards were implemented. This will be my focus in the following chapters. It is the combination of ideological and practical implications, both of which can be understood as discursive articulations, which constitutes Bankers' hegemony.

The end of western hegemony

On the 29th of September 2016, Bankers announced that the Chinese investment company, Geo-Jade Petroleum Corporation, had acquired all issued and outstanding common shares.[309] As a consequence, a Chinese senior management took over the direction of the company and the loans to IFC and the EBRD were repaid. Western corporate hegemony in Patos-Marinza was over.

It is Bankers' double-edged corporate story, about 'success' and 'conflict', 'clean up' and 'pollution', 'development' and 'exploitation', which I will continue to address in the following chapters. In this chapter you have been introduced to the hegemonic discourse of Bankers' activities as an 'investment' and the antagonistic, counter-hegemonic discourse that portrayed Bankers' operations as an 'invasion'. You have also seen how sustainability standards can be used to strengthen a hegemonic narrative of a 'successful' and 'responsible' company, as well as how they can be perceived as challenging corporate practices through the introduction of a point of reference for counter-hegemonic mobilisation. However, while sustainability standards may be a useful reference for criticising the company, I have also discussed (and will continue to discuss in the following chapters) their limited potential for creating a real alternative to the oil industry, that is, a new hegemonic project that would frame the region in other terms than an 'oilfield'. The sustainability standards thus seemed to strengthen the hegemonic view of the area as an oilfield, only to emphasise that a few amendments had to be made to make Bankers' project beneficial for all.

[309] Bankers (2016f).

By contrasting the concepts of the 'investment' and the 'invasion' I aim to reach a better understanding of how speeches, texts, actions and materialisations in Patos-Marinza can be understood as hegemonic and counter-hegemonic articulations. In the following chapters I will focus on three specific areas of company – community interactions. In each case, you will see how these two competing discourses were articulated and confronted with each other. Since I focus on areas in which IFC's standards were guiding Bankers' actions, I will show the practical implications of implementing concrete sustainability standards and how these functioned to strengthen corporate power.

CHAPTER 5
"They are inside our house"

Imagine that you live in an area surrounded by agricultural fields. In the morning you can sit on your veranda and smell the fresh air of dew before the sun becomes too hot. In the evenings the stars shine brightly as no city lights compete with their presence. Your family is not rich but the produce from your land is enough to keep you all well fed and properly dressed. You dream of buying a tractor and send your brilliant daughters to the capital for university studies. One day two men come to visit you. They tell you that they are trying to find a place for a new oil lease. You have heard rumours about this company from distant neighbours. The money they pay is more than lands could produce in a year. You also know what they want in order to rent your land. They want you to give them a share. But you are proud. You do not promise them anything. After a few visits they approach your neighbour instead. He is not so proud. His son is in prison. A new oil lease in built and equipped with roads, wells, oil deposits and rigs that frequent the area. Gases weighing down in heavy clouds now replace the fresh morning air. You have to eat your breakfast behind closed windows. In the nights the spotlights and noise from the oil lease scare away the brilliance and music of the stars. You think of moving but cannot afford it. Maybe the men will approach you again in the future. Next time you won't be so proud.

In this chapter I will look at Bankers' land rental process as the first of three areas of company-community interaction in which Bankers' hegemony was both enforced and challenged. From my time in Patos-Marinza I learned that the process of land acquisition, how land is rented by oil companies and how new oil leases are planned and developed, is key to understanding the struggles present when an oilfield on private land is expanding. While until now I have discussed Bankers' hegemony as asserting itself by means of a 'universally beneficial' narrative, land rental processes show how this corporate hegemonic discourse was articulated and stabilised in concrete material practices and with streams of money, while IFC's sustainability standards played a vital part in legitimising this entire process.

Similar to the previous chapter, I will describe Bankers' operations from two separate perspectives. The first is linked to the corporate hegemonic discourse of the 'investment', which describes the area as an 'oilfield' where problematical illegal residences have been built. In this perspective, Bankers' land rental processes are described as transparent and mutually beneficial market-based transactions based on IFC's sustainability standards.[310] In this discourse, land payments are depicted as making a substantial contribution to the local area while residents are portrayed as 'greedy' subjects, all of whom want a piece of the pie. The opposite perspective is linked to the counter-hegemonic discourse of the 'invasion'. In this discourse, the area of Patos-Marinza is described as a 'home' and an 'agricultural area'. Bankers' land rental process is in this perspective emphasised as informal and conflict ridden, and the construction of wells is associated with negative material effects on local residents and farmers.

My analysis in this chapter will highlight material and economic aspects of corporate hegemony, in particular the land on which the oilfield developed, and the streams of money that went into the pockets of dominant and subordinate groups. The focus on land acquisition shows that Bankers' dominance of Patos-Marinza was not simply predicated on the company's status as a legal concessionaire. In order to get access to land, money transactions were needed in order to make private landowners agree to sublet their land to the company. While Bankers described its land rental processes as voluntary, market-based, and implemented according to IFC sustainability standards,[311] it was also accompanied with grievances about impacts on adjacent landowners and rumours of clandestine practices. Now let us start from the 'investment' perspective where the 'oilfield' is defined and materialised, leading to the view that the local residents were the principal problem in corporate-community conflicts.

The spread of illegal residences in an 'oilfield'

Since the collapse of the communist regime, unregulated construction has been a widespread issue in Albania.[312] Hoxha's regime regulated the construction of residences within villages by residential borders, marked on maps as yellow lines. This system was abandoned with the collapse of the communist system in the 1990s, when new constructions without permits

[310] See Annex 3 for an outline if IFC's performance standards.

[311] Bankers Petroleum (2011a).

[312] UNEP (2000), p 14.

flourished, leading to an expansion of village borders and new residential areas formed on previously agricultural land.[313] A similar development was present in Patos-Marinza where villages within the oilfield spread outwards in all directions while squatters built houses with oil wells sometimes incorporated into their backyards.[314] The Albanian state did nothing to stop these developments, and therefore subsequent conflicts with the local population pertaining to land and impacts from oil wells became a matter for concessionary companies to handle. In one interview, a local government representative highlighted this proximity between oil industry and residences as the main issue in Patos-Marinza, complaining that the central government did not do its part in the concession agreement:

> The company and the [central] government have an agreement and each party should follow the obligations of the concession. The houses and the wells are so close to each other. When the company is extracting oil it is impacting on people. The company is doing its activity, but people live there.[315]

The view that the Albanian (local and central) government was responsible for letting local residences expand illegally was common within Bankers during my time with the company, and it was a view also expressed in many of the interviews. In one interview, the Bankers' representative, Rezart, explained:

> Because we [Bankers] are now, currently, suffering from the problems that are created from local government, from government in general. So, they [communities] have built houses all over the place, illegal houses, and now we are paying the consequences of that, which is not our fault. But if we would have taken a different approach, and would have local government involved in this process, I would say we would not have the problems we have right now.[316]

Rezart is thus placing the blame for the issues in Patos-Marinza on the government and the on lack of regulation. He provides an account in which Bankers is the victim of a regulatory 'vacuum' and 'suffers' the consequences of the lack of overall land planning. Another Bankers' represen-

[313] Hedlund & Sjöberg (2003).
[314] Bankers Petroleum (2012a), p. 10.
[315] Interview, local government representative, October–November 2017.
[316] Interview, Bankers representative, October–November 2017.

tatives, Jonida, gave a similar account about illegal residences and explained that the proximity between residences and oil wells led to conflicts, owing to a clash between residential and industrial standards:

> The problem is that we have this illegal building spree around the oilfield, so instead of having like old Marinza [village] of [19]58, now we have a new Marinza that is built, basically in the oilfield. And you have Belina [village] that is very close to the oilfield. Now, inside the village we are not operating but in close proximity to the village we operate. [...] sometimes what is industrial and what is residential is like four metres away, which is not the best of situations. [...] there are certain standards of operations in the oilfield which is industrial. And four metres away, on the other side of the road, you have residences, and these residences should apply [standards] to residential areas, the level of noise should be at the [level of] residential areas, but also the level of release [gas emissions]. So, when they [local residents] come and complain we show them we are within the norm and we *are* within the norm for industrial areas, but we are not within the norm for residential areas.[317]

Jonida thus attributes the conflicts between the oil industry and the local residents to the lack of government intervention and the expansion of residential areas. While Bankers can be described as complying with industrial standards, its own actions are insufficient, she explains, as residences are so close to the oil wells. The area is thus defined primarily as an area for oil extraction; it is not the industry but the presence of local residents in the area that is the problem.

Desirable land payments and community 'greed'

The hegemonic discourse of the 'investment' as beneficial to local residents, and the general development of the region, was strengthened by Bankers' land rental practices. These had an undeniable economic impact in Patos-Marinza where money was distributed to a fortunate percentage of the population. The importance of land rental payments from Bankers to local landowners was something that I experienced first-hand in my work. In the following autobiographical narrative, I describe my experiences from Bankers' land rental practices and the importance of land rental incomes to local communities.

[317] Interview, Bankers representative, October–November 2017.

A community survey that Bankers' Community Relations Department completed during 2015 showed that 10–20% of the households in Patos-Marinza villages were benefitting from Bankers' land rental contracts, meaning that the remaining 80–90% were not.[318] The practical and emotional implications of this distribution of land contracts were jealous residents who saw their neighbours getting rich from the generous payments that a land contract with Bankers gave. They themselves were stuck with a new well lease next to their land and the noise and smell impacts that came with it. With few other income opportunities in the region, signing a land contract with Bankers was like winning the lottery. A contract would pay between 2–4 dollars per square meter meaning that a contract for 5000 square meters of land would give an extra income of 20,000 dollars a year. Compared to the average annual salary for teachers (4800 dollars) or security guards (2400 dollars), an income from land rental could fund a brand-new life for the whole family. Photomontages posted in local Facebook groups revealed the economic importance that land contracts had for the fortunate few. In one of these pictures, a man with a large moustache and a huge bottle of Raki (home-made spirit) in his hand says: "For this day I had saved it, the day when the company [Bankers] rented my land". [319] In another, a little girl with a red scarf looks dreamily into the eyes of a little boy and says: "Why do you want to marry me, do you love me that much?", to which the boy answers: "I love you because you have land in Marinza my darling, and you have money because Bankers has rented your land. For you I don't care much".[320] The jokes in these community Facebook groups reflected the reality my colleagues and I were seeing daily in our meetings with residents in the area. Behind grievances about blocked drainages, air quality or dust were poorly hidden hopes that Bankers would rent a piece of land. Hopes that were often openly expressed when the formal grievance process was replaced by informal coffee breaks. The lack of employment opportunities and the poorly developed agricultural practices meant that renting a piece of land were the only imaginable way to improve quality of life for many residents. The importance of land rental incomes together with the complicated land ownership situation, where each plot could be owned by as many as ten different people, gave plenty of room for conflicts to arise.[321]

[318] Numbers varied between villages and should be read as an approximation. A representative sample was difficult to obtain in this context, due to lack of correct population registers and migration of residents.
[319] @vetvetdyhere (2014a, 23 July).
[320] @vetvetdyhere (2014b, 20 March).

In my autobiographical narrative I highlight the importance of land payments and the pressure felt by my colleagues and I from local residents who wanted to be part of Bankers' land rental scheme. In an area where few other income opportunities were available, land rental was perceived as something positive.[322] However, it was also a source of constant conflict in the villages. These conflicts were often disregarded as being about 'jealousy' or 'greed' within the company, a discourse that is articulated in the above autobiographical narrative where I refer to protests from those local residents not included in Bankers' land rental agreements. I do not describe these as valid claims for a more equal distribution of oil industry incomes, but I disregard them as a result of "jealous residents who saw their neighbours get rich".[323] In another section, I discount the grievances of residents from local communities as "hopes that Bankers would rent a piece of land"[324] and rather as related to project impacts. This resonates with the account from the Bankers' manager in the previous chapter who claimed that when residents "are unable to find employment in the company [...] they start to complain". Bankers' employment and land acquisition practices thus had a similar effect in the area both as promises that residents could be part of the corporate expansion and as reasons used to delegitimise residents' grievances caused by unfulfilled 'hopes' and 'jealousy'.

The perspective of local residents as 'jealous' and 'greedy' was also prominent in many of the interviews with corporate representatives. Lidia, a Bankers' contractor representative, described Bankers' land rental as:

> a good thing. Just letting money to people and the price was very good, so it helped people. But you must know that in a small area people feel jealous a little bit, like you know, even if they respect Bankers' standards, the criteria, people say "oh why did you rent that land", or "why did you rent that land and you did not rent my land as well". So this happens everywhere.[325]

Lidia thus describes land rentals as positive, a source of income for residents, but also as a source for conflicts to arise due to jealousy. Lidia describes the company "standards" and "criteria" for land rental as something that people "respect" but which do not hinder residents from com-

---

[321] Autobiographical narrative, written in 2016.
[322] Bankers (2015a).
[323] Autobiographical narrative, written 2016.
[324] Autobiographical narrative, written 2016.
[325] Interview, Bankers' contractor representative, October–November 2017.

plaining. Ervis, a former representative of one of Bankers' contractors, described conflicts with neighbours and family members as a continuous struggle in the land rental process:

> The problem was not the landowner who was giving Bankers the land for the [drilling] pad, [it] was his brother who was left outside, and his neighbour that he had on the left side, Sara, wow, it was hard over there.[326]

The conflicts between the company and communities are thus described as based on the greed of local residents, and of everyone else wanting to have their share of land rental incomes. A local government representative made a similar analysis of these conflicts.

> The main factor for the conflicts between the communities and the company is the mentality of the people, in my opinion. Before, during totalitarianism, it was another mentality. Now life is dependent on making money. [Before] there was more equality between people and people did not think so much about making money. The second is that the level of information that people had about the society and the world was very limited compared to now. People now have information and try to make money. A lot of land is rented by the company and this is a way for people to make money.[327]

According to the government representative, residents' access to information and their desire to make money are described as the two main factors causing problems. The period of communism is used as a point of reference in this statement. Life during communism was, according to the interviewee, more equal and people did not have access to information. Now people "have information and try to make money". It is thus the "mentality of the people" and not corporate practice that is the problem, at least, according to the interviewee.

In several statements from the 'corporate bloc', local residents are articulated as subordinate and problematic. This is connected to the designation of Patos-Marinza as an 'oilfield'. If the area is an 'oilfield' rather than a 'home', local residents are disturbances rather than legitimate subjects that can demand their rights. In an interview with Rezart, a Bankers' representative, this designation of the area prevails.

[326] Interview, former representative, Bankers' contractor, October–November 2017.
[327] Interview, representative, local government, October–November 2017.

> [Patos-Marinza] is special. So [local residents] are, they are our neighbours. But I would not say they are our neighbours, they are inside our house. We have an expression in Albania that "the person who rents the house makes the decisions when the house will be renovated even though the owner should make that decision". So, they [residents] were feeling like they have the right to force us to make the decision that they want, or that would be in their benefit.[328]

The Albanian expression to which Rezart refers is an ironic way to describe the difficulties that can arise from renting out your house to someone. All of a sudden it is the tenant who makes the decisions regarding the house rather than its owner. Bankers is renting agricultural land from residents yet, in this statement, it is the residents who are 'renting' and Bankers who are 'owning' the land. That the residents are "inside our house" spells trouble for Rezart; it means that they think they can tell the company what to do. It also means that they could potentially be thrown out since Bankers is portrayed as the owner. In this hegemonic discourse, Patos-Marinza is not a 'home' to residents. Instead it is Bankers' house, i.e. an 'oilfield' first of all and local residents are an obstacle for its expansion.

While my autobiographical narrative emphasises the economic importance that land payments had to the poverty-stricken area, it also highlights conflicts that arose as part of these payments. These conflicts were linked to the unequal distribution of land incomes and the impacts that followed when new well leases were built. Let us now turn to examine the counter-hegemonic discourse in which these impacts were articulated.

The construction of wells in a 'home' and an 'agricultural area'

The other side of this story is that Patos-Marinza is a place called 'home' where people live and farm, and where the oil industry has relentlessly expanded. Bankers' did not only take over old wells from Albpetrol, they also drilled new ones, constructed new leases and roads, expanded drilling pads and introduced new oil tanks and generators. The expansion of operations that Bankers' CEO described to potential investors in the video in the previous chapter – "when we started it was around 600 barrels [of oil] a day, its almost 20.000 barrels [of oil] a day now" – did not only provide an interesting investment opportunity, it also had social costs. Jonida, a Bankers representative, spoke of these costs during an interview:

[328] Interview, Bankers representative, October–November 2017.

> This period of time [between] 2008/2009 and 2014, was the best time for the company ever, like, you know, we increased the production, we increased profit, but at the same time we increased also the impacts on both environment and local communities. [...] In terms of you know, noise, in terms of traffic, and in terms of dust generated, there were like, more and more than it was before. Before we had one drilling rig, now we had six; and if we had two service rigs [rigs maintaining oil wells], now we had twelve. You don't have to be a genius to understand that these things make noise, these things operate, and in close proximity to residential areas, it's something that anyone can sort of witness by paying a short visit to Patos-Marinza.[329]

The growth of oil industry activities in Patos-Marinza, leading to an undesired proximity between houses and oil wells, is thus described as the foundation for conflicts between the company and the community in this statement. Jonida mentions noise, dust and traffic – impacts that have been created due to the oil industrial expansion. Even if these impacts may seem trivially expressed in this particular statement, it is nonetheless an acknowledgement of some negative effects from oil industry. Another of Bankers' representatives, Ditjon, similarly described how the expansion of Bankers' operations led to increasing community complaints:

> I think starting from 2011–2012, that was the time when the company was doing a lot of operations and started to get larger and larger, and as we we're becoming bigger, our operations expanded in different areas. I think that we were expanding in that size that we were going to close to the communities and the lands. I think that because of too many operations that we had during the time, too much traffic with the trucks and too many people moving around. So yeah, that was the time when we started to get complaints from the communities.[330]

The growth of the oilfield, that Jonida and Ditjon are describing, is shown on satellite maps from Patos-Marinza during these years.[331] A comparison of maps between 2010 and 2016 – the time span when Bankers greatly expanded its operations in the area and implemented IFC's sustainability standards – shows a dramatic increase in oil leases near Patos-Marinza villages.[332] That increase, based on renting privately owned agricultural

[329] Interview, Bankers representative, October–November 2017.

[330] Interview, Bankers representative, October–November 2017.

[331] See Google-Earth, search for 'Marinëz, Albania'.

[332] Leases are shown as white surfaces and villages as small red and brown dots on Google-Earth.

land, made Bankers one of the largest taxpayers and private employers in Albania.[333] But, it was also the source of tensions between local villages and the company. The same geographical area was designated to incorporate oil extraction and agricultural land, heavy trucking and health centres, lease constructions and private residences. Bankers' rental of private land was foundational in making this expansion of the oilfield possible.

In 2015, I was part of conducting a community survey for Bankers with the five villages in Patos-Marinza that were most impacted by oil industry.[334] The purpose was to evaluate Bankers' CSR programme and suggest actions going forward. As I refer to in my autobiographical narrative above, one of the main findings from the survey was the low percentage of households benefiting from Bankers' land rental contracts, as well as oil industry employment. During internal company discussions, I often heard claims that local communities should be grateful for oil industry operations; after all, had they not benefited from employment opportunities and land rental contracts? The community survey showed that around 10–20% of households in the area benefited from land rental payments while 10–20% had one or several persons employed in the oil industry.[335] While these numbers highlight that the oil industry was indeed an important source of income for many households, they also indicate that a majority of households were excluded from its streams of money.

During my time with Bankers, local communities often articulated an understanding of the land rental process that broke with the corporate narrative. Instead, the counter-hegemonic discourse emphasised the negative impacts from Bankers' land rental on residents who did not benefit from rental payments. One example is a news video from the TV-Channel Vizion Plus Albania, published in March 2015, showing a family protesting against the impact from Bankers' operations near their land.[336] The video shows a rural road near the city of Patos where Bankers' and Bankers' contractor trucks are lined up in a row. A man who sits in the middle of the road with a little boy in his lap blocks the trucks from travelling. The man and boy look distressed and worried; the former proclaims to journalists congregated that Bankers has destroyed his business since they built a new lease right next to his land. Now the land is being polluted with gases from

[333] Bankers Petroleum (2016d).
[334] Bankers Petroleum (2015a), p. 2.
[335] Bankers Petroleum (2015a), pp. 7-8.
[336] VizionPlusAlbania (2015, March 16).

oil extraction. This video thus shows the results of a land-rental process that seems far from beneficial to 'all'. The landowner who received money from the lease may be happy but his neighbour, the man sitting in the middle of the road with his son, has to carry the impacts of the change from agricultural to oil industrial land.

In interviews conducted with residents, many stories were brought up that described how the proximity between farming land, homes and oil wells impacted on their lives. A man living in Patos-Marinza, Taulant, and his son, Florenc, told us the following story when we visited their home:

> Florenc – We have a land plot over there [pointing], which is now destroyed. [...] It has slid down because they [Bankers] have been injecting [fluid into wells for enhanced oil recovery].
>
> Taulant – That well has been taken over by the Canadians. It was working during the old system [Albpetrol] for around 20–30 years. It is close to our land, next to our land. In the old system we did not have any problem with the works on the well, but as soon as the Canadian company came, they worked one or two years and the land started sliding.
>
> Florenc – Because they were injecting, they were injecting water.
> Taulant – It destroyed the land completely, it all slid, even the well slid downwards. The whole land [slide] and now it cannot yield crops.
>
> Florenc – It cannot be worked on; it has been like this for ten years now.
>
> Taulant – We made the request at your [Bankers] offices, and in the beginning they said good words, but then they changed their minds and said that the land had slid due to natural causes and they could not do anything.
>
> Taulant – You can come and see for yourselves and you will say that the farmer [referring to himself] is right. [The land] it's not workable, and the municipality says that they cannot convince the Canadians on this issue because the Canadians are very powerful.[337]

Similar to the man on the road, Taulant and Florenc articulate negative impacts from Bankers' land acquisition and operations. The change from the old operations during Albpetrol to the modernisation of the oilfield during Bankers is understood to have caused the land to slide, making their land useless. In contrast to the man in the video, Taulant and Florenc did

[337] Family visit, Patos-Marinza, September 2018.

not engage in road protests as a way to complain about their difficult situation. They instead went through Bankers' grievance mechanism, and contacted the local authorities. However, their disappointment with the lack of support given by these institutions is evident. Bankers blamed the landslide on natural causes while the municipality referred to the company as too "powerful". In either case the outcome was the same: there was nothing they could do.

Similar to Jonida, the Bankers representative who mentioned negative impacts from increased oil operations, many residents mentioned disturbances from Bankers' operations, for example noise, dust and traffic. In a group interview, the resident Berti described the noises from oilrigs operating close to his house:

> Those wells are close to the house, and when the service rigs come, they work 24 hours without stopping and there is a lot of noise. The noise travels, it flies, and in the summer, we leave the windows open because we do not have air-condition in the house, and the noise is unbearable.[338]

While noise, dust and the impact of traffic sound trivial when told from the side of a Bankers' employee, they are in Berti's account filled with meaning and connected to the daily life of the villagers. Berti uses his bodily experiences to describe how the noise "is unbearable", how it impacts on his ability to sleep during hot summer months. Another negative impact frequently mentioned by residents was connected to the drainage system in the area. In the same group interview, Armand described both the uneven distribution of land rental payments as well as the impacts on adjacent land and drainage canals:

> Why would someone get 1 million Leke [around 8000 Euros converted from old Leke] while I am left and the drainage canal is not excavated? So that this person can stay calm with 1 million Leke while I cannot work on my land? This is the problem, so the well is built on someone's land but next to that is [Ergys, Edison and Berti], they are all in a row. So, the company rents someone's land but at the same time they destroy the structure of the land and they block the drainage system. When the river floods the land gets flooded and it takes one month for the water to get drained but this guy who has taken the money for the

[338] Group interview, Patos-Marinza, September 2018.

> land, he is okay. But what about the other people who suffer the consequences? What about us?[339]

These stories show that for those who do not benefit from oil industry employment or land rental, Patos-Marinza remains primarily a home and an agricultural area. When Patos-Marinza is reclaimed as a 'home' and as a place to grow crops for incomes, Bankers' operations become a threat to human life and security, becoming an 'invasion' of the 'home' as the local area is, bit by bit, transformed into an 'oilfield'.

Performance standard 5 and voluntary land acquisition

When representatives of Bankers describe the issues surrounding expanding 'illegal' residential areas and the lack of land regulation in the area, they fail to acknowledge how the company has itself benefited from this unregulated environment, how it has provided Bankers with an opportunity to expand its operations. It is, in fact, the counter-hegemonic articulations by local residents that show how the unregulated environment has provided the company with an opportunity to expand very close to residences without government interference. Both the hegemonic and the counter-hegemonic discourses thus paint a picture of an anarchistic environment in which the construction of residences and wells flourish while government institutions remain passive. So how did Bankers' handle this conflictual environment in line with its CSR policy? When Bankers' signed the loan agreement with IFC and EBRD in 2009, the company agreed to follow the banks' social and environmental policies including detailed guidance notes for how companies should manage land acquisition processes.[340] The remainder of this chapter will focus on what these formal policies stipulated, how they were implemented and how residents perceived them.

As I underlined in Chapter One, when a company is responsible for a land-based development project, questions regarding environmental and social impacts are put at the forefront. Displacement or resettlement of project-impacted populations has been identified as one of the major effects of land-based development with large negative impacts on residents' socio-economic lives being a principal consequence.[341] Therefore, one of

[339] Group interview, Patos-Marinza, September 2018.
[340] IFC (2012b).
[341] Cernea (2003); Choi (2015).

the main areas of IFC's and EBRD's environmental and social policies relates to companies' land acquisition and recommendations to avoid the expropriation of land and the involuntary resettlement of people.[342] IFC's Performance Standard 5 gives detailed guidelines for compensation and mitigation when a project leads to involuntary resettlement.[343] The expropriation of land is thus a controversial use of government force that IFC and EBRD advise corporate clients to avoid. Instead, IFC recommends that free market-based transactions should be used when possible. IFC argues that when market-based mechanisms are used, mitigation measures described in Performance Standard 5 do not apply, since such transactions are based on the 'free will' of all parties. IFC writes:

> This Performance Standard [5] does not apply to resettlement resulting from *voluntary land transactions* (i.e., market transactions in which the seller is not obliged to sell and the buyer cannot resort to expropriation or other compulsory procedures sanctioned by the legal system of the host country if negotiations fail).[344]

Voluntary land transactions are thus seen as the ideal. In the cases where market-based transactions are implemented, Performance Standard 5 stipulates that no other mitigation measures are needed, since negative impacts are expected to be negligible. During the expansion of its operations, Bankers followed these advices and did not use expropriation as a way of accessing land. By not being able to rely on the Albanian government to expropriate land, the concession agreement was not enough for Bankers to ensure the expansion of its operations in Patos-Marinza. The company needed the 'voluntary' agreement of residents to rent pieces of agricultural land for the construction of new leases.

The result of introducing IFC's and EBRD's sustainability standards to Bankers was that a *Project Information Document* was written with the aim of informing landowners about Bankers' land rental processes. In the document it is stated that:

> Bankers Land Access Process is done according to Global and European Standards including: All Bankers Land Rental Agreements are voluntary; If residents are not willing to rent land, Bankers do not use the land; Bankers does not use any land if landowners will have to be

[342] EBRD (2014b); IFC (2002).
[343] IFC (2012b).
[344] IFC (2012b), p. 2, my emphasis.

> moved from their buildings or houses; Bankers makes every effort to minimize impacts on residents land or access and includes this in Project design.[345]

The information document states that Bankers does not use expropriation but that all land contracts are "voluntary", i.e. seen as based on 'free will'. Furthermore, even though Bankers' land acquisition is designated as 'voluntary', the leaflet describes how IFC's Performance Standard 5 applies to Bankers' land acquisition:

> Bankers Land Access Process complies with International Finance Corporation (IFC) Performance Standard 5 [...]. This ensures that Bankers reduces social and economic impacts of land access or restrictions on residents use of land by: Providing compensation for land use; Informing residents of Land Access Process; Conducting prior and inclusive consultation with all residents; and Ensuring no construction until compensation agreements are signed.[346]

According to the document, the formal procedure of Bankers' land acquisition can thus be understood as an exemplary process in line with IFC's sustainability standards, including avoidance of expropriation of land and houses, and consultation with landowners and their neighbours to minimise impacts. In terms of CSR, the company seems to be applying its land acquisition process in a way that brings benefits to the local population in the form of market-based land payments rather than harming them by forcibly moving people.

Informal land rental processes and control of community voices

In the corporate hegemonic discourse, the legitimate 'investor' Bankers is contributing to Patos-Marinza in the form of high land rental payments and in accordance with the guidelines of IFC's Performance Standard 5. In contrast, the counter-hegemonic discourse, according to which Patos-Marinza is a 'home' and Bankers' activities are an 'invasion', portrays Bankers as an actor employing clandestine practices alongside its formal procedures.

In the following autobiographical narrative, I describe a company-community meeting that took place in Patos-Marinza in the fall of 2015. In this

[345] Bankers Petroleum (2011a).
[346] Bankers Petroleum (2011a).

meeting, my colleague and I presented the results of a company survey for a group of men from one of the oilfield villages. Due to internal conflicts and a lack of transparency regarding land rental data within the company we did not have direct access to land contracts. Instead we had gone the 'back-route' trough a village survey to try and understand how the local communities benefited from the land that Bankers' rented in each village. Our interest in the land acquisition process was spurred by insistent stories among staff and residents about deals between Bankers' and governmental representatives during land negotiations. In the community meeting described below, the data we presented corresponded to these articulations about informal land rental processes, which were circulating in the company and within local communities at the time.

> The room was filled with tension as the dry statistics were projected on the wall in the small container office. Our survey among residents in one of the villages in Patos-Marinza Oilfield indicated that a sizable percentage of the land rented by Bankers belonged to non-residents. The reactions that my colleague and I had been waiting for materialised themselves. An upset murmur rose among the men in the room as the reality behind the statistics started to come alive. An older man stood up with a serious expression: "*We demand from the company to show us who is the owner of this land*". We explained calmly that the company land contracts were confidential and that such information could not be disclosed. I had become a full-fledged company representative during these years, as a coordinator at Bankers' Community Relations Department I was able to select my truths and argue in a way that could not be contradicted. However, I suggested, the man could ask the local government to show the cadastral map of the area that should include the names of landowners. I looked into his eyes and we both knew what the other was thinking, that this data was an indication of some accuracy behind the insistent rumours among residents and Bankers' staff members. The rumours were saying that actors within Bankers collaborated with the local government when rental agreements were signed. Ownership of communal land was privatised, names adjusted, and land contracts signed that benefited parties on both sides. The rumours said that huge sums of money were involved; hundreds of thousands of dollars, and the leases that were built on these lands were introducing batteries of oil wells closer and closer to residential areas. Residents had started to protest, claiming that the noise from service rigs at nights was disturbing elderly and infants in their sleep. The smell from gas released during oil extraction became so heavy during mornings and evenings that mothers and fathers worried for the health of their children. Another man at the meeting table

> raised his voice: "*Do you know that the lands on which your wells are built are designated as 'unproductive' ('pa frut') on the cadastral maps? This means that they were not distributed to village households during the 1991 land reform. How can you rent land that has not been distributed to private owners?*" We repeated the official mantra, that land contracts were confidential, that the men should approach their local government to get answers. The men accepted, realised that nothing more could be gained from arguing with us. We had done our job, showed them statistics from Bankers' community survey, adhered to IFC's Performance Standards about 'stakeholder engagement' and 'transparency'. Our presentation moved on to other survey results and the meeting ended in a friendly tone as our community meetings usually did; the men thanked us for the invitation and for listening to their experiences and opinions. "*We will approach the government about the landownership issue*", they said as they left the room. I agreed and encouraged the men to approach the local government, to hold them responsible for the situation in the village. "*We are just an oil company*" I explained, "*we cannot take responsibility for everything that is wrong in your village*".[347]

Based on the 'rumours' and statistics we showed on the wall, participants in the community meeting articulated anger that *their* legitimate benefits from land rental went to people who did not live in the village. They saw this as an indication of truth behind the stories about local government and corporate representatives collaborating to reap the incomes from Bankers' land rentals. This perception also frequently appeared in interviews with residents. Residents described the presence of 'outsiders' who had illegally 'bought' municipal land in the area in order to rent it out to Bankers. Ergys described this issue in a group interview:

> This land that was for pasture before [during communism], for livestock, communal land, now they have built wells on that land; who gets the money from this land rental? Why don't the community get that money for investments? No one knows who takes that money.[348]

Edison, in the same group interview agreed:

[347] Autobiographical narrative, written in 2016.

[348] Group interview, Patos-Marinza, September 2018.

> The biggest thieves here are the people who took the land. People from Durres and Tirana took the land.[349]

Flamur, in another group interview, reasoned in a similar way:

> They come from outside, they take the land from outside, from other villages, from the city. [...] The land is in the village but we do not know who owns the land.[350]

This story, about 'outsiders' being able to buy state owned land in the village for the sake of profiting from Bankers' land rentals, reveal perceptions of injustice among residents. Not only are residents *not* profiting from Bankers' land rental, but outsiders do, and the money, which is perceived as rightfully belonging to the village, lines someone else's pockets.

Another common narrative in relation to the land rental process was that of 'middle men', i.e. corporate actors who controlled the land rental process for their own gain. In the autobiographical narrative below, my colleague and I meet with a man who is angry because he feels deceived by the company. He perceive he has the right to land rental incomes that now goes to his neighbour instead, all due to the actions of 'middle men'.

> The man was standing steadily on the new drilling lease that Bankers had constructed adjacent to his land. He pointed to the access road crossing the river berm just next to the residential area: "*Your trucks pass here even during the night. Our houses are shaking from the vibrations and we cannot sleep. If you don't stop the traffic I will block the road*". My colleague informed him that we would talk to our contractors, tell them to enforce the speed limits so that trucks would not cause vibrations. The man did not look happy. "*I want Bankers to stop using the road. This lease was supposed to be built on my land, which is why I agreed to the road project. You did not keep your promise!*" His story left me confused: Why did we [Bankers] promise the man to rent his land and then change our minds? Different versions were told to me depending on whom I asked. One story was connected to rumours about corruption expressed by the photomontages circulating on Facebook saying that the "middle hand" took half of Bankers' land rental payments[351]. If landowners did not agree to give away that half, the area rented for lease construction would just be moved to another

[349] Group interview, Patos-Marinza, September 2018.
[350] Group interview, Patos-Marinza, September 2018.
[351] @vetvetdyhere (2014c, 20 March).

> piece of land, with the internal motivation to Bankers' management that ownership papers between family members were not in order. Another story was connected to the idea of the local population as poor and greedy, commonly expressed by company representatives and local authorities. This version claimed that when the man was approached about land rental, he wanted Bankers to rent one hectare of land or nothing at all. The man was thus trying to push the company to rent a larger piece of land and thereby receive a higher yearly payment. Since this pressure could not be accepted, Bankers simply moved the future lease to another location with a more collaborative landowner. The man in front of me was insisting on the first story, the one with the middleman, and asked me to raise the question internally about why the lease had been moved. When I did it was word against word. I realised then that grievances about noise and dust, blocked drainages and cracked houses often were hiding other storylines that in the context of rumours and distrust were impossible to delineate. Stories about poverty and unemployment, stories about unfair treatment and middle hands. As the oilfield continued to grow and leases were built closer and closer to residential areas, so did the stories flourish and with them a growing number of grievances to manage.[352]

This encounter, as well as continuous articulations of similar stories within and outside the company, indicated to me that the way land rental practices were implemented diverged from the official company story. According to official documents, Bankers' formal land acquisition process identifies a structured and transparent way to deal with the complex land ownership issues in the area, according to IFC's sustainability standards. However, the stories about middle-hands and clandestine payments suggest that other methods were also employed. In interviews with local residents many stories about informal land rental practices were brought up. One example is Berti, who in a group interview told me how he was approached by Bankers' representatives for a potential land rental but how this opportunity was later withdrawn:

> Berti – They approached me, I made the papers ready and then they left, they flew away.
>
> Sara - So they promised to rent your land?
>
> Berti – Yes, then they took someone else's.

[352] Autobiographical narrative, written in 2016.

> Sara – And why did they do that?
>
> Berti – I didn't pay, eh, they wanted money, instead I asked for the map from them, the map of the project [of the lease construction].
>
> Sara – And then they moved the project?
>
> Bert – Yes
>
> Sara – And what was the cost? How much did they want?
>
> Berti – The first half year of land payments, and afterwards I would get the payments.
>
> Sara – Okay.
>
> Berti – They told me "We will make a well on your land", "Do it!" I said. And then they came another time, "We will make a well on your land", "Do it!" I said. And then yet another time "We will make a well on your land", "Do it!" I said. Three times I said it. But I did not say "Take half of the payment", I could not tell them, I could give them a coffee [small bribe] but I could not say that. So they took their offer and they went to someone else.[353]

Berti's story aligns with the stories of 'middle-men' taking half of the land payments as well as the encounter described in my autobiographical narrative with a man who claimed that a planned Bankers' lease had been changed from his land to someone else's without a valid reason. Several residents in all three villages I visited depicted the same picture about Bankers' land acquisitions. In another group interview, Alban, Fatmir and Ermal explained the process:

> Sara – So how does the process for how the company rents land function here?
>
> Alban – Go and talk to [name of Bankers employee], they know.
>
> Sara – But I do not think they will tell me anything.
>
> Alban – Yes, they will not tell you that they have taken this much money from this person, this much money from another person [...]
>
> Sara – I understand, even in Belina and Marinza people are saying this. But why do people agree to this process?

[353] Group interview, Patos-Marinza, September 2018.

> Alban – So listen, in terms of corruption, this is the lower level. There is corruption in all institutions in Albania. At the prime minister there is corruption, at the company management there is corruption, with Sara there is corruption, it is a system.
>
> Fatmir – People [in the villages] do not agree but they agree to give money because otherwise they are excluded from the land rental incomes and the chance [to rent out land] is given to someone else.
>
> Sara – It's like pressure?
>
> Fatmir – Yes! If you don't give money they will find someone else.
>
> Alban – That's how things work here, even if you have decided not to give money someone else will. I would also do that I'm sorry to say.
>
> Sara – Okay, but do people know this is how it works? So, they offer [money] themselves?
>
> Alban, Fatmir, and Ermal – Yes
>
> Ermal – It's like routine, there is nothing people can do.[354]

The stories of 'middle-men' and pressures on residents' to give up half a year of land rental payments breaks the corporate narrative and strengthens the counter-hegemonic discourse in which Bankers' land acquisitions are portrayed as illegitimate and unjust. Together the stories of 'middle-men' and 'outsiders' paint a picture of Bankers' land rental processes being far from beneficial to the community. Instead Bankers appears to preside over a system in which corruption and injustice flourish.

Residents also described how land rental practices divided the community and prevented certain people from speaking out against the company. The resident Taulant, explained in detail about how company operations had impacted his agricultural land and told us that land rental contracts prevented people from speaking openly:

> Listen now, I will tell you something, if you go to a family who has rented land to the Canadians they will say good things [about the company]. Do you understand? It is because they have received money and if the company hear that they talk badly [about the company] they will take back the land contract.[355]

[354] Group interview, Patos-Marinza, September 2018.
[355] Family visit, Patos-Marinza, September 2018.

Taulant thus perceived that some of his fellow neighbours kept their mouths shut because of fear of losing incomes from land contracts. Even if they felt the same consequences as he did, they did not join him in the grievance process. In another village, Armand complained about the smell of gas from wells and conveyed a similar view about peoples' unwillingness to speak up:

> When the wind comes you can smell the gas. Some people do not complain because they have rented land to Bankers.[356]

These quotes tell similar stories about how land payments hinder communities from speaking with one voice, about happy landowners receiving large payments from Bankers and neighbours being left with the consequences. They indicate that land payments have ended up dividing the community into groups, separating 'winners' and 'losers' from Bankers' project and making community mobilisation harder to accomplish. A wide discrepancy thus exists between, on the one hand, the formal IFC documents where 'market-based' land rental processes are described as 'beneficial' and based on 'free will', and, on the other, the context of pressure and power imbalances that local residents describe.

Extending the corporate alliance through market-based land rentals

In the previous chapter I discussed the concept of the 'investment' as a nodal point in Bankers' hegemonic discourse, linking together other concepts such as 'development', 'clean-up' and 'technology' into a specific worldview. In this chapter, I have further detailed how this discourse, articulated by representatives from Bankers, IFC and EBRD, frame 'voluntary' land rentals in the 'oilfield' as beneficial to all. The link between the conceptualisation of Patos-Marinza as an 'oilfield' and Bankers activities as an 'investment' hides the controversial nature of the company's activities as a domination of a residential area. The articulation of these concepts thus covers over 'the political' nature of Bankers' activities and creates a context in which 'the oilfield' and 'the investment' are seen as objective truths. This is the hegemonic operation of the corporate discourse. The payments for land and the construction of leases, wells and roads are articulations of this

[356] Group interview, Patos-Marinza, September 2018.

discourse in which these activities and artefacts are connected to the nodal point of the 'investment' bringing 'development' and 'technology' to the area. The spread of wells can thus be seen as articulations that enforce Patos-Marinza as 'objectively' an 'oilfield' rather than a 'home'. The discourse around the 'investment' is thus articulated, not only by words but also by money and material artefacts such as leases and wells.

Bankers' representatives, including me, described the land rental process as ridden with conflict due to the 'jealousy' of local residents. In this corporate discourse the residents' 'mentality' was the cause of the conflicts while the company understood itself as a victim of poor state regulation and residential complaints. This discourse thus articulates a relationship between corporate representatives and community members, in which corporate representatives are seen as superior subjects working in accordance with IFC standards while community members are depicted as 'greedy' and 'jealous'. In this corporate discourse the hegemonic 'bloc' becomes a desirable position for subjects to identify with while those complaining about corporate practices are depicted as losers. The payments from land rentals enforce this division between 'winners' and 'losers', an articulation of the hegemonic discourse that takes the form of monetary payments.

But the context of Patos-Marinza also displays resistance and counter-hegemonic articulations. In the counter-hegemonic discourse, Patos-Marina is understood as a 'home' rather than an 'oilfield', and community complaints are instead articulated as legitimate protests held against company operations understood as an 'invasion'. Road blockades, filed grievances and Facebook posts are all examples of counter-hegemonic articulations. The narrative about the 'universally' beneficial land rental process is undermined by stories about damages to agricultural land, drainage problems, and disturbances to residents in the form of noise, dust and smell. The stories, grievances and protests are thus articulations of a counter-hegemonic discourse, which activate 'the political' character of Bankers' operations and question 'the objective' description of the area as an 'oilfield'. The stories from community members reclaim the area as a larger eco-system, rather than a patchwork of small administrative units (land plots) that can be rented on an individual basis. Noise 'flies', drainage systems are blocked and the air is polluted. These impacts make it harder for the incremental land-rental process to be portrayed as 'voluntary' and 'beneficial' to all. Instead, it is a wider residential and agricultural area that is impacted by the expansion of the oil industry.

While IFC's sustainability standards describe expropriation as a controversial process linked to the concept of 'force', private land rental is considered 'free' with potential benefits to all. But this market-based approach excludes alternative uses of Patos-Marinza as an area completely free from the oil industry. Farmers may be free to agree or decline land rental offers, but they do not have a choice when it comes down to living in an area altogether free from oil wells. The oil industry will be forced on them whether they like it or not. While expropriation of land for industry purposes is an openly violent process in which people are resettled from their land, market-based land-rental practices is a hegemonic operation which promises 'free choice' and 'development' but with the outcome that oil industry expands. While an expropriation process may open for a public debate about alternative uses of a geographical area, voluntary land-rentals sneak in behind the scenes and develop an area as it wishes through monetary power and material means, all under the banner of 'free choice'.

Even though Bankers' formal land rental process was communicated as adhering to IFC's sustainability standards, the community perspective on these processes tells another story. The details of Bankers' land rental process point to a clash between the grand neoliberal ideas of freedom and progress and local realities where force is masked as consent and the exploitation of weak land regulation is masked by international standards for 'voluntary' land rentals. It can thus be questioned how voluntary a transaction is when local landowners had few other income opportunities and were placed in competition with one another. When looking closer at Bankers' land rental process, the word 'voluntary' seems to hide more than it reveals. When the company approached residents, the 'choice' with which the residents were left was either to rent land to the company, and to receive a hefty sum of money, or say no and be left with their own agricultural land adjacent to smelly and noisy oil operations. In the discourse articulated by IFC and EBRD, which promotes private 'investments' and a 'transition' to market economy, this choice is considered free. The consequence was that the oilfield could expand on agricultural land without residents having the ability to resist the process. The 'weak state' of Albania is not a problem for Bankers in this context but rather an opportunity to expand an oilfield in close proximity to residential areas. Furthermore, the accounts of 'middle-men' and 'outsiders' indicate that the unequal economic power between the company and residents provided additional opportunities for company actors to pressure residents to agree with practices of corporate expansion and exploitation.

Even though residents were willing to speak openly and in detail about land acquisition practices during the interviews, these were rarely subject to open community grievance or protest during my time with Bankers. The residents' accounts of the silencing effects of land payments may be one reason for this. By applying Gramsci's thoughts, Bankers' land rental practices can be seen as dividing local residents into groups of beneficiaries and losers, into hegemonic allies and subordinates. Following the ideas of Ernesto Laclau, land payments move the antagonistic frontier within the social field and connect some residents to the 'winning side' of the corporate alliance. Potential chains of equivalence between residents are broken in this process, both through the satisfaction of land rental incomes and through what residents describe as fear of losing land incomes in the future. Residents with land incomes are afraid or unwilling to speak about injustices, with the implication that further community mobilisation is hampered.

Contrary to land acquisition practices, other aspects of Bankers' operations were more openly debated and the cause of constant grievances and larger community protests. In the next chapter I will discuss air quality grievances, which were filed in abundance through Bankers' grievance mechanism, alongside the corporate responses to these complaints. While community members identified land rental payments as effective means to keep the local community from mobilising, the company's grievance mechanism was another method to keep community members passive and isolated.

CHAPTER 6

"A bad smell does not harm your health"

Imagine that your five years old son is sick for the third time this winter. He has a horrible cough and when you open the window, to fill his lungs with fresh air, a heavy odour from the oilfield fills your nose. Imagine that you go to the local doctor to examine his lungs and the doctor tells you that the air you breathe is polluted and bad for your health. "Many people in this area have these problems," she says. She signs a prescription for medicine that you cannot afford as your debt at the local pharmacy is growing day by day. "You should move to the coast", the doctor says. "With what money?" you think. In the night your son has another fit of coughing and you desperately put him in the car and drive fast on dark narrow roads, away from the oilfield, away from the smell. Finally, you can open the windows, finally he can breathe again. The next day you visit the field office of the major oil company in the region. The man in the small container office is polite; he invites you for a coffee and listens to your concerns about your son. He has three sons himself he says and shows you photos on his cell phone. He tells you he will speak to the environmental department and ask them to measure gas levels at your home. He tells you that this is a company working according to European standards; he is a proud employee who can guarantee this. Your hopes are raised. The next day a polite young woman turns up at your door and says that she will place gas-monitoring equipment in your yard. She installs a small plastic tube on the gatepost to your house and tells you that it will stay there for 4 weeks before it is sent to the UK for analysis. You wait two months. The results come back and a company representative tells you that the gas releases do not cause health impacts even though they smell. You move your son to your parents who live in a distant mountain village. "The oilfield is not dangerous to his health," the experts say, "but mountain air is better".

In this chapter I will discuss the conflict between the residents of Patos-Marinza and Bankers regarding air pollution in the area. As you read in Chapter Four, the corporate hegemonic discourse depicted Bankers' takeover of the oilfield as a process which improved the environmental situation for the surrounding villages. Old Albpetrol equipment was removed and replaced by modern technology; oil sludge in agricultural fields and drainage canals were collected and placed in specific areas called Ecopits. IFC's and EBRD's loans to Bankers were motivated by this 'modernisation' and 'clean-up' of the oilfield. Here, local residents were framed as 'beneficiaries' of these wholesale changes. Since the area was defined as 'brownfield', i.e. with previous industrial development already in place when Bankers took over, the company could narrate a story which combined enhanced oil extraction with environmental restoration; a beautiful narrative indeed. However, as in the previous chapters, a counter-hegemonic discourse articulated by local communities undermined this corporate story of complete fullness and satisfaction. On the one hand, residents acknowledged that Bankers had removed pollution from soil and water resources, but on the other hand, they emphasised that air pollution had deteriorated with the increasing production of oil. Residents spoke of breathing difficulties, of children and elderly getting sick, of headaches and vomiting as common symptoms. While, as seen in the previous chapter, the land rental process was a practice that residents resentfully accepted in 'voluntary servitude'; the air quality situation was subject to constant complaints raised through Bankers' grievance mechanism.

In the second part of this chapter, I examine Bankers' grievance mechanism, designed in accordance with IFC's sustainability standards to handle community grievances "in an appropriate and timely manner",[357] but which also provided an effective way to isolate and control community demands. Community members registered their grievances by household rather than as part of wider community mobilisations. This meant that separate families could be dealt with in isolation. Bankers' grievance process thus worked as another hegemonic mechanism that prevented political mobilisation.

Bankers' clean-up of historic pollution

During the first years after the collapse of communism, the infrastructure and environment in Patos-Marinza was in a state of degradation. When Bankers signed the concession agreement with the Albanian government in 2004, a constant stream of black liquid filled the area's drainage canals;

[357] Bankers Petroleum (2016g).

rusting metal infrastructure, such as pipes and derricks, were a dominant part of the landscape. In a promotion video produced by Bankers in 2014, images of decaying oil industry equipment and pools of oil surrounding wells and tanks portray this development. Accompanying these images is a sober sounding voice-over that illuminates this part of Patos-Marinza's history.

> In the 1990s, there were 2400 wells in Patos-Marinza, most of which were depleted. In the first years of democracy, [oil] production fell drastically and investments were reduced, which caused degradation of the oilfield. The mismanagement of Patos-Marinza transformed the oilfield, that was once a symbol of the success of the [Albanian] oil industry, into one of the most polluted areas in Albania.[358]

Following this introduction of an oilfield in a state of despair, the video depicts a Bankers' manager who describe his memories from the pollution of the oilfield during the communist era:

> Frankly speaking, attention was not given to the environment or working conditions in the oilfield during that time [Albpetrol time]. Oil discharges from treatment facilities in Sheqishta and Marinza were two 'hot spots' that polluted the air, the soil and the water. Water contaminated with hydrocarbon was discharged in Ngjala canal and ended up in the Adriatic Sea. When I was swimming at Seman beach [beach downstream from Patos-Marinza] at that time, I was smeared with oil from Marinza.[359]

The promotion video thereafter frames Bankers' takeover of the oilfield in light of these historic levels of pollution. The takeover is depicted as an achievement, which both increased the oil production of the field and at the same time improved the environment. The video explains that when Bankers started taking over wells and implementing environmental clean-up activities, the field gradually transformed; old derricks and out-dated equipment were removed, leases were cleaned of sludge and gravelled. The watercourses became cleaner and Seman River, which runs through the middle of the field, was significantly improved. Moreover, the beaches along the Adriatic Sea could once more be used for recreational swimming

[358] Albania Oilfield (2014, January 24).
[359] Albania Oilfield (2014, January 24).

and sunbathing. The video shows another Bankers' manager who explains to the viewers in a proud voice:

> As you can see the water flowing along the coast of Seman is clean. We are pleased to say that this is a major benefit for the community and for the entire city of Fier. They can now use the beach of Seman without any fear of coming out smeared with oil.[360]

The video voice-over then explains Bankers' efforts to improve the environment in Patos-Marinza:

> To create a healthy and safe environment, and to develop a good rapport with the community, Bankers took over the cleaning of pre-existing pollution in Patos-Marinza although this was not a contractual obligation for the company. Bankers operates according to an Environmental and Social Action Plan (ESAP), which is monitored by international institutions EBRD and IFC. Bankers is transforming Patos-Marinza into a western standards oilfield. Bankers has invested in the reinjection of polluted produced waters. Bankers has built Ecopits and have installed a network to monitor the pollution level of the environment. Bankers also monitors the level of H2S [hydrogen sulphide – a poisonous gas that smells like egg in low concentrations] in the air and keeps it regulated. The company has also installed a facility for treatment of contaminated soil. By the end of 2012, Bankers investments in environmental projects reached 20 million [dollars].[361]

The video thus portrays Bankers as a company that not only cares about the extraction of oil but also adheres to a serious commitment to improve the environmental conditions in the area. The positive transformation of the oilfield, which the video depicts, was a narrative that most employees, government representatives and international stakeholders acknowledged. In a monitoring report by IFC from 2013, the health and safety improvements of Bankers' takeover activities are discussed:

> Health and safety risks to community members are mainly related to derelict Albpetrol equipment, abandoned facilities and pre-existing pollution in the field. Bankers' progressive interventions in the Patos-Marinza field have steadily reduced these health and safety risks to the communities. Old abandoned Albpetrol wells are generally uncapped,

[360] Albania Oilfield (2014, January 24).
[361] Albania Oilfield (2014, January 24).

> unfenced and in a poor state, often surrounded by pools of leaked oil and associated sludge. As Bankers takes over these wells, they are substantially remediated and made safe, reducing associated risks to neighbouring community members.[362]

The IFC report thus depicts the gradual improvement of the oilfield as a positive impact from Bankers' takeover, and that, over the course of several years, the local population are said to have directly benefitted from. The state-owned company Albpetrol becomes the villain in this narrative while Bankers is portrayed as the foreign hero that has brought salvation. The resulting change from historic degradation and pollution to a modern and clean oilfield was underlined in many interviews with Bankers' employees and partners. Lidia, a Bankers' contractor representative, who lives close to the oilfield, explained:

> I used to walk [to Patos-Marinza], when I was young, my brothers used to play football with the villagers there, [...] I can remember that it was like a forest with those, how are they called... derricks [Iron towers used to pump oil]. Yeah, it was like a forest. And remembering that picture, that I have in mind, and seeing it now, it is a great, great change. Like you know, so all the area is cleaner now and things are well organised. Big changes they [Bankers] have done within the area.[363]

Lidia is thus describing a change from an iron 'forest' of derricks to a 'clean' and 'organised' environment. In another interview, Bankers' representative Rezart underlined how the communities' perception of the company during the initial phase of the investment was influenced by the change from a polluted oilfield to a modern one.

> It [Bankers' takeover] was seen as positive. Because they [local communities] were seeing changes, so when we opened Pad D and Pad H [areas for drilling wells constructed by Bankers in 2004] you see... and I have photos from that time, you would see that they were brand new, clean, so they were seeing positive changes, they were seeing that we [Bankers], foreign investors, came to the oilfield with different standards compared to Albpetrol. We were taking over wells and cleaning them, so that's why.[364]

[362] IFC (2013).
[363] Interview, Bankers' contractor representative, October–November 2017.
[364] Interview, Bankers representative, October–November 2017.

Rezart thus expresses the view that community members, just as the employees themselves, saw the positive changes that the new investment brought, which in turn made them positive towards the company. Gramos, another Bankers representative who worked in Patos-Marinza during the communist era, described his memories of the situation when he first started in the field.

> Marinza was an oilfield but at the same time there were residents living there, only they were not living as close to the wells as now. Nevertheless, the pollution of the environment with natural gas affected their health. But they did not complain because they understood that this was how the work in an oilfield was. The state knew what it is doing, because it was a communist state at that time, and the residents did not protest and they did not make all kinds of requests.[365]

Gramos thus refers to the poor conditions in the past, but he emphasises that the residents did not complain at that time as they were living under a communist regime. The complaints, he underlined, came after communism when foreign companies took over the oilfield and started to improve the environment:

> When Saxon [later renamed as Bankers] started its project the residents and the workers could see that Saxon's director and managers cared for the environment. The residents, and quite rightly, then started to ask: "But what about us who live here, for the children who live here, that live in the air polluted with hydrocarbon, you should do something for them!" They started to raise requests for employment opportunities; that the air quality should be within acceptable limits; that pollution should be controlled; and for various kinds of compensation. And this was unthinkable before [during communism]; the residents did not request anything and the state, Albpetrol, and other state institutions did not think like this. [...] If you go to other oilfields in Albania to Gorisht, Cakran or Ballsh, you can see pollution there still. It is very different from the zone that Bankers operates within now.

The clean-up of pre-existing pollution is thus articulated as a vital part of Bankers' narrative about the universally positive impact of its takeover in Patos-Marinza. Complaints from local communities are in these articulations placed in relation to the poor living and working conditions of the

[365] Interview, Bankers representative, October–November 2017.

past, and through this, complaints are framed as less valid owing to the improvements made to the environment. "*Residents were living in horrible environmental conditions in the past but then they never complained*", this narrative stipulates, "*Now they complain even though Bankers has made huge improvements*". This frames residents as ungrateful or ignorant of the positive changes that Bankers achieved. At the same time, it portrays them as exploiting the possibilities to speak their mind, which democratic change brought with it.

While this corporate narrative would not have been possible in a green-field [without previous industrial development] operation, a brownfield takeover provided the base for the idea of an 'environmentally friendly' oil company to be articulated, not only by words but also by the practical clean-up activities that Bankers performed. The 'modern', 'western' oilfield was thus articulated not only by words but also by concrete practices, such as with the use of machinery transporting sludge into secure areas, the implementation of a Social and Environmental Action Plan and the instalment of air monitoring stations.

New air pollution from expanding operations

While concrete practices strengthened the powerful narrative of Bankers' improvement of the environment, residents articulated another side of Bankers' ever-expanding operations. Bankers did not only take over old Albpetrol wells but also drilled new wells in new areas of Patos-Marinza. Oil extraction increased, and with this wells and tanks multiplied, along with traffic from the transportation of crude oil on local roads. The increased oil production led to new detrimental effects on the local population, including a persistent smell of gas. Residents had temporarily been relieved of the smell from old sludge pits, which Bankers' had removed. But soon they were introduced to gases from new wells, engines, oil deposits and Ecopits. Community concerns about air quality impacts were expressed already in the Environmental and Social Impact Assessment (ESIA), which I was a part of implementing in 2011. In Bankers' public disclosure document, which conveyed the results from the ESIA process, it can be read that:

> Stakeholders expressed concerns about possible health impacts and odours related to vent gas emissions from Bankers holding tanks in the main Patos-Marinza operations area, as well as odours from Ecopits.[366]

Vent gases from tanks and odours from Ecopits were thus a main concern for residents when we started the ESIA process in 2011, and this continued to be the case during my time as an employee. Grievances about air quality concerns were constantly filed through Bankers' grievance mechanism, and residents made jokes with reference to Patos-Marinza 'gases' in community Facebook groups. One example is a post that shows a man on a beach dressed in swimwear and diving equipment. Instead of an oxygen tube, the man has a red gas tube on his back, labelled "gas" and "H2S", providing him with gas through a green pipe that is inserted in his mouth. The text accompanying the picture reads: "If you are from Marinza and go on vacation, you cannot separate yourself from the gas smell", and the man thinks for himself "Without gas there is no life".[367] The joke thus refers to how the residents of Marinza are trapped within this gaseous smell, indicating that this is a state they have become so used to that, when diving, they chose to breath H2S instead of oxygen. Another Facebook post shows a man with a gas mask and the Bankers logo behind him. The text on the picture reads "Bankers Petroleum Ltd. – causes serious damage to your health".[368] The joke refers to the warnings placed on the side of cigarette packages, but here the picture suggests that it is Bankers, and not cigarettes, that seriously damages one's health.

The air quality issues in Marinza were thus a constant concern and were subject to jokes among local residents, even though Bankers' promoted a narrative in which the area was now clean and the air quality monitored. In my role as a company representative I often heard concerns about health impacts from both Patos-Marinza residents and colleagues at Bankers who argued that it was bad for one's health to work in Patos-Marinza for too long. Artur, a previous Bankers' representative, expressed a perception that deviated from the formal company's narrative, even while acknowledging that the clean-up activities had been carried out. He recalled that:

> Artur – [When Bankers' operations started to expand] you could see the changes on the oilfield. If it was a mess before, now you could see

[366] Bankers (2012a).
[367] @vetvetdyhere (2014d, 15 April).
[368] @vetvetdyhere (2015b, 25 September).

> that the place was cleaner and it was becoming cleaner every day. Even before on those irrigation ditches, where it was crude oil, after they were clean they were filled with water and you could see people fishing. So it was that clean. The only problem right now is the release of gases. The gases released into the air. This is a health issue for the people living in that area or people working in that area. Even though the Canadians had a very good technology. It's actually the most advanced technology for heavy oil. It's quite difficult to contain all the gases; different gases are released from crude oil. So, this affects the people that live in the area and people who work in that area for a long period of time.
>
> Sara – And what do people who work there say about all this?
>
> Artur – Actually everyone that works over there, no one wants to work in that environment. But they say that "we have to work because without working we cannot maintain a family", so basically people will do anything to feed their families.

Similar to Artur, residents generally acknowledged that clean-up activities had been carried out by Bankers, while at the same time emphasising that air pollution had become worse due to expansions in oil extraction. During a family visit, Besa and her husband Fatjon acknowledged that the clean-up had been carried out by Bankers but emphasised at the same time that the air quality in the area had deteriorated:

> Fatjon – When they [Bankers] started to clean up I thought that now they will do something to improve the environment here. […]
>
> Besa – Yes, cleaning they have done, clean-up, but the air is worse.[369]

In another village, Taulant underlined that Bankers had cleaned up sludge pits but stressed that the environment was cleaner during communism than at present:

> Taulant – During Enver Hoxha, it was clean, everything was clean, the machinery was clean, the place was clean, there was no pollution and no earthquakes.
>
> Sara – So there was no air pollution, no earthquakes? But how was the oil field?

[369] Family visit, Patos-Marinza, September 2018.

> Taulant – It was clean without smell. There were sludge pits [with oil residue] beside the wells but the machinery came and took the sludge to collect it in one place. [...]
>
> Sara – But the Canadians had a project to clean the oil field, have you heard about it?
>
> Taulant – Yes, they have cleaned the sludge pits but the environment is polluted. For the new generation things are very bad, for my grandson I mean. They have been severely impacted by the environment, from all kinds of diseases, [...] with stomach pains, vomiting, cough, and all those things.[370]

When Taulant compares his memories of communism with the present situation he draws the conclusion that it was cleaner before. He also brings up health issues surrounding his grandson and draws a direct connection between these symptoms and present levels of air pollution. In another interview, Lisa, a Patos-Marinza resident, also described the poor all quality and drew parallels to the communist era and how health impacts from the oilfield were discussed during that time:

> If you come here to stay with me one night you will see how heavy the gas is in the morning. Come and stay just one night. A lot of people are sick in the area and have to take medicines because of the environment. In the communist time the workers got milk to drink because of the pollution. Is it possible that the company can pay for medicine for people? People are poor and without work they cannot afford to buy medicines.

Lisa is thus convinced of the link between oilfield pollution and health issues in the area and asks for free medicines from the company in a similar way as milk was provided to oil workers for free during communism. During my time with Bankers I was often told that when people visited the hospitals and health clinics, health professionals confirmed peoples' perceptions that the air quality in Patos-Marinza was bad for their health. Similar accounts were raised during interviews, for example by Edison who explained that:

> I went to hospital two weeks ago because my head was hurting, I took paracetamol but it did not go away. At the hospital I had an injection

[370] Family visit, Patos-Marinza, September 2018.

> and the doctor asked me "where are you from?" "I am from Patos-Marinza," I answered and the doctor replied: "You people from that area are all like this, you are all are sick from the polluted air".[371]

Even though this account comes after the Canadian era, similar stories were very common during my time with Bankers. The general perception about air quality health impacts thus seemed to be confirmed when residents went to health professionals who also believed that the air was unhealthy.

Residents also mentioned economic impacts relating to poor air quality, especially with respect to their ongoing agricultural activities. During a group interview, Shkelqim explained:

> We are the worst impacted in this village; for example, I have an oil lease [with wells and tanks] next to my land, and when it was time to harvest, the workers came to help but then they left, they left two or three times during the work because it smelled very bad. I had planted watermelon but the workers did not stay to finish the harvesting work because I of the well next to me. I had to finish the work with the help of family members.[372]

Shkelqim was thus negatively affected by oil industry on his neighbour's land, giving the neighbour a regular income from land rental payments while his own agricultural production suffered due to the poor working environment. In another village, Fatmir explained that the agricultural production in the area was considered less valuable due to air quality issues, which had been a problem for residents for many years.

> Our production, our livestock and crops, are pre-judged in the markets around Fier. They call it 'contaminated production': the seeds, the fruits, the vegetables. The salesmen come and say "those are products from Patos-Marinza, no, no, no we don't want them because they are contaminated, they contain gas, they are polluted". [373]

The buyers of agricultural produce in the area thus seemed to have the perception that produce from Patos-Marinza was contaminated from the poor air quality there. It mattered little if the residents agreed with this per-

[371] Group interview, Patos-Marinza, September 2018.
[372] Group interview, Patos-Marinza, September 2018.
[373] Group interview, Patos-Marinza, September 2018.

ception or not; on point of fact of finding it harder to sell their produce, they experienced direct negative economic impacts.

All these accounts indicate that stakeholders in the area were not convinced by Bankers' narrative about a clean oilfield. Health professionals told employees and residents that they were getting sick from spending too much time in the polluted air, temporary farm workers left when gaseous smells became to intense, and agricultural salesmen refused produce from the area. The narrative of poisonous gases and a polluted oilfield thus seemed to maintain a dominant position among several stakeholders, providing the ground for strengthening the counter-hegemonic discourse surrounding the company's 'invasion'. In the counter-hegemonic discourse, the poor air quality situation was linked to 'genocide' and 'risks' to human health, as described in Chapter Four. This was thus a situation that Bankers had to manage in order to maintain its hegemonic position, and enforce its narrative of an extraction industry that would benefit everyone. Luckily for the company, IFC's and EBRD's sustainability standards provided helpful guidance in this endeavour.

Bankers' air monitoring programme

Prevention of air, water and soil pollution is an integral part of IFC's environmental and social policy, and detailed guidelines to clients are stipulated in IFC's Performance Standard 3. There it is stated that:

> During the project life-cycle, the client will consider ambient conditions and apply technically and financially feasible resource efficiency and pollution prevention principles and techniques that are best suited to avoid, or where avoidance is not possible, minimize adverse impacts on human health and the environment.[374]

In line with this standard, and in accordance with the commitments outlined in the company's Environmental and Social Action Plan (ESAP), Bankers commissioned an air emissions inventory monitored by IFC and EBRD representatives. In the report from a review visit by EBRD and IFC representatives in 2013 it can be read that:

> Bankers commissioned an air emissions inventory as part of its ESAP commitments following the original IFC-EBRD supported project. Air

[374] IFC (2012b).

> emissions from Bankers' operations at the Patos-Marinza field are principally related to three treatment facilities; soil storage areas; waste sludge pits ('Ecopits') containing hydrocarbon wastes; wells and well batteries including well burners, oil tank vent pipes, pumps and generators; and diesel engines on drilling and service rigs. The final draft air emissions modelling report (January 2013) indicates fairly widespread exceedances of applicable air quality standards for NO_2, $PM_{2.5}$ and total reduced sulphur and more limited exceedances for SO_2, PM_{10} and benzene within parts of the Patos-Marinza oilfield. As per the attached ESAP, Bankers will develop and implement a field-level air emissions management programme to systematically address these findings and ensure that its air emissions comply with relevant Albanian, EU and IFC EHS [Environmental Health and Safety] Guidelines limits within a reasonable period of time. The company will also confirm that emissions do not pose health and safety risks for workers or community members in higher risk scenarios and take further precautionary measures if and where necessary.[375]

EBRD and IFC representatives thus state in the report that air emissions in Patos-Marinza exceed air quality standards for some gases, and they outline Bankers' commitment to implement an air emissions management programme to reduce this environmental impact from operations, ensuring that emissions do not pose health and safety risks for workers or community members. An air emission management programme was therefore developed and implemented by Bankers,[376] including participatory air monitoring practices to include community members and to improve levels of trust in monitoring results.[377] Bankers informed residents about this programme in a leaflet:

> As part of our ongoing commitment to improve environmental conditions in the Patos-Marinza area, Bankers will set up air quality monitoring points in vicinity to residential areas. The location of the monitoring points will be determined by Bankers environmental specialists in collaboration with local residents. [...] Once locations have been determined, the monitoring equipment [plastic and metal tubes] will be in place for 4 weeks to absorb samples of the air at the specific

[375] IFC (2013).
[376] Bankers Petroleum (2016h).
[377] Bankers Petroleum (2015e).

> locations. […] Once the samples have been collected the tubes are sent to specialist laboratories in UK for analysis.[378]

However, even though Bankers put in place both an air emissions management programme and participatory monitoring practices, local residents continued to file their grievances. The grievance mechanism thus became another way for Bankers to manage residents' concerns.

Bankers' grievance mechanism

The Bankers' website notes that the company established its grievance mechanism in 2011, with the commitment to respond "in an appropriate and timely manner" to comments or questions "from any project stakeholder, including local/regional authorities, residents of nearby communities, and other interested parties".[379] IFC emphasises the importance of a grievance mechanism in one of their *Good Practice Notes*: "since it creates opportunities for companies and communities to identify problems and discover solutions together" and "are part of a broader framework for businesses to address human rights issues in their operations".[380] In Patos-Marinza, residents could file their grievances at the Bankers' field office. They would then be approached by a grievance officer, responsible for investigating the validity of the grievance. If the grievance was found to be valid, the community member was compensated for negative impacts from Bankers' operations. Several issues were raised through Bankers' grievance mechanism; for example, blocked drainage canals, damaged roads, crops destroyed by dust, noise disturbances and poor air quality. To illustrate how this mechanism can be understood as a hegemonic articulation, let me tell you the story about Arber, an air quality grievance case that I was involved in 'solving'.

The story of Arber

> We were sitting around the table on the veranda next to the small business, below the brick house surrounded by wines. His eyes were red with fury and his cheekbones distinctive as he pressed his teeth against each other. His whole body was tense, shaking as if he was fighting to keep

[378] Bankers Petroleum (2015e).
[379] Bankers Petroleum (2016g).
[380] IFC (2009b).

> himself from throwing my colleague off the porch. "I cannot keep my children here for another day! My daughter threw up from the smell the other night and my parents are old and sick and cannot sleep. You need to stop this smell or move us away from here! This is our home but we cannot live like this!" We had brought maps from our environmental department specifying the air monitoring results of the area. The data showed that all air emissions (H_2S, SO_2, NO_2 and CO_2), were at acceptable levels and therefore not dangerous to the health of the communities. The maps showed reference data from the centre of Fier city, and the data revealed that air emissions were much worse in the city centre than in the oil field. The conclusion from these figures was that the family could safely continue to live in their house. When disclosing these maps we normally announced standardised phrases from the senior management: "Just because it smells bad does not mean that it is bad for your health." "H_2S smells a lot even in very low concentrations but according to WHO no correlation between small concentrations of H_2S and health implications has been shown." "Our company is taking health and safety very serious and would not let staff members work in environments that could damage their health. Since they are working safely at the well leases you can safely live at this distance from the field." For some reason I could not repeat these phrases this time, maybe it was the insane look in the man's eyes, or maybe it was the fact that I myself started to feel slightly nauseous by the smell from the oilfield stretching out behind me. My head was hurting and in my colleague's red face I could see desperation to leave as soon as possible. Maybe it was also the realisation that this type of communication would mean very little to the man as I had heard concerns from several Albanian staff members working in the field. "You should only work in the field for a couple of years, otherwise you will have health problems when you are old", a staff member had told me earlier. How could we communicate that the oilfield was safe to live in when not even our own staff members were convinced about the lack of health impacts from infield air quality? We did not unfold the maps on the plastic table in front of us, nor did we repeat the worn out standardised phrases. We told the man "we will speak to the senior management" and left the scene as soon as we could. My head was banging as we entered the air-conditioned car and drove back to the city office on the dusty roads leaving the wells and houses behind us.[381]

In the narrative I recall a situation in which Bankers' air monitoring results failed to convince the resident that the air quality was good enough for

[381] Autobiographical narrative, written in 2016.

adequate living. Technical figures from monitoring results and maps, showing air pollution levels in different parts of the region, would not help in the slightest. Arber referred to his own, as well as his family's, bodily experiences as a way of resisting the reports. 'International standards' were thus placed against residents' experiences of the pungent odours and poor health symptoms. My colleague's and my own experience from sitting on the veranda that day made us reluctant to show the air monitoring maps; we also felt sick. In my autobiographical narrative I continue to recall the events after this meeting with Arber:

> A few days later at the central field office I was standing outside the main entrance with a senior management representative. "People feel the smell and immediately think that it is dangerous for their health. We just need to give them more information about how an oilfield smells and that they don't need to be concerned" he stated as a response to our discussion about the air quality grievances in the area. I sensed the underlying assumptions of this statement, that I, with an educational background in social science, had no idea about the technical particularities of an oilfield or how gases are supposed to smell. In my mind, what the senior manager really was saying was: Are you sure *you* understand the oilfield? Are you sure you are explaining the air quality data properly to the residents? No, I guess I did not understand completely. I just knew that people were desperately worried about their children and elderly parents, and that they were mentioning headaches, vomiting and dizziness. I also knew what an unpleasant feeling it was to sit on the porch the other day and to feel sick from the smell. I gathered my courage and explained to him how the smell was more intense now than previously, how particular days were especially bad, and that mornings and evenings were the worst. I also explained that this group of houses just next to the oilfield were especially vulnerable; the air from the field seemed to gather there when the wind was blowing from northwest. "I sat on their veranda the other day and I felt like I could not stay there for 10 minutes" I ended my speech; feeling satisfied that my voice sounded firm and convincing. He looked at me with doubt in his eyes and smiled as he responded: "But you know better than me that people are poor and are hoping to get compensation from us. We cannot pay for one family to move because then the rest will ask for the same." He appealed to my years of experience in the oilfield, managing grievances and community engagement. At the same time, I knew that he was seeking to question whether my experience had taught me how to judge people, if I was still too empathic and naive to make an objective conclusion. I knew very well that many of the grievances we received were opportunistic and groundless.

> I had spent countless hours arguing with people over cracks in worn down houses and blocked drainage canals that had not been maintained for decades. Those grievances had nothing to do with our operations and were easy to dismiss. But the man with the burning eyes did not look like an opportunist; he looked genuinely concerned about his family. Did I misjudge his intent? Was I still too "Swedish" and "feminine" to handle the harsh realities of the field? Was I just a sensitive office worker who couldn't handle an hour in the smell of gases that operators worked in daily? We ended our conversation and I left with a feeling of uncertainty about my own capacity and competence. Back in the office I told my colleagues about the conversation and they quickly dismissed the senior manager. "Those people have no idea about the reality people live in here. They live in five-star hotels and fly first class to Canada every month. They would never let their children live in this environment for a minute." I realised that while I had reasons to feel insecure, so did the senior manager and the feeling of uncertainty left me. We had to continue our struggle to let the residents' voices be heard in the internal management debate. Air quality grievances were not about small damages to properties or minor disturbances. This was peoples' health we were discussing and nothing could be more serious than that.[382]

In the narrative I recall my own feelings of insecurity and confusion. Did I understand the air emission impacts? Was I just fooled by the expressive grievances of 'greedy' residents? The senior manager's referral to residents' complaints as a game that was played to pressure the company for money was, as has been seen in previous chapters, a common articulatory practice within the corporate discourse. So was the notion that people did not understand oilfield technicalities, and thus were worrying due to ignorance. With no reliable third party involved that could monitor air quality on behalf of residents, the technical expertise of the company was the only reference point to which their bodily experiences could be compared. But while they continued to complain about headaches and dizziness, the company experts continued to claim that air quality was safe. My colleagues' dismissal of the senior manager gave me strength to put my own insecurities to one side. Many Bankers' employees were also concerned about the health impacts from air emissions. Air quality might have been within oilfield standards but would the senior managers let their own precious

[382] Autobiographical narrative, written in 2016.

children live beside an oil tank? I did not believe so, and so we continued to pressure for Arber's and his neighbours' case internally:

> The little girl in our office looked terrified at her mother who was screaming at the top of her lungs. "I am going to leave my child with you, she is sick from your gases and you have to take responsibility!" I looked at the girl who has started to run around the room with one of her toys; she did not look sick. Her mother on the other hand looked like she was about to have a nervous breakdown. After months of internal discussions the company had finally decided to move the families from that particular area by providing compensation for alternative lodging in Fier or Roskovec cities. An incident in the field involving a whole rig crew visiting the company clinic in the middle of the night due to headaches, dizziness and vomiting strengthened our case internally. When we read the email in the morning about the incident that had occurred during the night it was hard not to relate staff accounts to the symptoms described by residents in the area. The man with the burning eyes signed an agreement which made his small business part of the group of Bankers' generously paid sub-contractors. Thereby he could make enough money each month to rent an apartment in Fier for himself, his wife, parents and children. This also generated some much-needed additional incomes. His tense appearance had been transformed to the most generous smile imaginable and our visits to his veranda, which he used during the daytime as part of his business, were now truly pleasant experiences including Turkish coffee, caramels and jokes about the general situation in the country. Whenever we came by, he and his wife were working frenetically to serve customers, and I felt so proud for our agreement, for the way it had transformed their lives and for how they were honouring their commitment by working hard and expanding their business. "This is how it feels like to be part of an oil company that is acting according to the slogan to be a good neighbour", I was thinking. But then, as the senior manager had anticipated, air quality grievances started to increase. Residents further away from the field heard the rumours about generous compensations and wanted a piece. The woman sitting in our office was another example of this, now loudly expressing her worries not only for the health of her child but also for how the poor air quality had caused her to have a miscarriage the previous year. We had visited her as well as the other households complaining, installing special tubes to measure the air quality thinking that, as the performance standards stipulate, a transparent air monitoring process would promote trust in the monitoring results. The results came back with all parameters safely within acceptable limits. This made the residents even more furious and visits to our office like this one were now part of our daily routine.

> The woman suddenly stood up and ferociously proclaimed: "I'm leaving now! You will have to take care of my child!" The little girl stopped her games and stared terrified at us. "Don't worry", I told her with a smile, "your mum is not going to leave you". Then I called the security guard and asked for support to escort the woman and her child out of the office building. "I am the kind of person who defends oil companies against women who had miscarriages", I thought to myself as I closed the gates behind her.[383]

In my narrative I recall how Arber and his neighbours finally received a solution that allowed them to move their families from the area. Bankers made agreements with each family, renting their agricultural land or contracting their businesses which gave them sufficient remuneration for apartments in nearby towns. But I also recall how the air quality grievances continued to flood our grievance mechanism and to these we continued to respond with 'participatory air monitoring' and 'disclosure of monitoring results'. This situation, I often felt, was intense and unbearable. And yet no larger community movement emerged; Bankers was allowed to continue its operations unopposed. The woman and her child in our office was removed by security guards and silenced. When I returned to Patos-Marinza a few years later to make interviews, I met Arber in Bankers' reception and wrote in my field diary:

> When I visited Bankers' main office [to make interviews], I met [Arber] in the reception. He still works with his [small business] as a sub-contractor to Bankers and he looked happy, satisfied, well dressed and well groomed. I asked about his family and work and he said that they were all good. When I talked to [my old colleague] afterwards [the colleague] said that [Arber] works very hard with his [small business]. When coming to the office to hand in his invoices, he is always cleanly shaved and well-dressed. So amazing that something we did actually worked![384]

From my point of view the story of Arber and his family was a success, a case that was solved and a family that became happy and managed to escape oil gases and poverty at the same time. But, when looking at this case through Laclau's theory of popular mobilisations, it is a clear case of isolation and satisfaction of community demands – a method that hinders

[383] Autobiographical narrative, written in 2016.
[384] Field diary note, 5 November 2017.

the growth of a 'community' in which demands can be linked together into a local 'popular' resistance movement. When I first met Arber he was angry and ready to fight for his rights. Indeed, if he worked together with his neighbours in similar situations, a larger community protest could have been staged, and, moreover, air quality grievances could have been linked to grievances about dust, noise, a lack of jobs and seismic tremors, etc. Bankers' hegemonic position as a 'hero' and 'beneficiary' to the local community would have been threatened. Instead Arber and his neighbours were isolated and dealt with individually by Bankers' grievance mechanism. This was something I was part of implementing. Each received an individual 'solution' from the company, which meant that they could relocate from the area. As IFC's *Best Practice Note* stipulates, Bankers' grievance mechanism allowed the company and the community members to "discover solutions together".[385] Bankers' grievance mechanism worked in the same way in many different cases; individual solutions were found and money was transferred. During the village chats and interviews, this division of community members became apparent, as those who were positive to Bankers had received various forms of compensation or employment. One example is Alkeida, a Patos-Marinza resident who told me that her family was happy with Bankers:

> Our family has nothing to complain about. My husband work with Bankers and is satisfied with the company. There is a bad smell in [village name] but we as a family are used to it, we have no problems with the environment or the health. We have been compensated by Bankers and have an apartment in Fier but go to the house in [village name] regularly. If the company would rent our 2000 square metres of land that we have in the middle of Patos-Marinza it would be even better. It is in the middle of leases and is like a hole where the water collects which makes it very hard to plant. And of course at our land it smells a lot because it is in the middle of the oilfield. But we have no complaints as a family. Though, if the company rented our land we would be happy.[386]

As the examples of Alkeida and Arber shows, and just as in the cases with land rental payments, discussed in Chapter Five, flows of money strengthened the narrative of Bankers as an 'investor' and contributor to local

[385] IFC (2009b).
[386] Interview, Patos-Marinza, September 2018.

development. The air in the field did not bother Alkeida's family, as they had received compensation and rented an apartment in the city. Similarly, Arber and his neighbours became part of the satisfied corporate alliance. Five households were successfully relocated while thousands of residents remained in the smelly oilfield where air emissions continued. And so the company could continue to promote the idea that its operations were beneficial to all.

Breaking chains of equivalence through grievance management

In this chapter I have described the corporate hegemonic discourse, which connected Bankers' takeover of a degraded oilfield with signifiers such as 'clean-up', 'modern technology', and 'environmental management systems'. These signifiers are brought together with the nodal point of 'investment', which stabilises the signifying system within which Bankers is seen as a 'good neighbour' to local communities. This discourse was not only verbally articulated in promotional videos and IFC's monitoring reports, but also through concrete clean-up activities, removal of out-dated equipment and an extensive air monitoring programme. Similar to the articulations related to land acquisition, this discourse also framed Patos-Marinza residents as 'greedy' and 'ignorant', and accused residents of using air quality grievances as a way to pressure the company for money. The company thus portrayed itself as a victim of the local context; a context framed as problematic where 'ignorant' residents dismissed the 'technical facts' from air monitoring stations.

The air quality situation in Patos-Marinza fuelled increasing community demands on the company to change the situation. Although Bankers' clean-up activities were acknowledged, the residents spoke about expanding operations and vent gases from new tanks, Ecopits and wells. While the company described the environment as cleaner than before, residents describe a situation in which air pollution led to health impacts among their family members as well as to economic losses in their agricultural production. Compared to the land acquisition process, which residents quietly accepted and participated in, the air quality issues made women and men raise their voices and demand change. However, these vocal protests never led to a larger counter-hegemonic movement, and so Bankers' could continue its operations and air-monitoring programme. The grievance mechanism was an effective way for Bankers to meet some of the most vocal voices, transferring money through 'joint solution' agreements and bringing residents over to the corporate alliance. The grievance mechanism is thus another example of how the antagonistic frontier between the company and the community was dispersed through corporate hegemonic articulations such as money transfers. The grievance mechanism also broke potential chains of equivalence between community members through the isolation of individual cases from wider community demands. This isolation of demands kept them on what Gramsci called a 'corporative' rather than a 'universal' level thus preventing further community mobilisation.

Through my autobiographical narratives it is clear that I saw my participation in Bankers' grievance mechanism as a way to support community members, to raise their voices internally and to create solutions they were happy with. While I viewed these acts as moments of transgression, as ways of breaking my alliance with the company, in order to work on the other side of the antagonistic frontier, it is clear that my actions in reality strengthened the very corporate alliance I saw myself working against. Through my participation in implementing IFC's sustainability standards, some community members were moved to the company side; they became 'well dressed' and 'well behaved'. Community resistance had effectively been weakened. These processes also upheld my own fantasmatic ideal of myself as an inside antagonist, working to change the company from within. My participation thus supported the narrative of the good oil company that could be beneficial to all residents. All we had to do was to work a little bit harder, make further 'joint solutions', and move some more people from the oilfield. Consequently, I became the friendly face that the 'good' western corporation needed in order to maintain its image as a 'partner of choice' for local communities.

Contrary to land acquisition practices, the air quality issues in Patos-Marinza caused residents to verbalise their grievances and thus apply pressure on Bankers. However, a larger community movement failed to mobilise. In the next chapter I will discuss a further intensification of community resistance in relation to the conflict about seismic events. This conflict led to open community protests such as residents forming blockades and vandalising oilfield infrastructure. Community reactions to the seismic events were thus the most intense articulations of the counter-hegemonic discourse I encountered during my years as a Bankers' employee. They required that the Albanian state use force against its own citizens to quell the unrest.

CHAPTER 7

"They are using earthquakes to attract attention"

Imagine you wake up in the middle of the night from a sensation that the whole world is shaking. You freeze in you bed before you realise that you have to put your children in safety. You run to the living room where they are sleeping and they weep as you pull them out of their beds and push them out into the front yard. The street is already filled with people; women and men shouting with angry voices, children crying in fear. Your neighbour comes by and asks if you are ok. "The company did this," she shouts, "they have to pay for the damages they have caused!" Your children sit on the veranda with confusion and anxiety written on their faces. You will not let them sleep in the house tonight; another tremor might happen at any moment. You enter the house to bring them some blankets and food. Large cracks have appeared on the living room wall. In the kitchen, a class cabinet is broken and the fridge is quiet, as the electricity cord has been cut. "The company did this," you think, "they have to pay us compensation". In the following days the government promises to open an investigation about the cause of the tremor. Experts from abroad will be brought in to make the assessment. "An earthquake," the experts say and no compensation is paid. "Corruption", your neighbours declare. The company continues to drill wells only a few hundred meters from your cracked walls. You buy a new fridge on credit and repair the cracks by hand. Your children sleep in your bed during the following months. You are too tired to join your neighbours, who plan to march all the way to the capital to protest. "This time we won't let them get away with lies," they tell you before they leave, "we demand compensation".

In this chapter I will discuss the conflict regarding seismic events in Patos-Marinza. The trembling earth, causing fear among residents and damage to their houses, led to protests on local streets and vandalism of Bankers' property. As in previous chapters I will start by examining how hegemonic and counter-hegemonic discourses provided opposing narratives regarding what was happening during these events. While Bankers' representatives designated the seismic events as natural 'earthquakes' caused by movements of the earth's tectonic plates, community representatives described them as 'tremors' caused by oilfield activities. It is in this competing understanding of reality that the conflict takes its starting point. For what is true and what is false is a matter for societal institutions to determine. When no trust in joint fact-finding institutions exists, society as a radically contingent place discloses itself: word stands against word, structures of meaning compete for recognition.

The struggle surrounding seismic events is the last area in my investigation of the relationship between Bankers and Patos-Marinza communities. While Bankers' land acquisition processes caused little resistance, complaints about air quality raised the level of antagonism between the company and local residents. However, it was the seismic tremors that brought the communities of Patos-Marinza onto the streets. The company as well as the government was forced to act. As a short-term strategy, the government sent representatives from local authorities as well as the police to calm down residents in the midst of protest. As a long-term strategy, Bankers addressed community unrest by disclosure of technical information and by participating in joint 'dialogue groups' which were set up by the Compliance Advisor/Ombudsman (CAO) of the IFC.

In the second part of this chapter I will look at how the CAO dialogue groups were played out. Similar to Bankers' air monitoring programme, discussed in the previous chapter, the dialogue groups aimed to find a 'common solution' to the seismic conflict through discussions and 'participatory fact finding'. Even though no common solution was found, Bankers' continued the expansion of the oilfield while the local population remained terrified as the earth trembled beneath their feet. This chapter thereby highlights how dialogue-based methods aiming at finding 'consensus solutions' end up maintaining corporate legitimacy by way of incurporating opponents in dialogues that are discursively set in the corporation's favour. I will start my exploration of the seismic conflict by presenting how media outlets portrayed the events.

Community protests and media reports

Several media reports from national TV channels show the chaos that took place after each seismic event in Patos-Marinza. These reports include interviews with residents and government representatives in the midst of mass protests on the streets of Patos-Marinza.

A news video produced by the national digital TV channel Kanali Shtate in November 2013 starts with pictures of what appears to be a damaged house. Large cracks can be seen on the white walls of the dilapidated house and an older woman and small girl with worried facial expressions are standing at the entrance. The video changes to a night setting were a group of men are gathered on a street, hardly visible in the dark. A video voice-over explains:

> Tremors of the ground in Marinza and Zharrza in Fier [region] have caused panic amongst the residents who live in this zone. After the tremors, they have abandoned the night in their houses and have gathered on the street. They are blocking the access between Fier and Berat.[387]

The video zooms in on the men in the street and shows their backs dressed in dark winter jackets. A murmur of loud angry voices dominates the night. The voice-over continues:

> A group of irritated residents are walking towards the community relations office of the foreign company Bankers. They claim that the earth tremors are not earthquakes but tremors created by explosions underground.

The video focuses on a representative from the Fier prefect (the regional government), who tries to reason with the group of men. He tells them to calm their families and explains that the government will assess the houses that have been made dangerous by the tremors. The voice of the government representative is thereafter drowned by a wall of upset murmurs from the group of men surrounding him. The voice-over explains that the Fier prefect, Fier police department and local municipalities have mobilised to handle the situation and that the Fier prefect have announced they will take the help of a specialist to assess the claims of the residents. A journalist interviews the prefect representative who explains: "...people are psychologically terrified. We have mobilised our emergency plan to handle the situation. We will investigate and uncover the cause of the large explosion that happened today". The journalist continues to interview some of the protesting men. A man proclaims in an upset voice "...a big explosion until the house started cracking". Another man with deep wrinkles between his eyes argues: "...it is not an earthquake! It is from the oil, seismic tremors from the oil industry". Another man with bright grey hair explains that:

[387] Kanali Shtate (2013, November 22), my translation.

"...earthquakes cause vibrations [showing movements with his hands from side to side] not up and down [waving his hands up and down]". The journalists move on to visit a family living in the area whose house has been destroyed. The woman of the house argues in an upset tone: "What earthquake is that?! It is a tremor from Bankers, the Canadians! We are scared to stay in our own home".[388]

This media report is a clear articulation of the counter-hegemonic discourse in which the 'tremors' are connected to Bankers and the oil industry. The notion of 'tremors' is connected to 'damaged' houses, 'terrified' residents and 'explosions'. The media channel emphasises residents' accounts by reporting about the events as 'tremors' rather than 'earthquakes'; so does the local government representative who speaks about 'explosions' and a government assessment that will find the cause. The video also shows a resident talking about the difference between a tremor and an earthquake: the earth moves side-to-side during an 'earthquake' but up-and-down during a 'tremor', according to the man. This was a common account in the area in which residents used their own bodily experiences of tremors as 'proof' that the company was lying.

In this report, media, government representatives and residents are all contributing to a discourse in which Bankers is framed as a dishonest villain. However, Bankers' hegemonic discourse was also articulated by some news agencies. In a media report called "Fier protest against earthquakes" from the national TV broadcaster, Top Channel, aired on the 3rd of March 2014, another community protest is documented. The voice-over explains that the residents of Zharrza are again protesting and blocking the road between Fier and Berat. The voice-over brings up residents' claim that Bankers have caused the tremors but underlines that the company has denied these allegations. Instead, the voice-over explains that Bankers claims that an earthquake with an epicentre 10 kilometres away from the oilfield has caused the seismic events. The video continues to show the webpage of the National Institute of Geoscience, which has registered an earthquake of 4.2 on the Richter scale with an epicentre 5.4 kilometres from Roskovec, a town near the oilfield. Thereafter, the report shows a man being interviewed by a Top Channel journalist. Behind him is a crowd of young boys, men and a few women. The man explains in a calm but determined tone:

[388] Kanali Shtate (2013, November 22), my translation.

> We have gone out to protest, the whole population, because the representatives of the local communes, the government, lied to us the first time. They said, "we will place the equipment [seismometers] to measure and to determine if it is tremors caused by Bankers or if it is earthquakes." We don't know anything about where they have placed the equipment. No representative from the community has been able to see the equipment. The equipment was bought by Bankers and installed by Bankers.[389]

The video ends with the voice-over explaining that government representatives are taking measures to assess the incident and will reach a "final conclusion" whether the seismic events are caused by "nature" or by the oil extraction of the "concessionary company" (Bankers). By framing the event as a "protest against earthquakes" and by including statements from Bankers as well as reports from the Institute of Geology, this media report in part feeds into a narrative in which the company is seen as a victim of unfounded accusations. On the other hand, the interviews with residents, alongside accounts about how the government seek to reach a "final assessment", leave the nature of the seismic events an open question.

As these examples show, the Albanian media reported various views surrounding the seismic events; some framed them as tremors caused by Bankers while others left it an open question that, in the fullness of time, would be properly ascertained by the authorities. Internal to Bankers, the media's attention was usually discussed as problematic, since it often framed the company as the cause of the seismic movements. The view of media being problematic is also something that I articulate in the autobiographical narrative below, which describes my feelings and thoughts during one of these seismic events.

Earthquakes as seen by a western expat

> I was sitting in our living room sofa when the pendant lights above me began to swing in larger and larger movements. I looked at the frames I recently had arranged on the wall behind the TV and they too had started to move with a disturbing frequency. We were living on the 12th floor in an old apartment building that was not able to stay straight but leaned carelessly towards its neighbouring edifice. I always thought that if the structure would start to fall, at least its neighbour would stop its collapse, and I could jump from our terrace to the roof of the other

[389] Top Channel (2014, March 3), my translation.

building. The story behind the adjacent buildings, which were separated by a distance of 2 metres on the ground floor but less than half a metre at the top, was a conflict between builders and a typical consequence of the lack of legal enforcement in the Albanian construction industry. As I realised that I was trapped on the 12th floor in an earthquake, having knowledge about this construction history did nothing but add fuel to my worries.

After happily concluding that our building did not collapse, I started to think about the consequences that this earthquake would have on Patos-Marinza oilfield operations. Local communities had from the day the company started consultations in the area in 2010[390] emphasised the frequent tremors as one of their major concerns in relation to the oil industry. Some rumours in the communities claimed that the company was using explosives in its extraction activities while others speculated that decades of oil extraction had created cavities in the ground with tremors being the direct consequence. Residents were upset as the tremors led to damage to their properties and made them concerned about the safety of their children. Even though Albania is part of a wider earthquake zone, with earthquakes occurring frequently all over the country,[391] residents in Patos-Marinza were convinced that they were caused by the oil industry. The issue was so sensitive that we, as company representatives, had to refer to all incidents as tremors (*lëkundje*) in our conversations since just using the word earthquake (*tërmet*) could ignite protests; it was perceived as a way for the company to refuse responsibility. The situation was further worsened by the Albanian authorities and media, who did nothing to clarify facts behind the tremors but with various statements, used as tools in the political debate between opposition and government, sometimes even fed into the rumours by accusing the company of using inappropriate technology. Even staff members and sub-contractor staff were doubtful about the origin of the tremors, as many oil industry workers had family and friends in local communities and sometimes even lived there themselves.

I was right about the social consequences of the earthquake. The following days, protests and roadblocks took place at several places in Patos-Marinza and some of the company's oil deposits were vandalised by an angry mob. Bankers had to close down the Public Information Centre for some days, because it was not considered safe for staff to work there. Media embraced their usual role of fuelling the conflict and

390 Bankers Petroleum (2012a), p. 28.

391 Institute of Geosciences, Energy, Water and Environment (2016).

> for some days afterwards our Community Relations team could not resume our usual stakeholder meetings. Even though we disclosed company documents explaining the frequency of earthquakes in the area, the details of the oil extraction technology we employed and how unlikely it was to produce such massive tremors,[392] the general public would not believe a word we said. In the aftermath of this and several other earthquakes in the area, I realised that successful stakeholder engagement had little to do with disclosing 'facts' and more to do with building trust. If trust was missing to begin with, disclosure of information documents would never work to calm stakeholders in a time of crisis. As the company engineers and geologists complained over how their attempts to communicate facts were misread and disregarded, I learned that 'truth' was relative and never stable in a context where rumours circulated freely from village farmers, via media outlets and members of parliament.[393]

In this autobiographical account of the seismic conflict I describe the position of local communities with words such as 'rumours' and 'speculated'. My account thus undermines the validity of residents' claims and dismisses them as perceptions enforcing a relation between 'Bankers' staff' and 'local residents' where the group 'Bankers' staff' is articulated as superior. In another passage, I also delegitimise Albanian authorities and media by picturing them as compliant in the production of 'rumours' and for 'fuelling' the conflict.

The portrayal of local actors' 'ignorance' and 'lack of trust' is further underlined in my description of the frustrations with disclosing technical information. This account is based on the idea that information documents could be a solution to the crisis *if only* there were trust among local stakeholders. The conflict is thus viewed as being fuelled by the lack of trust rather than on the potentially doubtful content of the information disclosed. I describe the narrative of the company as the objective truth and articulate Bankers' advanced 'technology' in a positive light. Furthermore, I articulate the processes of disclosing information about Bankers' technology as an act of CSR, a way in which the company takes responsibility not only for the technology used but also for addressing the complicated situation with distrustful local stakeholders. I place this company effort in opposition to the behaviour of local authorities, which are instead described as worsening the situation.

[392] Bankers Petroleum (2012b).

[393] Autobiographical narrative, written in 2016.

I end my narrative with a sentence that summarises my frustration with the context and with local actors' dismissal of the 'truth':

> I learned that 'truth' was relative and never stable in a context where rumours circulated freely from village farmers, via media outlets and members of parliament.

What this sentence shows is that I view the context of Patos-Marinza as different from the 'western' (Swedish) society in which I lived previously. In my experience of this foreign context, 'rumours' circulated freely, and 'truth' was never stable. This is based on a view of 'western' society, in opposition to Albanian society, as rational and objective where the road to conflict resolution is based on expert accounts and technological information. What I say is that truth in Sweden *can* be established while truth in Albania is flexible. Based on my accounts, the hegemony of technical information and expert accounts is challenged in Patos-Marinza since various stakeholders do not see these as objective. It is apparent how I find this frustrating since *I* view experts and technology as objective. This shows that among Bankers' expatriated staff, the subject position with which I identified, technology and experts had achieved hegemonic status; they *were* the objective truth. This view was also confirmed in interviews with my former colleagues.

Corporate accounts about earthquakes, technology and politicians

In the interviews I conducted, some of Bankers' and contractors' staff discussed the seismic issue with certainty: the 'earthquakes' were 'natural'. Bankers' representative, Jonida, expressed her conviction that the earthquakes were not caused by company activities:

> The earthquake conflict is, I believe, totally exaggerated. I believe it's a form of claiming opposition, more than anything it's an excuse that communities have. Because they have always used grievances to communicate, and this is the biggest grievance they have, that we [Bankers] are causing earthquakes. It's not possible by [extracted] volumes, and by [the] pressure that we are disposing [through injecting fluid], to cause huge movements of the earth. Because the earthquakes are felt in Fier, they are felt in Berat [a city located 46 kilometres away from Fier] as well, it is not possible. People continue [to protest] because they believe that they have a natural resource, which is being used, and cer-

> tain people are making money, and they are not making money. And they are using earthquakes as an excuse to attract attention, because they want a share of the pie.[394]

This account starts with Jonida describing the technical information from corporate engineers and geologists 'proving' that the 'earthquakes' are not caused by company activities. At the same time, she frames residents' protests as their way of showing disapproval of the distribution of benefits from the oil industry, and as attempts to receive money from Bankers. Local residents are, according to Jonida, only "using earthquakes as an excuse to attract attention". She thus depicts residents as strategic and manipulative and thereby delegitimises their expressed fear and anger by disregarding these as theatrical moves. Residents have, according to Jonida, "always used grievances to communicate", a statement which portrays the protests as just another community strategy to make Bankers act in their favour. Another company representative, Rezart, blamed the conflict on the government authorities and their political influence:

> There was a lot of talk about earthquakes and honesty I don't know where to start [...]. I cannot say that overall in Albania democracy is understood as it is in other countries. So, we are an underdeveloped country, and here politicians have a lot of influence in our communities, not only in Patos-Marinza but all over the place. The [Canadian] management came with the perception: "we are a foreign company, we have different standards and we implement our standards" but we forgot the power of politics, the influence of politics in our communities.[395]

Rezart argues that the conflict is a result of government authorities and their political influence in Patos-Marinza communities. He is critical towards the Canadian management and depicts them as incapable of handling the political pressures and influences in Albanian society. This frames the company as a 'victim' of local circumstances whose attempts to implement higher standards failed due to local actors. A former contractor representative, Ervis, pointed to a similar picture of the company as a 'victim' of local politics and rumours:

[394] Interview, Bankers representative, October–November 2017.
[395] Interview, Bankers representative, October–November 2017.

> Sara – And during this time [2008], what did people say about Bankers?
>
> Ervis – Not much, we had small operations at that time. We had an incident in [one village], they were saying that our injection caused the earthquakes, and this was supported by some local politicians like [the] Mayor at the time, […], who were confusing the fracking operations with water disposal operations. And they also produced some leaflets, distributed to the communities that were describing fracking, […] and they were not mentioning that this [Bankers operations] is not fracking, this is only water disposal.[396]

Ervis points out that even though Bankers never used fracking as an extractive technology, local politicians and community members brought the notion of fracking to Patos-Marinza by comparing Bankers' activities to oil operations in other contexts. Ervis is thus blaming the conflict in a local village on misinformation and political influence from the Mayor. Another of Bankers' representatives, Ediona, pointed to similar issues with the political environment and the company's lack of information management:

> I think we as a company, we are not talking a lot about this, we are not informing people, we are not teaching people, […] and then we are leaving room to the people, like organisations, politicians, others, to do or to say what they think is the right thing. […] or in case they are experts they are politically affiliated so unfortunately our institutions are not doing a good job. So for us as a company it is a very bad thing.[397]

Ediona underlines that Bankers should do more to manage information about its operations and not leave room for others to define what is happening. This again rests on the assumption that the company is right, that the earthquakes are natural and that all that is needed is a proper process of information disclosure. Ediona also points to politics as influencing the process by claiming that government authorities are doing a bad job and accusing experts of being 'politically affiliated'. Hence Ediona emphasises the entire context as highly problematic and difficult when it comes to creating a public understanding of how the company is operating. These accounts clearly align with my autobiographical narrative, depicting the company version as 'true' and the community version as 'rumours'.

[396] Interview, Bankers representative, October–November 2017.
[397] Interview, Bankers representative, October–November 2017.

Employee and community voices about tremors

The previous accounts from managers and staff of Bankers clearly align with the hegemonic discourse. However, some of Bankers' affiliated actors also expressed contrasting views. A Bankers contractor representative, Lidia, who also lived next to the oilfield, explained her impression of the issue in a careful manner:

> I didn't have much information about the [Bankers] operations. Like you know just hearing the people who blame the company, you know protesting. So, I don't want to be part of that, but knowing and listening to some specialists as well, it wasn't only Bankers' operations who created [the earthquakes] I think. So, I don't want to be part of that, but I think it wasn't the company which caused what they [the community] think or what they protested for.[398]

This account contains a certain insecurity with respect to the issue; Lidia first says that "it wasn't *only* Bankers" and later that "it wasn't the company which caused" the earthquakes. In a later account, Lidia jokes about the earthquakes as a phenomenon that was not present when operations were smaller.

> I think that you must know that the operations weren't that big that time, so, I mean in 2008, and 2009 and 2010 it wasn't that big, [...] it was a good time even for people because there were no earthquakes [laughing].[399]

This sense of ambiguity (heightened by the telling of jokes) was something I recognised from my time as a Bankers employee. From various actors, definitive accounts regarding how earthquakes were not caused by the oil industry were paralleled with equally committed accounts that the tremors were the responsibility of the oil industry. A former Bankers contractor representative, Ervis, brought up a commonly referred to theory, saying that cavities created by oil extraction caused imbalances in the geological formation:

> Talking to many [Canadian] drilling guys, because I stayed with them for many years, they told me, "this technology", but this was confidential, "is not that good for the formation", because if you pull a

[398] Interview, Bankers contractor representative, October–November 2017.

[399] Interview, Bankers contractor representative, October–November 2017.

> bottle of water of the oil from the down [ground], you have to put another bottle. Do you know how much we [Bankers and contractors] pull out and how much we put in? Yes, because we have the papers, yeah but this is 'paper' – and the dark side over there? And they want the production to always go up – with that technology the production went up.[400]

Ervis insinuates that Bankers' extraction techniques caused imbalances in the geological formation by pulling more liquid from the ground than what was later replaced. Ervis also hints that improper reporting about extraction techniques obscured these practices. This account resonates with the counter-hegemonic discourse that circulated in the company in parallel to the dismissals of community claims as 'greed' and 'lack of information'. One of the most common theories about why earthquakes happened was the one to which Ervis refers; that years of oil extraction had created imbalances in the geological formation that caused the ground to shake. Artur, a former Bankers representative, also referred to this theory:

> My opinion for earthquakes is, if you take something from the ground, like crude oil, which is heavy, it's like glue and supposed to stay there. It will be a hole and this hole will be filled for example with water. But if you replace crude oil with water, it's not going to be the same because the ground is going to be hollow and if a real earthquake happens this area will be in more danger because the impact in that area will be more, because something is missing in the ground.[401]

It was this internal uncertainty, combined with the residents' terminological difference between how an 'earthquake' and a 'tremor' feels, that fed into my own hesitation about the causes of seismic tremors. During the years in the company I oscillated between these two discourses; while at some moments I felt convinced that all 'earthquakes' were 'natural', at other moments I hesitated and started to think that extraction induced 'tremors' also took place in the area.

While the hegemonic and counter-hegemonic articulations were both present within the company and among its contractors, community members expressed with certainty that the company's operations caused the tremors. As can be seen in the media reports described previously, community members voiced their anger over the lack of information, the

[400] Interview, former representative, Bankers' contractor, October–November 2017.
[401] Interview, former Bankers representative, September 2018.

government's inability to do something about their collective situation, and the way Bankers would use the word 'earthquake' in order to evade responsibility. Similar views were conveyed during the interviews. When my translator and I visited residents' homes for interviews, several of the interviewees showed us cracks in their homes that they said were caused by the tremors. They complained that even though state authorities had promised compensation, no payments had been forthcoming. Several residents also expressed their perception that the seismic events started when 'the Canadians' started operating in the area. Taulant, who had lived in Patos-Marinza all his life, described how the environment changed after Bankers took over the oilfield.

> So with one word, they did that, the tremors: when the Canadians came the tremors happened.[402]

In another interview, Fatmir stated that the tremors had stopped since the Chinese took over the oilfield.

> Sara – Have you noticed any difference between the time of the Canadians and the Chinese?
>
> Fatmir – There is a change, they [the Chinese] work but we don't feel it. There have been no more tremors.[403]

These accounts thus show that residents have made their conclusions about the tremors in the area based on a correlation between the Canadian takeover and the frequency of tremors. While Bankers communicated that earthquakes had always been occurring in the area, residents claimed with certainty that they started when oil operations expanded. Other residents complained about the media and emphasised that news agencies had reported about 'earthquakes' rather than 'tremors'. The resident, Alban explained:

> It is censorship from the state. The media said straight away that this was an earthquake without analysing if it was really an earthquake caused naturally or caused by the work that the company was doing.

[402] Family visit, Patos-Marinza, October 2018.
[403] Group interview, Patos-Marinza, October 2018.

> The media took the same line as the state and said straight away that this was an earthquake.[404]

Similar to the corporate hegemonic discourse, residents expressed their lack of trust in the media and state institutions, indicating that state authorities had their own agenda and that the media was controlled by the state. Similar community voices were also reflected in the social media groups that local residents had initiated. In one Facebook post a man in a helmet, depicting a rig worker, thinks to himself: "Why do I work with the drilling rigs when this company is damaging my house? The money I earn I invest in the house and then they destroy it. I should do something".[405] This post thus strikes a cynical note about the seemingly vicious circle in which local residents are stuck; having to work for a company that at the same time is destroying the houses they live in. Another post from the same Facebook group shows a photograph of the former Albanian prime minister, Sali Berisha, who says: "That was not an earthquake, no, it is Edi Rama [Albania's current prime minister] transporting drugs underground".[406] This post can be interpreted as poking fun at the authorities' lack of responsibility regarding the seismic events; in this example, they blame each other for drug trade as part of a political game, instead of taking seriously residents' concerns. The notion of fracking taking place in Patos-Marinza was also circulating in community Facebook groups. One example shows a map of Patos-Marinza underlined with red letters saying "residential prohibited – Fracking Zone",[407] referring to the perceived dangerous situation in which residents live.

As you will have understood from the first part of this chapter, the earthquake conflict escalated and attracted much media attention, and street blockades and protests went beyond the company's or state authorities' control. While Chapter Six described how Bankers dealt with air quality grievances through its grievance mechanism, the seismic events mobilised residents into protests that could not be isolated and dealt with on an individual level. In the next part of this chapter I will describe how dialogue groups, set up by the CAO, became one of the company strategies to handle the seismic conflict. These dialogue groups are an example of

[404] Group interview, Patos-Marinza, October 2018.
[405] @vetvetdyhere (2014e, Mach 31), my translation.
[406] @vetvetdyhere (2014f, May 19), my translation.
[407] @nopetroleum (2015, August 7).

'stakeholder engagement', emphasised as one of the main features of IFC's sustainability standards,[408] and as vital to any CSR programme.

Bankers' stakeholder engagement and information disclosure

In line with the consensus ideal of deliberative democracy, stakeholder engagement has emerged as one of the key elements of social and environmental sustainability management in land-based development projects including the extractive industry. As part of their sustainability standards, IFC and EBRD promote stakeholder engagement activities as a method to resolve conflicts between companies and local communities.[409] As described by IFC in their *Stakeholder Engagement Handbook*:

> our continued experiences in working with our clients in emerging markets have significantly advanced our thinking about the centrality of stakeholder engagement to all other aspects of environmental and social performance. We are not alone in this shift. The risks associated with poor stakeholder relations – and the opportunities provided by constructive ones – are now better understood by the private sector and financial investors alike.[410]

When Bankers received the loan from the IFC and the EBRD, a process of stakeholder engagement was initiated, including meetings and interviews aimed at an improved understanding of community frustrations and expectations. Ongoing stakeholder engagement activities were thereafter a vital part of Bankers' CSR programme. In a report from IFC and EBRD after their review visit to Patos-Marinza in 2013, the seismic conflict and its consequences are addressed as well as Bankers' strategy to handle the conflict:

> The occurrence of earthquakes has created a number of concerns amongst certain community members, who attribute tremors to Bankers' sub-surface activities. This has at times resulted in acts of vandalism affecting company property and production. In response, Bankers has compiled a Public Information Document dealing with the nature of earthquakes and disseminated this to communities. The Community Relations team also met with local leaders in all of the

[408] IFC (2007).
[409] IFC (2007).
[410] IFC (2007), p. 1.

> affected areas of operation to discuss related matters, including analytical findings from Bankers' geologists.[411]

Bankers thus first tried to handle the seismic conflict through meetings with local leaders and by disclosing the specifics of company technology in a Public Information Document. This Public Information Document also focused on explaining the frequency of earthquakes in Albania stating that:

> Albania is located in an active seismic region where small earthquakes are very common. The Institute of Geosciences, Energy, Water and Environment of Albania[412] recorded 247 separate, small earthquakes in Albania between January – April 2012. Earthquakes have also been measured near Fier.[413]

By emphasising that earthquakes are a common feature in the Albanian landscape, including the region of Fier, and by referring to statistics from the Institute of Geosciences, the company appeals to an understanding of the seismic events in Patos-Marinza as 'natural'. The information document also explicitly underlines that Bankers' drilling techniques do not cause earthquakes:

> Bankers' operations are conducted according to Western operating and Health, Safety and Environment standards. Unlike old techniques used by other operators, no high level explosives or blasting techniques are used during any of Bankers' operations. [...] Bankers occasionally use a technique called perforation when recompleting old wells. During perforation, small charges are used to burn through the steel casing lining of the well and connect it to the underground oil reservoir. [...] In the Patos-Marinza area, perforation typically occurs between 1200–1500m below surface. Perforation cannot be heard or felt at the surface and does not cause tremors.[414]

Thus, by referring to their operations as conducted according to 'western standards' and by describing the specific techniques used as not harmful, Bankers underlines that its activities have not caused the tremors. However, regardless of Bankers' communication efforts, community protests continued after each major seismic event. As part of the Community

[411] IFC (2013), p. 6.
[412] Institute of Geosciences, Energy, Water and Environment (2016)
[413] Bankers Petroleum (2012b).
[414] Bankers Petroleum (2012b).

Relations team who implemented these stakeholder engagement activities, I often experienced the communication efforts as fruitless. In 2013, the situation took a new turn when one of the communities lodged a formal grievance with IFC's Compliance Advisor/Ombudsman (CAO).

The CAO assessment report

In March 2013, the CAO received a complaint from an environmental leader representing Zharrza community in Patos-Marinza.[415] The resulting *CAO Assessment Report* reads as follows:

> The complainant raises concerns about the extraction techniques of Bankers Petroleum Albania Ltd., and alleges several incidents and accidents may potentially be associated with those techniques.[416]

When the CAO receives a complaint from affected communities in an IFC client project area, they start an assessment to decide on the next steps. The concluding assessment report outlined the perspectives of communities, Bankers representatives and state authorities in relation to the seismic events.[417]

Articulations connected to the relationship between 'western technology' and the 'local environment' can be clearly found in the CAO's description of the company perspective. The report states that Bankers' representatives "described a series of company-initiated steps undertaken since mid-2009 to better understand, document, and communicate seismic activity at the project site".[418] Based on these efforts "they [Bankers' representatives] believe the area's earthquakes are naturally occurring, and not caused by the company's extraction methods".[419] The report shows that company representatives who met with the CAO were referring to the superior skills and technologies applied by the company to 'prove' the company standpoint on the 'earthquakes' as natural occurrences. As no counterpart with equal knowledge about the company technology could stand against this assessment, the company framed itself as the most knowledgeable actor in the conflict. Furthermore, company representatives explained that Bankers had undertaken a "Seismograph Installation

[415] CAO (2013a).
[416] CAO (2013a), p. 5.
[417] CAO (2013a).
[418] CAO (2013a), p. 7.
[419] CAO (2013a), p. 7.

Project" with the purpose of "supporting national and regional seismic monitoring networks [...] to better understand and communicate information on earthquakes in its operating area".[420] While this refers to the advanced technology of the company it also goes beyond that and portrays the company as a responsible actor investing in infrastructure, which was originally a government responsibility. The company is thus not only claiming to use its technology to ensure safe operations of the oilfield but also investing in technology that will improve the government's capacities to handle earthquakes. This articulation frames the company as superior to the Albanian government in terms of responsibility and technical capacity. Finally, the CAO report shows how company representatives described themselves as superior to the local population.

> The company says it has made multiple efforts to engage the residents of Zharrza in dialogue and information sharing about the science and causality of the tremors, but has been frustrated by ongoing mistrust and residents' lack of willingness to engage constructively or to accept technical findings.[421]

As I have noted before, company representatives thus describe residents as 'distrustful' and 'lacking willingness' to understand the company's technology. This positions residents as subordinate subjects and removes the legitimacy from their claims by discrediting their standpoint as based on false information and lacking a healthy dose of pragmatism. Here company representatives gain their legitimacy in relation to their view of the local population; the 'knowledgeable' company representatives are trying their best to communicate 'the truth' while the 'uninformed' and 'distrustful' local population actively prevent common solutions.

The CAO report also describes the position of community representatives, who explained to the CAO team that: "they believe the extraction techniques of Bankers Petroleum are responsible for earthquakes felt throughout their village".[422] Residents challenged the company's articulation of 'western technology' as beneficial to Albania and used their own bodily experiences as 'evidence' that the 'tremors' were induced by Bankers' technology rather than being natural. As has previously been shown, they did this by describing to the CAO team how the "ground

[420] CAO (2013a), p. 7.
[421] CAO (2013a), p. 7.
[422] CAO (2013a), p. 6.

moves 'up and down' instead of 'side to side', and that loud and unnatural explosions seem to precede the earthquakes".[423] Similarly, by emphasising that "these earthquakes have resulted in structural damage to their homes and to a perpetual sense of fear and anxiety"[424] the residents challenged the company's attempt to discursively articulate the position of local residents as subordinate and misinformed, thereby establishing their legitimacy as victims of company operations and as subjects with rightful claims. The report also describes how community representatives told the CAO team that "they do not trust Bankers Petroleum assurances that earthquakes are a natural phenomenon" and that "the government has failed to provide an adequate judgment or solution".[425] This challenges the corporate articulations that depict the company as a responsible actor working together with the 'weak' government to improve society. Instead, residents articulate the company's 'responsible actions' as a façade, something that cannot be trusted, and frame both the company and the government as jointly negligent and ignorant regarding residents' rights.

According to the CAO report, local and national government representatives hold varying perspectives on the earthquake issue. Two of the interviewed government representatives align with the counter-hegemonic articulations, claiming that "the intensive extraction method utilised by Bankers is a likely cause of earthquakes around Zharrza".[426] The local Mayor and representatives of Albania's National Seismological Institute (NSI) and Natural Resources Agency (AKBN) emphasise the need "to improve scientific cooperation in order to verify what is happening geologically".[427] Indirectly, this position also challenges the company's articulations of 'western technology', since it emphasises the need for further investigations and thus does not fully support the company claims that the 'earthquakes' are natural and were not caused by extraction techniques. Engineers from the National Institute of Geosciences are the only government representatives who disregard the community's claims as "not supported by scientific evidence", emphasising that they had registered "an increase in seismic acidity across Albania and cracking to homes was likely

[423] CAO (2013a), p. 7.
[424] CAO (2013a), p. 6.
[425] CAO (2013a), p. 7.
[426] CAO (2013a), p. 8, citing the former Deputy Minister of Energy.
[427] CAO (2013a), p. 8, citing a NSI representative.

along fault lines".[428] Thus supporting the view that locals were less educated and ignorant about building techniques and seismic activities.

The CAO team concluded in their final assessment report that there "was broad agreement" among residents, Bankers and state authorities "that this question could be answered more definitively through better, more trusted technical information" and "that any such inquiry should be cooperatively designed and should involve trusted, independent experts who specialise in seismology in the context of oil and gas development".[429] This conclusion became the start of ongoing dialogue groups led by the CAO where both community members and Bankers' representatives attended to collectively discuss and find solutions to the seismic issue. The perception of the government as either a collaborative partner with limited capacity (the company's position) or as a company compliant exploiter (the community's position) was not addressed by the CAO recommendation. The CAO concluded that the "composition of any potential working group should be decided collaboratively by the company, appropriate public sector representatives, and the complainants".[430] The responsibility of the Albanian government is thus generally undermined by this conclusion, depicted as an equal partner to the company and the community for finding a solution. In the following CAO dialogue, government representatives only played a minor role and rarely participated in further discussions.

The CAO dialogue groups

The following autobiographical narrative is situated in the CAO dialogue groups where company and community representatives discussed the seismic issue and where I was present as a company representative. An analysis of these narratives provides further insight into the dynamics between antagonistic positions as they interact in the same room:

> As a participant in the CAO-led dialogue groups, the different levels of conversations that seemed to flow along in parallel during the meetings continually amazed me. There was the official level of Bankers' senior managers and the CAO representatives, which involved actors writing down action items, paraphrasing the corporate policy and adhering to the CAO guidelines for successful mediation. On the official level spoken in, or translated into, English, community representatives and

[428] CAO (2013a), p. 8.
[429] CAO (2013b), p. 1.
[430] CAO (2013a), p. 10.

local staff members were actors, playing along to impress the managers and to make their voices heard. The Albanian spoken on an unofficial level was excluded from the ears of the top managers and was comprised of jokes on a more personal level, references to events taking place outside office hours and discussions about political and family affiliations which were not expressed openly. On paper the CAO process was formulated as an ambitious attempt at solving company-community conflicts through dialogue and 'participatory fact finding' but it looked to me more as a series of incoherent meetings where the process itself seemed more important than the actual outcome.

"Can you find a specialist who can look into how the oilfield has impacted ground stability over time?" the young woman on the other side of the room asked with a firm voice. She had read about the theory that cavities can be created as a result of oil extraction, resulting in tremors. *"I believe that we have to find a specialist who knows about our technology"*, the senior manager responded calmly, *"and since it is heavy oil we are producing here there are not many such specialists in the world"*. He suggested that Bankers could do some research and come back to the dialogue group with suggestions of experts but emphasised that the company could not do this if there was a lack of trust in the process. *"If we suggest experts to you there may be people who will claim that we have selected them and thereby the experts would not be trusted. We are thus in a dilemma here, no matter how we proceed people will not trust the technical results"*.

The conversation shifted to the seismometers that the company had bought and installed in the field in order to improve the national system for monitoring earthquakes. With the two seismometers located in Patos-Marinza, the National Geophysical Institute would have increased their capacity from three to five seismometers on a national scale. This would have made it easier to assess whether or not tremors originated from the oilfield. But the Albanian government continued to ignore the company's request to connect the seismometers to the national grid and as long as they were not connected, the data gathered was useless. The dialogue group had written a joint letter to the government requesting them to connect the seismometers and to start measuring the data but without success.

"I'm going to apply for a work permit in Germany," the young woman told me in the coffee break. She seemed tired of the endless discussions in the dialogue group and the lack of concrete results. *"It is a long application process, but it is worth it"*, she said, *"there is no future for me in Albania"*. As the dialogue group was continuing, I thought about the exodus of young Albanians leaving the country due to lack of employment possibilities and rampant corruption. We would need years to

> agree on a technical expert that everyone in the group could trust. *"Maybe a coffee in the sun would do more to improve the relationships"*, I thought, as the discussions continued in the CAO format.[431]

My account from the CAO dialogue group shows that the focus on technology dominated proceedings, a natural consequence of the conclusion of the CAO assessment – that the conflict could be solved through "better, more trusted technical information" and with the involvement of "independent experts".[432] The focus on technology strengthened the position of the company in these dialogues as it had superior access to the knowledge and skills to understand oilfield technology. The community members tried to reinforce their position through reading up on oil technology, such as the young woman asking for a long-term impact study. However, the company easily dismissed such attempts by referring to the special technology used by Bankers and the few experts available worldwide. This skewed the balance of power balance, something also visible from the summary reports of the meetings. The *CAO Case Progress Report* from 2016 lists action items discussed in the dialogue groups and details how the company offered to organise "joint field trips", to "provide information and documentation", and encouraged community members to "identify international experts with experience in the specific type of technology".[433] These types of actions can be seen as hegemonic articulations that frame both Bankers' 'western technology' and CSR activities as positive and beneficial to Albania. The company's focus on technological disclosure and the need for fact-finding can thus be seen as a strategy to shift opponents from a position of direct resistance to a process of finding mutual solutions. Bankers needed the community's good will to continue its operations and thus had an interest in incorporating demands into efforts that seemed collaborative. The goal of consensus, of finding a solution in dialogue, can thus be seen as a hegemonic articulation in which other solutions and views were excluded.

Controlling the 'truth' through experts and stakeholder dialogues

In the above sections you have seen how Bankers' staff and contractors, including me, used the word 'earthquake' to equate the seismic movements

[431] Autobiographical narrative, written in 2016.
[432] CAO (2013b), p. 1.
[433] CAO (2016), p. 5.

in Patos-Marinza to similar occurrences in other parts of the region and the world. The word 'earthquake' emphasises that tectonic plates, i.e. the earth itself, causes the seismic movements. On the other hand, the term 'tremors' was used by local residents, who said that 'earthquake' is a false attribution, that the company is lying, and the 'tremors' are the direct consequence of Banker's extraction techniques. Here, 'tremors' is used to equate the occurrences in Patos-Marinza with discussions about earth movements and extraction techniques in other parts of the world, for example fracking.[434] The prevailing definition of reality is what creates a temporary hegemonic structure, a frame which steers future words and actions. It is thus not a mere play with words, an analysis for the sake of analysis. It has social consequences. The conflict surrounding seismic tremors shows how community members held protests and wrote satirical comments on Facebook pages as part of their counter-hegemonic discourse, establishing their legitimacy as subjects with rightful claims as victims of corporate exploitation. The company focused on communicating their technological and societal initiatives, reinforcing the discourse of the company as a contributor to Albanian development. At the same time the company continued to expand the oilfield even though no solution to the seismic issue had been found. The company participation in the CAO dialogue groups can thereby be seen as a way to maintain its hegemonic position, expanding its operations on Patos-Marinza soil while at the same time showing willingness to hold dialogues with local residents in the area.

The conflict regarding earthquakes/tremors in Patos-Marinza clearly exemplifies Laclau and Mouffe's rejection of a separation between the discursive and non-discursive,[435] highlighting how a conflict regarding what can be seen as based on a 'natural' phenomenon is actually a conflict between discursive structures. It is the competition to define reality that is highlighted through the analysis of how various terms are articulated in the conflict. When there is a lack of consensus regarding the processes and the institutions producing facts, a 'joint fact finding' solution is deemed to fail. The CAO conclusion did not address this underlying issue but was framed as a neutral, objective position focusing on finding answers through technological expertise. This is thus a classic example of the "depoliticisation of politics", a process that Peter D. Thomas describes as "the conversion of formerly expressly political debates into purely bureaucratic or technical

[434] Alba Leaks (2015, May 11); @nopetroleum (2015, August 7).
[435] Laclau & Mouffe (1985/2014).

questions".[436] The technical focus in the CAO dialogue groups enhanced the powerful position of Bankers as the party with the best access to technological information about oilfield operations. By not addressing the general lack of trust for state institutions, the CAO process contributed to a situation in which the company could continue to act in a 'vacuum'. In addition, by ignoring that community members were portrayed as ignorant in the hegemonic discourse, the CAO contributed to a conflict in which community members remained as the subordinate party. From the conclusions made in the assessment report, the 'objective' standpoint of the CAO can thus be seen as reinforcing corporate hegemony rather than challenging it. Corporate technology gained a dominant position over the bodily experiences of residents. Here it also become important to highlight the characteristics of the CAO as a 'western' organisation with headquarters in Washington DC and reporting directly to the President of the World Bank Group.[437] The 'neutral' position of the CAO as a mediator can be seen as ways for western institutions, such as IFC, to criticise themselves on their own premises, incorporating critique in order to maintain power.

So, where did I stand as a company representative? On the one hand, I believed the engineers' accounts that the 'earthquakes' were 'natural', and that the community members were misinformed about the relationship between oil extraction techniques and tremors. However, as a company representative, I also went to numerous meetings with community members who stated that the earth moved and sounded differently during induced tremors when compared to natural earthquakes. This, for me, opened up the possibility that both natural and induced tremors took place in the area. Some of my Albanian colleagues also expressed convictions that the earthquakes were induced by extraction activities, which further challenged my belief in the company's story. The articulations by residents and staff members connected to the counter-hegemonic discourse that the company was hiding something. This antagonistic discourse described 'western technology' as damaging the local environment and the company's CSR efforts were a way of hiding the facts. I wondered, then: what incentives were needed for the company to stop certain activities or to change technologies if extraction techniques were indeed causing tremors? In a context with low governmental control and with no environmental NGOs present, such incentives were negligible. Instead, participating in

[436] Thomas (2009/2010), p. 151.
[437] CAO (2017).

information disclosure and the CAO dialogue groups would be in line with IFC's and EBRD's sustainability standards and a workable way to mitigate stakeholder demands while its operations were expanded as planned. The underlying issue in this conflict, the lack of trust which hindered any joint fact-finding mission from being successful, was not addressed in the CAO dialogue groups. Instead the groups allowed Bankers to continue producing oil in a governance 'vacuum' while the residents wasted their time in endless company – community discussions. With no reliable third-party institutions available to solve the conflict, I was left wondering how 'truth' could ever be achieved.

A summary of findings

I have now completed the analysis of the three company-community conflicts that I set out to investigate in the introductory chapter. While Chapter Five showed how residents reluctantly accepted Bankers' land acquisition practices, Chapter Six showed how the air quality conflict created stronger articulations of the counter-hegemonic discourse in Patos-Marinza communities. In this chapter you have seen how the conflicts regarding seismic events further fuelled discontent in Patos-Marinza. However, a larger community movement failed to mobilise, and Bankers continued to expand its operations. The discursive configuration of the CAO dialogue groups allowed the company to reinforce its hegemonic narrative, namely that it was actively working together with community representatives to find a 'joint solution'. The use of experts and technology was a vital part of this hegemonic articulation, which at the same time dismissed residents' bodily experiences as valid evidence in the discussion.

In the next chapter I will summarise the findings from Chapters Four to Seven and discuss how these can contribute in answering my question regarding the role of sustainability standards and CSR in Patos-Marinza conflicts. I will also discuss my role as a CSR professional and how my shifting and contradictory subject positions contributed to conflict dynamics. In addition, I will link this discussion to the wider question regarding how discourses around 'sustainability' and 'CSR' in the corporate sector can be understood as hegemonic articulations.

CHAPTER 8

Corporate sustainability as a hegemonic practice

Now you might ask: so what really happened in Patos-Marinza? Were corporate representatives using land acquisition for their own gain? Was the air quality dangerous to residents' health? Did Bankers' operations cause the earth tremors? It has not been my intention to solve these puzzles, but instead to highlight how 'truth' and hegemony are linked. My aim has thus been to show how opposing discursive configurations struggled to define what was happening in Patos-Marinza and how verbal, monetary and material articulations, enforced by IFC's sustainability standards and Bankers' CSR practices, created a hegemonic 'bloc' of actors that made possible Bankers' continuous expansion of the oilfield. No matter what the facts behind these struggles were, Bankers' operations and hegemonic definition of the field continued to expand.

In the following sections I will summarise and deepen my analysis of Patos-Marinza in order to answer the three research questions, which I first specified in Chapter One:

- What role did sustainability standards and CSR practices play in the conflicts between Bankers and the communities of Patos-Marinza?
- How can I understand my own role as a CSR professional in this dynamic?
- In what way can corporate discourses around sustainability and CSR be understood as hegemonic articulations?

I will start this chapter by discussing the configuration of Bankers' hegemonic discourse and relate this analysis back to my theoretical framework. Next, I will briefly address the role of the Albanian state in Patos-Marinza and discuss what can be understood as 'force' in this context. I will then move on to discuss the role of sustainability standards and CSR practices in the conflicts between Bankers and local communities. This analysis highlights how Bankers' CSR activities helped to extend the corporate alliance, break potential chains of equivalence between various community demands, and control truth claims through dialogues, technology and experts. I will continue the chapter with an analysis of my own role as a CSR professional and how I participated in Bankers' hegemonic articulations. Finally, I will conclude by discussing 'sustainability' as an empty signifier and the potentially pacifying role of 'sustainability' and 'CSR' in conflictual relationships between the corporate sector and society. I will also describe how the framework of three hegemonic mechanisms – transformism, corporatisation and depoliticisation – developed from the dynamic in Patos-Marinza, can be used as a guide to scrutinise other corporate contexts where 'sustainability' and 'CSR' are applied.

A hegemonic alliance around the 'investment'

Based on what you have read so far about the struggles in Patos-Marinza, you might ask: *Is it right to frame Bankers' discourse as hegemonic in a context where many actors opposed it?* With this question in mind, I want to start by emphasising that Political Discourse Theory defines hegemony as never fully constituted and the conflicts in Patos-Marinza is an example of this. The concept of hegemony thus highlights a power relationship, but one that is under constant negotiation and which needs to be continuously reinforced to be sustained. Some actors, in local communities, among Bankers' staff and government representatives, did not buy into the corporate discourse but challenged it through continuous counter-hegemonic articulations. By sharing stories that disclosed cracks in the corporate narrative these actors created a foundation for protests against Bankers and negative media attention regarding the company's operations. Regardless of this forceful resistance, western actors (such as IFC, EBRD and Bankers) continued to promote company activities as beneficial to Albania. The framing of the Albanian state and society as lacking capacity and skills was one way of legitimising Bankers as the only and best option for the development of the oilfield, in particular towards western stakeholders such as investors and international control organs. One can thus understand the corporate hegemonic discourse as a way of gaining legitimacy on the international arena, that is, it appeals to the international 'hegemonic bloc' comprised of investors, international banks, and global financial institutions. Although many local actors did not buy into this discourse, it provided a possible way for the company to continue its operations in Patos-Marinza, highlighting the power of international institutions vis-a-vis local actors.

But the hegemonic discourse was also accepted by many local actors and enforced by various material hegemonic articulations that drew local stakeholders into its hegemonic bloc. In the period between 2004 and 2016, when a Canadian senior management team directed Bankers, 'the west' appeared at the doorstep of Patos-Marinza and filled 'the social' with hopes and dreams of a better future. Let me summarise the hegemonic discourse that my empirical material portrays in the voice of a constructed 'western alliance'. The alliance smiled and held out its hand to residents while whispering:

> *Leave behind the poverty of your communist past and your tiresome agricultural tasks. You can become a well-paid employee, a wealthy landowner or an appreciated contractor. Join us in the quest for a free life in which wealth flourishes and happiness is within reach. We are your opportunity for success. We are rich, well organised, technologically advanced and socially responsible. If you join us, your life will never be the same again. The complaints you hear are from people who are stuck in the past. They are jealous, ignorant and greedy. They are not capable to take advantage of the opportunities that we are providing. But you are different, you see, you can become one of us.*

This hegemonic discourse was articulated by the 'historic bloc', consisting of IFC, EBRD, Bankers' investors and managers, satisfied employees and contractors. Discursively, it was stabilised around the nodal point of the 'investment'. It defined Patos-Marinza as an 'oilfield' and stated forcefully that a 'western investment' would be a blessing to the degraded area. It promised that the 'investment' would be an opportunity for all, a universal development project in which everyone could participate. Bankers' corporative project – that is, the project of this particular group – was thus by this hegemonic articulation extended to include a broader alliance, to make the project a vision for society at large. The 'investment' became what Laclau and Mouffe call an 'empty signifier' – a concept that each aspirational group of actors filled with their own dreams of economic progress. When this narrative was disrupted by actors speaking about an 'invasion' and 'genocide', the 'western alliance' sighed with impatience: *this local area does not know what is in its best interests and, with its ignorance, laziness and rumours, it is so difficult to handle.* The alliance thus diminished the critics by depicting them as 'ignorant' and 'greedy'; in contrast, it personalised the dream by showing examples of happy employees who were making a decent salary, a subject position that potentially was within reach for anyone who made the effort.

But wait – you may contest – *Bankers was investing in Patos-Marinza. This was not only a verbal proclamation but the reality; an 'invasion' is something different.* This thought is what makes the nodal point of the 'investment' central to Bankers' hegemonic configuration. It is a signifier which allows us to define certain activities in a specific way, and this definition is seen as objective. To frame something as neutral and objective has a particular meaning in Political Discourse Theory. Laclau emphasises that a discourse has achieved a hegemonic position when it can be viewed as objective: "it is what appears to be given with the effect that it hides contingency and hegemonic struggles".[438] The 'investment' can thus be seen as such a hegemonic articulation that legitimised and naturalised 'the truth' about Bankers' operations in Patos-Marinza. Through its connections to other signifiers – such as 'economic growth', 'technology', 'skills', 'sustainability' and 'corporate social responsibility' – the 'investment' was framed as beneficial to the region and as a process from which everyone would win. In this powerful higher 'truth', contradictory examples of how the corporation caused harm to the local environment and people did not fit and thereby were covered over. An 'investment' is in the current societal configuration something legal, legitimate and economically beneficial. An 'invasion' on the other hand is brutal, illegitimate, and destructive. When corporate activities are designated as an 'investment' they therefore gain legitimacy, support and admiration. They are seen as activities that create 'economic growth', 'development' and 'prosperity'. This hegemonic articulation covers over 'the political' logics constitutive of these social activities, they make these descriptions objective and true. What is covered over is the illegitimate nature of corporate practices; the violence, injustices and damages that were all prevalent in Bankers' operations.

Force – undesirable subject positions and an expanding oilfield

My analysis of Patos-Marinza also shows the contingent subject positions of the actors themselves and how groups are fluid and subjected to transformations by hegemonic articulations. Just as Laclau and Mouffe explain in their framework,[439] there are no pre-existing groups. Rather, the subject positions of the actors are articulated in competing discourses. As described by Gerber: "material transformations of places create different

[438] Laclau in Gerber, Gunnarson Payne & Lundgren (2012), p. 3, my translation.
[439] Laclau and Mouffe (1985/ 2014).

opportunities and limitations in peoples' daily lives, as well as which identifications that become possible and attractive".[440] Accordingly, the hegemonic intervention of Bankers' alliance rendered some subject positions desirable while others became synonymous with a 'losing' and 'subordinate' side. Patos-Marinza is yet another example of the classic division of the population where the 'winners' (the rich) are considered strong, superior and desirable while the 'losers' (the poor) are considered weak, inferior and undesirable. This shows what Glynos and Howarth call the 'fantasmatic' dimension of the hegemonic narrative; the 'beatific' dimension of the 'investment' promises a "fullness-to-come" while the 'horrific' dimension is represented through "images of impotence or victimhood".[441] Those Patos-Marinza residents who complained about Bankers were frequently described in the hegemonic discourse as ignorant, greedy and jealous; descriptions that de-legitimised their grievances and placed them in an inferior position. This narrative has often been repeated throughout history, for example in Gramsci's description of how the rural Italian south was framed by the industrial north,[442] or in John Gaventa's description of the degradation of the Appalachian mountain culture in favour for the new industrial order.[443] The creation of winner–loser, superior-inferior, strong-weak, educated-ignorant dichotomies make an alliance on the 'undesired' side less likely as various segments of the population would rather define themselves as being on the winning side. Counter-hegemonic tendencies are thus connected to the 'horrific' dimension of the hegemonic narrative in which specific bodies become degraded as 'impotent victims'. This discursive definition of counter-hegemonic subject positions then opens up for the legitimisation of violence against these 'inferior' bodies. When Gramsci wrote "force can be employed against enemies"[444] he emphasised that hegemony is a blend of force and consent.[445] While Gramsci saw the creation of consent as vital for a hegemonic bloc to gain and remain in power, force, he argued, would always be present, it would lurk behind the scenes. In Patos-Marinza, the hegemonic bloc created the 'enemy' through logics of difference; making dissatisfied residents and farmers the impossible subjects to include in an otherwise 'benevolent' and 'inviting' hege-

[440] Gerber (2012), p. 55, my translation.
[441] Glynos & Howarth (2007), p. 147.
[442] Gramsci (1929-1930/ 1992), p. 144.
[443] Gaventa (1980), pp. 65-68.
[444] Gramsci (1929-1933/1999).
[445] Thomas (2009/2010), p. 194.

monic formation. The hegemonic bloc was continuously creating this 'enemy' by systematically discrediting residents' claims as 'ignorant' and 'greedy'. As a consequence, the violence that sometimes showed itself in Patos-Marinza through the intervention of state police was directed against this antagonistic group. Force was used towards those defined as 'losers', who protested and continued to demand that they be included as beneficiaries.

Regardless of the brief interventions by state police, the actors in Patos-Marinza mainly described state authorities as 'absent', but from different angles. Company representatives complained that the state has been absent and had not performed its regulatory role. 'Illegal' residences, lack of air monitoring and 'rumours' of oil operations causing tremors could thus be blamed on irresponsible state authorities, at least according to company claims. This echoes the descriptions of regulatory 'vacuums' in the CSR literature in which multinational corporations are 'suffering' from a lack of government control. Bankers' claimed to fill the gap of a 'weak' Albanian state through its CSR initiatives, investing in responsible land acquisition, air monitoring and seismometers. The consequence of this 'gap filling' was that it hindered a necessary conversation about the role of state authorities and their societal function to control company operations. Instead, the company could engage directly with the local communities, in dialogue groups and through its grievance mechanism, without the meddling hands of state authorities. On the other hand, the accounts from residents indicate that they were also experiencing a situation where they lived in a 'vacuum', where neither state nor media were on their side and the company could "do whatever it wants". However, in contrast to company representatives, residents perceived this lack of state intervention to be due to an alliance between state and corporate representatives, a situation in which this 'bloc' of actors gained money from oil operations while residents were left with the consequences. According to residents' testimonies, the governance 'vacuum' in Patos-Marinza was thus not a problem for Bankers but a condition that allowed the company to "do whatever it wants", that is, to further expand its operations. The lack of regulation, which Patos-Marinza actors described, provided a situation where Bankers' 'market based' land acquisition and the expanding oilfield itself can be understood as a 'force' directed towards residents. This force towards bodies in Patos-Marinza showed itself as a direct effect of Bankers' expanding operations in the form of poor air quality, noise and blocked drainages. This force was linked to what residents signified as an 'occupation', an expanding oil operation that changed their living environment in the form of underground tremors, wells next to their lands and gas emissions that filled the lungs of their children and elderly. For what is force if not the physical threat to bodies working on their lands to survive? The accounts of residents indicate that this threat made residents accept corrupt land rental practices as the only way for them to live a tolerable life in an environment where the oil industry was perceived to threaten them on all fronts: from below, next to their land and from the air. The 'horrific' dimension of Bankers project was thus also connected to these physical threats to those persons living in Patos-Marinza. The 'horrific' dimension stipulated that those who did not win, who were not part of Bankers' alliance, were left to experience the physical force of Bankers expansion in an area they continued to call home.

The role of IFC's sustainability standards and Bankers' CSR practices

I have now summarised my findings from Patos-Marinza in terms of the hegemonic discourse promoted by Bankers and the force directed towards undesirable subject positions. I will now proceed to deepen my analysis of the role of sustainability standards and CSR practices in this dynamic by answering my first research question that I formulated above and in chapter one:

- What role did international sustainability standards and CSR practices play in the conflicts between Bankers and the communities of Patos-Marinza?

The ways in which Bankers' applied IFC's sustainability standards in relation to the three corporate-community conflicts, which I have discussed in the empirical chapters of this study, are expressions of the ideals advanced in the academic discussion on deliberative democracy and consensus driven CSR. The standards were applied in order for the company to 'understand' and 'respond to' community demands as a way to achieve a fullness; working towards a 'beatific'[446] ideal in which all actors were satisfied. Through these empirical examples my aim has been to illustrate how sustainability standards and CSR, based on ideals of deliberative demo-

[446] Glynos & Howarth (2007), p. 147.

cracy, can be used to dominate stakeholders and strengthen corporate power through slight amendments in the corporate structure, all the while preventing more fundamental change to the dominant order and its underlying injustices and violence. My findings from Patos-Marinza point to three specific hegemonic mechanisms, made possible through the implementation of IFC's sustainability standards and Bankers' CSR practices:

Transformism – extending the corporate alliance

The first hegemonic mechanism that was active in Patos-Marinza is what Gramsci called 'transformism' – an "absorption of the elites of the enemy classes" that "results in their decapitation and renders them impotent".[447] This 'absorption' moved community members over to the hegemonic side, and created new chains of equivalence between company and community interests, blurring any potential antagonistic frontier dividing the social.

Market-based land acquisition promoted by IFC's standards and in Bankers' communication material allowed for this first type of hegemonic articulation. While IFC's sustainability standards describe expropriation as a violent and damaging process at risk of creating community resistance, privately negotiated land rental processes are promoted as 'beneficial' and 'free'. Accordingly, Bankers' land rental processes were dealt with each landowner individually, thereby allowing a larger transformation of the geographical area without the formation of any widespread community resistance movement. As formulated by Laclau, chains of equivalence between community demands can be prevented from being established if the institutional system satisfies claims, i.e. "to absorb them in a *differential* way (each in isolation for the others)."[448] Market-based land rental meant that each community member could potentially become a beneficiary of Bankers 'investment', meaning a chance to be part of the corporate alliance. As Patos-Marinza residents testified to, their fellow neighbours were silenced as they received money for their land and were afraid that the company would cancel these incomes if they complained. Money thus worked to silence community members and divided them into winners and losers; IFC's sustainability standards were legitimising devices that framed these market transactions as 'beneficial' and 'voluntary'.

'Transformism' was also made possible through Bankers' grievance mechanism. By satisfying aggrieved parties, Bankers' grievance mechanism

[447] Gramsci (1929-1930/ 1992), p. 137.
[448] Laclau (2005), p. 73.

helped to extend the corporate alliance; for example, households receiving generous compensation packages were brought over to the side of the Bankers' beneficiaries. The example of Arber's air quality grievance served as such a case. His grievance was addressed and satisfied, and subsequently he was included within Bankers' hegemonic bloc. The threat of an antagonistic frontier between the company and the community was thus diffused by this move; lines of conflict were blurred and potential opponents incorporated into the corporate alliance. This move, which may look like an admirable approach – a company that 'listens to' and 'understands' community demands –, was essentially a way to prevent larger protests movements being formed as chains of equivalence were constructed between the company and those actors benefitting from 'investment'.

Corporatisation – the prevention of a 'community'

The second hegemonic mechanism that was active in Patos-Marinza is what I will call 'corporatisation', a term based on Gramsci's separation between 'hegemonic' and 'corporate' groups. To recapitulate what was outlined in Chapter Two, a 'hegemonic group' is, for Gramsci, one that can articulate general demands towards the institutional system, and that moreover can incorporate the demands of other groups, creating a sense of 'community' or a 'people'. A 'corporate group' is, on the other hand, a group that articulates only those demands relevant to itself. As emphasised by Laclau, those in power have an interest in isolating demands and groups, thus actively preventing the formation of a general community demand, which could threaten the current hegemonic order. To reiterate a formulation by Laclau: "The anti-political move par excellence consists in obtaining, as much as possible, a situation in which all interests become corporative, preventing the formation of a 'people'".[449] Those in power can use various techniques in order to keep community interests 'corporative', preventing chains of equivalence forming between groups. Bankers' grievance mechanism, which allowed community members to file their complaints individually, was one such mechanism through which community demands were isolated. Instead of protesting against the company as a group, community members could be dealt in isolation. Bankers' grievance mechanism can thus be seen as an example of consensus driven

[449] Laclau (2006), p. 113.

CSR, in which the political nature of corporate actions is hidden under buzzwords such as 'stakeholder engagement' and 'consultation'.

Market-based land acquisition worked in a similar way; strong incentives were introduced for each household to consider their own well-being before the general community. Land payments (or potential land payments) were thus used to isolate community members, making them afraid of losing their current or potential future benefits. The narrative of the 'investment' that would benefit all, coupled with money flows that strengthened this hegemonic discourse by means of land and compensation payments, thus effectively silenced community actors by isolating each landowner and aggrieved resident as an actual or potential beneficiary. This strategy kept residents' interests on what Gramsci called a 'corporate' level.[450] Whereas the mechanism termed 'transformism' describes how community members were brought over to the side of the corporate alliance, 'corporatisation' describes a process in which community members remained on the antagonistic side of the frontier, but were isolated from each other. 'Transformism' thus describes the creation of chains of equivalence between the corporation and community members while 'corporatisation' describes how chains of equivalence on the antagonistic (community) side were broken or, in fact, never formed.

Depoliticisation – controlling facts and 'truth'

The third hegemonic mechanism active in Patos-Marinza was depoliticisation; a process to control what is discussed in the public debate and what can be considered 'truth'. This was highlighted in Chapter Seven about the seismic conflict and the CAO dialogue groups. Political Discourse Theory emphasises truth as contingent and continuously created in political struggles dependent on the cultural and historical context. As described by Gabriella Nilsson: "What we see as objective is in this view the result of these power struggles where the traces of power have been wiped out".[451] The conflict of earthquakes/tremors in Patos-Marinza was based how various actors understood what was happening, in accordance with which discursive structures the actors had access to and which discourses appealed to their group. Jenny Gunnarsson Payne emphasises that when we look at political articulations, we need to understand their relation to the wider societal context and ask ourselves from which discourses "they gather

[450] Gramsci (1929-1930/ 1992), p. 147.
[451] Nilsson (2012), p. 42, my translation.

inspiration, oppose or are part of".[452] To understand the conflicts in Patos-Marinza it is thus important to look at how 'investments' in oil extraction activities, and opposition to such 'invasions', have been framed in other contexts. The actions of project stakeholders become easier to understand in light of external discourses and how the subject positions of actors are linked to them. The word 'earthquake', used by company representatives, was linked to concepts such as 'tectonic plates', 'the earth', 'seismic monitoring' and 'building techniques'. The word 'tremors', used by community members, was linked to a different discursive structure with relations to concepts such as 'extraction techniques', 'fracking', 'irresponsibility', and 'exploitation.'

While transformism and corporatisation highlight material and economic aspects of hegemonic articulations, depoliticisation shows how the construction of 'truth' is used for domination and how this prevents unifying 'empty signifiers' to be formed on the antagonistic side. As formulated by Spence, hegemony means that "...meaning can be relatively fixed and is so when certain discourses come to dominate others and become the main guide for action".[453] In constructing 'truth' in local places, we contribute to a particular side of a hegemonic struggle, that is, to the particular interests of a particular group or alliance. My analysis of the seismic tremors and the company-community dialogue groups are in line with previous research that show how stakeholder engagement and deliberation can become primarily a tool to control the discourse about company-society conflicts.[454] As Cederström and Marinetto describe, a core feature of CSR is: "that all problems are of practical nature, and hence best solved by corporate engagement".[455] Bankers' addressed the conflict surrounding seismic tremors through dialogue groups where experts and technology were used to enforce the company's view on the conflict. Bankers' representatives were frustrated that the general public did not believe in the 'facts' and framed this opposition to corporate 'truth' as politicised and based on poor education. Modern science, technologies and experts were thus framed as 'responsible' and 'objective' and were used to silence the bodily experiences of community members. In the 'vacuum' left by Albanian state authorities, the company became the producer of 'facts' and

[452] Gunnarsson Payne (2017), p. 258.
[453] Spence (2007), p. 858.
[454] Fooks, Gilmore, Collin, Holden & Lee (2013).
[455] Cederström & Marinetto (2013), p. 416.

'truth' while community members had no third party to turn to, and thus no epistemic and scientific support for their own claims. While we today speak frequently about the dangers of the 'post-truth society' – Patos-Marinza highlights the dangers of the 'truth society' to those in subordinate positions who do not have access to the skills, education, technology and social networks necessary to produce 'facts' or higher 'truths'.

The production of 'facts' through Bankers' technology and appointed experts was not only used to undermine residents' bodily experiences of poor air and earth shakings, but also to control the general agenda for the public debate and to avoid larger political issues. The question addressed in the dialogue groups became focused on whether or not the oil industry was causing earthquakes. This question hides other questions, such as if the oil industry is beneficial for the local population and if oil industry should continue to expand or exist at all? This can also be seen in how Bankers addressed grievances related to air emissions and land acquisition with technical information and 'stakeholder engagement'. The depoliticisation of the debate in Patos-Marinza was thus accomplished both by producing 'facts' regarding specific technical issues and by avoiding more fundamental questions that challenged the nodal point of the 'investment'. As a result, Bankers 'investment' could continue without being challenged by an alternative empty signifier that could unify heterogeneous community grievances within the wider area. Dialogues and technical references thus continuously undermined the counter-hegemonic discourse based around the nodal point of the 'invasion', while the 'investment' could continue to expand through both verbal and material means.

To sum up, the implementation of IFC's sustainability standards and Bankers' CSR practices in Patos-Marinza supported the articulation of three specific hegemonic mechanisms – transformism, corporatisation and depoliticisation. The result of these articulations was: (i) the incorporation of community members into the company alliance through land-rental payments and compensation arrangements; (ii) the isolation of dissatisfied community members through the processing of grievances on strictly a corporate level; and (iii) the depoliticisation of debates surrounding Bankers' operations by focusing on technical issues rather than fundamental questions, such as the existence of the oil field or the distribution of oil revenues.

My role as a CSR professional

Having answered my first research question, regarding the role of sustainability standards and CSR practices in the conflicts between Bankers and Patos-Marinza communities, I now turn to my second question, which concerns my own involvement in the conflicts in Patos-Marinza:

- How can I understand my own role as a CSR professional in this dynamic?

With this research question, my intention is to use my own experience as an example to discuss the involvement of sustainability workers and CSR professionals in corporate – community struggles. This is in line with my autoethnographic approach, in which the personal can be used as an asset in order to understand society. In my role as a CSR professional, I implemented the sustainability standards and CSR practices that the previous section describes. While understanding myself as an internal critic at the time, I can in hindsight see how my participation supported the expansion of the three corporate hegemonic mechanisms I now have identified.

The relatively fluid character of subject positions is a core feature of Laclau and Mouffe's theoretical framework. This means that our conceptualisation of ourselves in relation to our surroundings may change when we come in contact with new discourses.[456] Different discourses position me as an expat employed in the oil industry, a PhD student, a daughter or a mother. Sometimes we inhabit these various positions without conflicts while at other times they come into conflict with one another. Mats Lindqvist argues that in times of cultural and social change (what Laclau calls *dislocations*), previously harmonic subject positions can become antagonistic: "The freedom that dislocations open converts individuals (independent of their will) to political subjects, as they seek solutions through identification with new discourses".[457] A similar process of dislocation happens when a person moves from one context to another and thereby gets access to new discourses. When I moved from Sweden to start working in the Albanian oil industry, new discourses became available to me, which forced me to reinstitute myself as a subject. My fantasmatic ambition to 'change the oil industry from within' soon clashed with the 'lived reality' and the tasks I needed to carry out as an employee within this industrial

[456] Laclau & Mouffe (1985/2014), p. 101.
[457] Lindqvist (2012), p. 19.

sector. My certainties and doubts about Bankers' operations, which I express in the autobiographical narratives can thus be understood in this way; in my professional role I continued to shift subject positions between a resentful but loyal company representative to an internal antagonist and back again.

So, let us return to where we started this story, with me standing in the middle of a community protest, sent out by Bankers to calm down resistance and demobilise a growing crowd. When I analyse my past verbalisations and actions I ask: How did I contribute to a specific hegemonic configuration which made certain social actions and structures possible while hindering others? What 'truth' did I reproduce through my articulations? What did I tell myself in order to keep working in a system that I saw as failing? Based on my analysis in the previous chapters I can see how my own involvement was an integral part of Bankers' CSR programme, which functioned as a hegemonic tool. Regardless of my conscious views and hidden hopes to change the company from within, I was, when all is said and done, part of the articulation of corporate hegemony. By including myself in my analysis of this phenomenon in Patos-Marinza, I want to underline the importance of analysing the consequences of our specific articulations rather than our intentions. By this I want to avoid discussions about a capitalist or western 'conspiracy'. The concept of hegemony highlights the importance of awareness regarding how we are all a part of reproducing certain truths and structures and how our speech and actions challenge or maintain a specific dominant order. It is the consequences from how we speak and act that are highlighted through this analysis, not our internal motivations. Spence writes:

> There may be some value in the Gramscian conception of how ideas develop and are disseminated throughout society. Ideas are not pumped out by some central "ministry of truth". Rather, they are constructed and reproduced at various levels throughout society, and by a variety of social groups.[458]

In this way, local articulations related to CSR may be both, as Spence writes, "the reproduction of an existing ideology" and "the construction of ideology that in some way, however marginally, feeds back into wider dis-

[458] Spence (2007), p 876.

courses".[459] The relationship between local articulations and wider discursive structures is thus highlighted in this process.

When looking at my experiences in Patos-Marinza from a distance, I can see how my own shifting subject position was influenced by the hegemonic mechanisms of 'transformism' and 'corporatisation'. The imagination of the CSR worker as an 'internal critic' or a 'Trojan horse'[460] is a narrative that allows corporations to include critics on the corporate hegemonic side and prevent them from forming potential chains of equivalence with other critics. Positions linked to discourses around 'CSR', 'sustainability' or 'social and environmental management' thus allow the process of transformism to take place when previous antagonists are included to work for the corporate alliance, softening its image, and making it appear responsive towards demands that critics hold. This is the mechanism that I carried out in my daily role as a CSR professional, communicating with residents, NGOs and international control organs with a soft and pleasing voice, convincing them that Bankers' management were committed to changing corporate behaviour as a result of their critique. At the same time, these positions also allow the process of corporatisation to take place, on point of fact that critics are isolated from each other when corporate money is directed towards their livelihood, preventing alliances to form. While I was frustrated when corporate activities did not live up to their own stipulated sustainability standards and CSR policy, I did not contact critical NGOs in order to forge antagonistic alliances, nor did I instigate a community movement to raise stronger demands. When taking the position as an 'internal critic', I left a potential position as an external critic vacant and quiet. This also highlights the importance of understanding how flows of money work as articulations of specific subject positions; our dependence on the capitalist system for our livelihood makes the subject position as an 'internal critic' more attractive, since (after all) the external critic is often unpaid.

The analysis of my autobiographical narratives also shows how, as a company representative, I contributed to the mechanism of depoliticisation, by reinforcing certain discourses that I took for granted. I often took the subject position of a western expat with a view of Albanian society as difficult and frustrating. My articulations of 'western technology', 'CSR' and 'locals' can be linked to the corporate hegemonic discourse, pointing to

[459] Spence (2007), p 876.
[460] Kvarnström (2016).

Bankers' 'investment' as the best option for local development. In my narratives, I describe Albanian society as frustrating and lacking rational 'truth' mechanisms, a view which places the blame for corporate-community conflicts on local residents rather than the company. In my participation in stakeholder engagement activities, I reproduced this discourse by aiming for a consensual agreement based on 'participatory fact finding', a process that was aiming to convince residents of the corporate 'facts' that experts had produced. It is only by distancing myself from this corporate discourse, through my movement in time and space, and through the availability of new discourses, that I can see how I was part of reproducing certain 'truths' about Bankers and Patos-Marinza, even though (or maybe because) I saw myself as an internal critic. Similarly, through the continuous movement between theory and the empirical context in my PhD process, I look at my actions as a researcher in a new light. The PhD process has been a journey in which my subject position has shifted several times. For example, in my introductory letter to interviewees, I described Patos-Marinza as an 'oilfield'[461] and not a 'home'; and in the first interviews, I asked about seismic events as 'earthquakes' and not as 'tremors'. My research process was thus one in which I continued to produce Bankers' hegemonic view of the area and only later came to realise how these specific words strengthened the corporate version of the 'truth'.

Ellis emphasises that: "Autoethnography requires that we observe ourselves observing, that we interrogate what we think and believe, and that we challenge our own assumptions, asking over and over if we have penetrated as many layers of our own defences, fears and insecurities as our project requires".[462] To get a deeper understanding my contradictory feelings and behaviour as a CSR professional, I draw on the concepts of 'fantasmatic narratives' and 'enjoyment', which have been introduced to Political Discourse Theory from Lacanian thought.[463] These concepts allow me to dig deeper into my own thoughts and motivations when implementing CSR practices in a highly conflictual context. As I outlined in Chapter Two, several organisational studies have pointed to the fact that workers' transgressions and 'cynical distance' can provide effective means for organisations to function, for these provide an outlet for workers'

[461] See Annex 1.
[462] Ellis (2013/2016), p. 10.
[463] Glynos & Howarth (2007).

frustrations and allow them to continue performing their tasks.[464] As Stavrakakis writes:

> to retain its grip, every hegemonic ideology needs to take into account in advance its own failure, its own limits, and to condition its own (partial) transgression. Here, we see the lacking Other, an incomplete power structure, indirectly acknowledging this lack, allowing a certain degree of dis-identification, providing a breathing space for its subjects, on the condition, of course, that this remains under control.[465]

Stavrakakis thus underlines that transgressions and dis-identification are a vital part for a hegemonic regime to retain its grip over subjects. In my diary notes and autobiographical narratives, I describe a struggle through which I saw myself as continuously questioning and working against the corporate regime while at the same time being very much a part of it. The notion of 'CSR' and 'sustainability', that I was part of introducing to Bankers, allowed my fantasmatic narrative of the 'internal critic' to be maintained, providing me with daily doses of enjoyment while carrying out my tasks. In the larger picture, my acts allowed the continuous production of the contradictory concept of 'the sustainable oil company'. I told myself that if our team could just make social actors in the current order behave differently, the fantasmatic narrative of the ideal oil operation would materialise. It also gave me enjoyment in the fact that I could work for something higher and better; the company management became the bad 'other' in this narrative while those promoting sustainability and CSR became 'good'. If only this hindering Other could be changed or removed, then the ideal about the completely responsible corporation could be achieved. In this way I could enjoy my position within Bankers' regime through my transgressions. The enjoyment and transgressions are what allowed me to stay within Bankers for so long. When, as a CSR professional, I worked to maintain good relations with local residents, and sometimes worked against company policies in order to meet their demands, I was both sustaining my subject position as the 'insider antagonist' and maintaining the hegemonic order by making residents less hostile to the corporation.

I have now shown how the sustainability standards and CSR activities implemented in Patos-Marinza functioned to reinforce corporate hege-

[464] Burawoy (1979); Fleming & Spicer (2003).
[465] Stavrakakis (2010), p. 70.

mony over allied and subordinate subjects and how I participated in this dynamic as a CSR professional. In the last part of this chapter, I will address my third research question by reflecting on how corporations may use 'CSR' and 'sustainability' to make amendments to the current economic system and business models, and how that may hinder more fundamental change or the carrying out of a 'sustainability revolution'.

Pacifying a sustainability revolution

Having answered my first and second research questions, I now turn to my third one, in which I aim to expand my reasoning beyond Patos-Marinza and examine how the results can be applied to examine other corporate contexts. I ask:

- In what way can corporate discourses around sustainability and CSR be understood as hegemonic articulations?

To recapture what I explained in Chapter One, my intention here is not to generalise the results from Pats-Marinza to *all* corporate contexts but rather to describe how the hegemonic mechanisms I have identified above can be used to examine other corporate operations in which discourses around sustainability and CSR are applied.

In order to further discuss how CSR and sustainability operates as hegemonic articulations, I will return to Laclau's work on populism. What I want to do here is to imagine that 'populism' is a movement which allows an alternative vision of society to exercise its grip over the social, a transformation which dismisses the possibilities to mitigate or compensate for corporate harms and unsustainable businesses models and instead imagines the need to replace current business models by alternative modes of production. In order for such a transformation of society to take place (what Laclau calls 'populism' but what I will call a 'sustainability revolution'), Laclau details three conditions which have to be fulfilled. First, "the formation of an internal antagonistic frontier separating the 'people' from power"; second "an equivalential articulation of demands making the emergence of the 'people' possible"; and third, "the unification of these various demands [...] into a stable system of signification".[466] As you may notice, the hegemonic mechanisms which I have identified in Patos-

[466] Laclau (2005/2007), p. 74.

Marinza are directly opposed to these three conditions; transformism hinders the formation of an antagonistic frontier between the corporation and the community; corporatisation hinders links between community demands to be established; and depoliticisation hinders an alternative stable system of signification, that is, an alternative vision of society, to be formed. Let me elaborate on these necessary revolutionary conditions and hegemonic mechanisms one by one in order to describe how corporations may use 'sustainability' and 'CSR' to pacify a 'sustainability revolution'.

Blurring the antagonistic frontier

Firstly, an antagonistic frontier separating people from power, or, in this discussion, critics from the corporation, requires the formulation of the corporation as 'the problem' to be opposed to. In this sense, various sustainability measures taken by corporations will hinder such formulation by presenting the corporation as willing to change and by incorporating opponents into its realm. As I explained in Chapter One, international banks created sustainability standards in order to mitigate the harms that their investments in land-based development projects were recurrently creating. Standards were thus designed, not as a new 'sustainable' way of doing business, but as a measure to reduce the harms that the various projects were creating. The definition of 'sustainability' and 'CSR' as implemented in Patos-Marinza follows this idea of the mitigation of harms, something that is linked to the idea of the 'triple bottom line',[467] as discussed in Chapter One. This implies that win-win-win situations can be found, that prevailing business models can remain intact if only adjustments are made to compensate for social and environmental damages. Through this corporate definition of 'sustainability', the group of win-win-winners can be enlarged by all sorts of means, motivated by international performance standards for environmental and social sustainability. In Patos-Marinza, the mechanism of transformism, supported by IFC's sustainability standards, enlarged the 'winning' side of the antagonistic struggle; the winners were employed, contracted and benefited from land and compensation payments. A similar dynamic can be seen in other corporate contexts. When mitigation measures are presented under the concept of 'sustainability' it does not often mean that the corporation in question contributes to a new way of doing business that would lead to

[467] Elkington (1994); Kuhlman & Farrington (2010).

social and environmental improvements; rather it means that the corporation in question will attempt to do less harm but maintain its current business model. In Patos-Marinza, the mitigation of harms were articulated through land rental contracts instead of expropriation, participatory air monitoring programmes instead of relocation, dialogue groups instead of police force. Measures were thus presented as a way for Bankers to listen to the communities. It was a way for the company to be a 'good neighbour'. The result was however that oil extraction could continue as planned. Mitigation measures in other industries could be everything from recycling, minimising waste, replacing materials and designing projects in order to limit disturbances to nearby communities. One example is retailers encouraging consumers to recycle used clothes in order to receive a discount on their next purchase. Another example is airlines providing CO_2 compensation packages to their consumers. These measures make the corporation appear receptive to criticism from environmental groups and receptive to customers' needs for products that do not harm the environment. Such mitigation measures may also mean that specific 'critical' actors are employed or contracted as 'change agents'. In Bankers this work was carried out through the recruitment of a community relations department. The incorporation of 'critical' actors on the side of the corporate alliance may include various 'sustainability' positions as well as contracts with NGOs or state agencies. However, no matter how many harms are mitigated, the mitigation of harms is not the same as the creation of an alternative vision, of a socially and environmentally 'sustainable' mode of production. When mitigation is dressed in the veil of sustainability, the 'unsustainable' production system is portrayed as receptive to grievances of social and environmental degradation, showing willingness to mitigate these and work together with opponents. Yet, these changes do not often address the larger issues of production systems that rely on unaccounted externalities, which are paid by society in the form of social and environmental costs. Instead mitigation measures allow the production system to continue with claims that corporations are part of the 'sustainability transition' undertaken by an alliance of societal actors. A potential antagonistic frontier between critics and the corporation is thus blurred and the first condition for a sustainability revolution prevented.

Dispersing a sustainability movement

If a clear frontier has been established, and various demands are made against the corporation, then a second condition for a sustainability revolution is the formulation of links between these demands so that a 'sustainability movement' can be formed; what Laclau calls "the emergence of the 'people'".[468] Sustainability measures taken by the corporation may prevent such movements from appearing by isolating and satisfying demands, making them stay on a 'corporate' level without expanding any unifying links. This is the second hegemonic mechanism active in Patos-Marinza, which I call corporatisation. Corporatisation may be active through money distributed by the corporation, which makes actors depend on the corporation and keep their demands to themselves. This may be carried out by compensating for harms caused to specific individuals or groups, or by sponsoring various projects in civil society, which make actors dependent on corporate willingness. In Chapter One it was described how sustainability standards proclaim that harms perpetrated by IFC projects should be compensated for, if mitigation is not possible. 'Sustainability' in this sense is thus used to allow for compensation for the harms that a corporation causes, so that damaged parties are satisfied. Here sustainability is thus not about avoiding harm but to cause harm, where corporate resources are used to pay impacted parties until they can accept the harm that has been caused. In Patos-Marinza this was done through the grievance mechanism and by means of market-based land acquisition. In other contexts, compensation dressed as 'sustainability' could be everything from payments for environmental pollution or land use, donations to civil society and investments in local communities. One such example is corporations donating money to environmental NGOs while at the same time continuing to pollute the environment. Another is corporate projects to support economically vulnerable groups while at the same time opposing increased taxation or labour rights. Compensation packages allow corporate resources to be distributed to a wider range of actors, thereby making them less likely to complain about corporate practices. It thus hinders any alliance to form between counter-hegemonic forces and instead contributes to the corporatisation – isolation – of company opponents. As seen in Patos-Marinza, corporate promises of employment or contracts may prevent people from raising critique, since they may fear sacrificing any potential future income possibilities. Hence, the mechanism of corporatisation does not move actors from one side of the antagonistic frontier to the other, as in transformism, but rather it makes certain that links between demands are never formed. Chains of equivalence between demands are

[468] Laclau (2005/2007), p. 74.

thus dispersed or never created and the second condition for a sustainability revolution is prevented.

Suppressing a unifying signifier

If an antagonistic frontier between the corporation and its critics has been formed, and if a sustainability movement has been created through links between various demands, the third condition for a sustainability revolution is a unification of demands into what Laclau calls "a stable system of signification".[469] This means that demands are unified under an 'empty signifier', a signifier that each group of corporate opponents can fill with their own hopes and dreams and thus create an alternative vision of society opposing the corporate hegemonic order. The hegemonic mechanism of depoliticisation is active through sustainability measures that prevent such a unifying empty signifier to be articulated by corporate opponents. Various corporate communication efforts promoted under the umbrella of 'sustainability' or 'CSR' (and other given labels, such as 'stakeholder engagement' or 'community dialogues'), are examples of how the process of depoliticisation takes place in practice. Just as in Patos-Marinza, the conversations that take place under such labels risk being dominated by the corporate agenda, shifting focus from questioning the existence of an industry to how harms caused by the industry can be mitigated. The corporate definition of 'sustainability' thus covers over its radical potential as an idea that may open up alternative ways of envisioning both the economy and society. This can be seen in Patos-Marinza where corporate critics failed to envision an alternative to the oil industry. 'Sustainability' and 'CSR' can thus be defined as tools that corporations can use to prevent the underlying 'political' struggle – i.e. the redefining of society – from appearing. 'Sustainability' and 'CSR' is in this way used to cover over 'the political', to hide corporate failures through promises of improvements and to maintain the ideal of the 'sustainable' corporation. Corporations that actively engage in sustainability dialogues and collaborations, such as those promoted under Agenda 2030, is one way in which the private sector can continue to emphasise the need to maintain current economic structures and business models and instead promote small changes as 'sustainability transitions', while larger more existential and foundational questions get pushed to the margins. Even though sustainability is discussed in all

[469] Laclau (2005/2007), p. 74.

spheres of society today, the lack of alternatives to current 'unsustainable' economic models is glaringly obvious. Even the promising movement "Fridays for future", which has been able to articulate demands, create an antagonistic frontier between 'the young' and 'the powerful' and link demands under the empty signifier 'future', still lacks articulations of alternative visions of society. The mechanism of depoliticisation thus supresses a unifying signifier to form, which could otherwise have worked to mobilise a 'sustainability revolution'. Corporate hegemony, and the neoliberal order we all depend on for work, education, health and retirement, maintain its grip over our ability to think differently and daringly.

The risk and radical potential of the empty signifier 'sustainability'

For scholars who are interested in understanding and critiquing the hegemonic capitalist order, 'sustainability' and 'CSR' are important concepts to follow since they are widespread in today's business community. As emphasised by Stavrakakis:

> it is obviously impossible to analyse and effectively critique capitalist hegemony without closely following its often revolutionary and unexpected mutations, without locating the shifting distributions of form and force securing its reproduction within the broader anthropological, historical and moral picture. [...] Indeed every age, every historical conjuncture, every socio-political order, will institute its own blend of coercion, symbolic authority as well as fantasmatic and self-transgressive jouissance.[470]

Stavrakakis thus underlines that the capitalist economy changes and transforms over time and space. This needs to be closely examined to understand how capitalist hegemony is maintained. 'CSR' and 'sustainability' can in this picture be seen as an important part of the current configuration of capitalist hegemony. As I have argued above, they may represent a way for the capitalist order to integrate opponents into its realm and thereby diffusing the antagonistic frontier that threatens to grow stronger based on claims for environmental justice and the prevention of climate change. Just as the hegemonic discourse in Patos-Marinza shows, 'sustainability' and 'CSR' are umbrella terms that promote heterogeneous activities with a

[470] Stavrakakis (2010), p 73.

common universal endeavour; to picture the interest of the corporation as the interest of us all. Consequently, they have a hegemonising effect; they conceal the particularity of the group and support the creation of a system in which the corporate project becomes the project of and for society. As formulated by Cederström and Marinetto:

> the naturalization of CSR, as combining the interest of businesses with that of the wider public, supresses questions of the nature of the corporation and the systemic damage the latter may have committed.[471]

'CSR' and 'sustainability' thus hide the particular interests of the corporation and the potential harms it may have caused. This makes it harder to formulate an alternative project for society, both in particular project areas, such as Patos-Marinza, and in the economy in general. Through the vagueness of 'sustainability' and 'CSR', the corporation can take over activities that previously belonged to the realm of the state or civil society with the proclaimed benefit to the wider society. 'Sustainability' and 'CSR' makes this possible through their open-ended character; they are 'overdetermined' and 'empty' concepts that are hard to define and therefore open to an alliance of actors to identify with.

As was explained in Chapter Two, Laclau argues that the formation of a popular identity needs an 'empty signifier', a concept that can be filled with the hopes and dreams of several groups and thus function as a mobilising centre around which an alliance can be formed. It is important here to underline that the word 'empty' does not mean that the concept is a void without meaning; on the contrary it is overfilled with meaning; 'over-determined' in terms of that various groups attach their own visions and ideas to the signifier in question. I think of empty signifiers as 'black holes', places that contain more matter than any other locality we know of but which are still thought of as 'holes' as they are invisible and continue to absorb new matter in its vicinity.[472] While 'CSR' can be thought of as an umbrella term, which makes the corporation expand its influence over society, it still contains a particularity in its combination of signifiers, specifying that it is the *corporation* that is responsible. 'Sustainability', on the other hand, is truly 'empty' and 'universal' as a signifier; it encompasses the whole earth, all humans, and so behind 'sustainability' the corporation

[471] Cedertröm and Marinetto (2013), p. 429.
[472] NASA (2018).

can hide safely, claiming to be a part of a movement that works for the benefit of 'all'. As argued by Carroll, while 'CSR' "implies trying to pinpoint 'responsibility' [...] [s]ustainability is somewhat neutral in that it seems so logical – take care of the present, take care of the future – that virtually no one opposes it as a concept".[473] Similarly, Kuhlman and Farrington argue that sustainability, when combining economic, social and environmental benefits (rather than trade-offs), "becomes a concept that is equivalent to 'good' and thus devoid of any specific meaning – a blanket concept to assure stakeholders of the policy's good intentions".[474] As the signifier 'sustainability' increasingly replaces 'CSR' in corporate reports and policies,[475] discursive space thus opens up for corporate hegemony to expand. Sustainability can be thought of as an empty signifier that constantly absorbs new meanings and visions, an 'overfilled' concept, ideal for creating alliances and absorbing antagonists into its realm. While this 'emptiness' presents an opportunity in terms of unifying actors for progressive change towards a new type of society, which does less harm to social and environmental systems, it also presents the risk of being taken over and redefined by corporate interest. Kulman and Farrington argue that the consequence of the Triple Bottom Line perspective is that the environment becomes almost weightless, as economic and social issues constitute two thirds of the equation and thus "violate the Brundtland requirement that development should not take place at the expense of future generations".[476] It is also evident that the economy (i.e. the capitalist system) is given more weight in this equation, being equally important to environmental and social concerns, and that hinders formulations of a possible future where these other issues could be put at the forefront, standing over and above the (capitalist) economy. When sustainability is aligned with the idea of the Triple Bottom Line, the concept thus loses it radical potential and instead becomes a terrain in which capitalism extends its tools of dominance over society. In this version, 'sustainability' loses its position as a nodal point to which subordinate subjects can connect their visions of another future. Instead it becomes an arena where radical elements can be made passive or compliant.

[473] Carroll (2015), p. 93.
[474] Kuhlman & Farrington (2010), p. 3439.
[475] Carroll (2015), p. 93.
[476] Kuhlman & Farrington (2010), p. 3439.

On this gloomy note I end my answer to my three research questions. But yet, I cannot finish here, since questions regarding resistance and alternative visions linger in my mind. *What is to be done?* In the next chapter, I briefly take on this daunting question, starting with an analysis of the resistance movement in Patos-Marinza and continuing with a general discussion about 'sustainability revolutions' linked to Mouffe's concepts of agonism and radical democracy.

CHAPTER 9

Resisting corporate hegemony

Maybe you now, like I do, wonder: if 'sustainability' and 'CSR' is not the solution to corporate irresponsibility, social injustices and environmental degradation, then what is to be done instead? If we disregard these corporate initiatives as hegemonic articulations and criticise attempts to make corporate practices more 'sustainable', what is the road to improve corporate practices, which we see as damaging to our social and environmental surroundings? In this chapter, I will address the above question by first analysing what can be learned from the resistance movement in Patos-Marinza, and then move on to discuss alternative routes to encourage community mobilisation and new hegemonic visions, based on Mouffe's notions of radical democracy and agonistic pluralism. Thereafter, I will briefly discuss what this study may add to the field of Political Discourse Theory, and lastly, I will elaborate on how insights from my autoethnographic approach can be used in other research contexts to critically analyse 'sustainability' and 'CSR'.

Resistance in Patos-Marinza

As concluded in the previous chapter, sustainability standards and CSR practices can be used by corporations as tools to: (i) incorporate demands into the alliance of the corporate hegemonic bloc and thus diffuse the antagonistic frontier between the corporation and its adversaries; (ii) isolate demands in order to prevent the formation of chains of equivalence between adversaries; and (iii) define the corporate project as a project 'beneficial to all'. However, as with all social orders, Patos-Marinza shows that the corporate hegemonic project is never fully completed; 'investments' by corporations does not meet all demands in local communities. New demands constantly arise and haunt the corporate order and so the battle for hegemony continues, as it does in Patos-Marinza. Political Discourse Theory emphasises words, actions and objects as fundaments in a discursive structure and a hegemonic formation. Thereby, resistance against hegemonic formations, counter-hegemonic articulations, can also be understood in this way. It is not only what we say that forms resistance but also what we do and the materialisations that we create. In the first part of this chapter I will take a closer look at the various forms of resistance in Patos-Marinza and discuss how internal constraints may have hindered a wider mobilisation. Based on lessons from this empirical context, I will thereafter discuss resistance to corporate hegemony in a wider sense.

From subordination to oppression

Laclau and Mouffe present the democratic discourse as the beginning of the conditions under which various forms of subordination could be discursively framed as oppression and by which social agents could be gathered as part of an antagonistic frontier against their oppressors. In their theoretical framework, 'subordination' is defined as a relation "in which an agent is subjected to the decisions of another", and 'oppression' as "relations of subordination which have transformed themselves into sites of antagonisms".[477] 'Oppression' is thus a signifier that transforms a relation of subordination, which is framed as objective, into a relation that is questioned and challenged. The signifier 'oppression' thus brings 'the political' back into a structural social relationship that has previously been covered over as objective.

Laclau and Mouffe bring forward two ways in which antagonism emerges in a social formation and discursively transforms relations of subordination to relations of oppression. Firstly, the emergence of an exterior discourse – for example the democratic discourse proclaiming the equal rights of humans – may put into question previous relations of subordinations and thus frame them as illegitimate oppression. They write:

> 'Serf', 'slave' and so on, do not designate in themselves antagonistic positions; it is only in the terms of a different discursive formation, such as 'the rights inherent to every human being', that the differential positivity of these categories can be subverted and the subordination constructed as oppression.[478]

What they mean is that the relationship master-slave could be seen as a natural and objective social order if not the discourse about 'universal

[477] Laclau & Mouffe (1985/2014), pp. 137-138.
[478] Laclau & Mouffe (1985/2014), p. 138.

human rights' had been available to formulate this relationship as 'oppression'. They argue that:

> it is only from the moment when the democratic discourse becomes available to articulate the different forms of resistance to subordination that the conditions will exist to make possible the struggle against different types of inequality.[479]

Inequality, they mean, can thus be seen as 'natural' or as 'oppression' depending on which discursive configurations are available to define a relationship of subordination. Secondly, they describe how antagonism can appear through periods of social transformations that question previously established identities of social agents and thereby create new forms of subordination in which acquired rights are challenged.

The introduction of the democratic discourse and the transformation of society and relations of subordination happened simultaneously in Patos-Marinza through the Albanian transition from communism to both democracy and a market economy. The introduction into a market economy, and the entry of foreign corporations, changed the relations of subordination that had previously existed within the communist system. The ability to make money became a 'potential possibility' for everyone and the connection to the communist party was (at least in theory) no longer necessary to reach higher societal positions. At the same time, exterior discourses appeared in the local communities as the country opened up to the world and democratic ideals started to spread. As you have seen in the previous chapters, government representatives and Bankers managers referred to this transition as the reason why people complained about current oilfield operations. One Bankers representative stated that people complained even though the oilfield had dramatically improved and mentioned peoples' 'mentality' as a principal reason why company-community conflicts were so prevalent. Another Bankers representative saw IFC's sustainability standards as a reason why people "thought that they had the right to influence our business". In one of my autobiographical narratives I describe the company's fear when stakeholder engagement activities commenced in the villages, since company representatives perceived this as giving residents 'ideas' about their rights. However, in my meetings with residents during my time with Bankers, and

[479] Laclau & Mouffe (1985/2014), p. 138.

later during the interviews for this study, community members did not use IFC's sustainability standards as a reference but compared Patos-Marinza to conditions in other countries and protests movements in other contexts. Residents used signifiers such as 'fracking' and 'genocide' to describe Bankers' operations, words that were clearly brought into the context from other parts of the world. As Laclau and Mouffe write: "…there is no relation of oppression without the presence of a discursive 'exterior' from which the discourse of subordination can be interrupted".[480] Residents' accounts show that exterior discourses were an important part of their ability to form counter-hegemonic articulations against Bankers, but that these came from other sources, provided by the democratic progress in the country and the availability of information from other places, and not from our implementation of sustainability standards.

The discourse linked to the concept of 'subordination' is in the case of Patos-Marinza the hegemonic discourse stabilised around the nodal point of the 'investment'. The 'investment' naturalises a social configuration in which some people make a lot of money while others are forced to live with the consequences from oil operations. It makes these inequalities 'neutral' and 'rational', referring to the neoliberal promise of a market economy in which 'everyone' gains through the 'trickling down' of opportunities and prosperity. It is through the counter-hegemonic discourse, verbalised by actors within the local communities and stabilised around the nodal point of Bankers' operations as an 'invasion', that a relation of 'oppression' can be formed. The verbalisation of Bankers' operations as an 'invasion' delegitimises corporate actions and connects them to signifiers such as 'exploitation', and 'genocide'. Verbalisations, actions and materialisations of actors in Patos-Marinza that connect to the nodal point of 'invasion' are articulations which strengthen this counter-hegemonic discourse as an alternative way of understanding society and the social relations within it. This counter-hegemonic discourse involves a re-articulation of 'local residents' which, rather than 'beneficiaries' of the 'investment', become 'victims' of the 'invasion'. This also changes the meaning of 'Bankers managers'; if 'local residents' are portrayed as victims of company operations, 'Bankers managers' are defined as the villains, and a relation of subordination has been transformed into a relation of oppression. Another source of counter-hegemonic articulation that residents used was their own bodies and bodily experiences. They felt the ground shaking and the air

[480] Laclau & Mouffe (1985/2014), p.138.

smelling and used this as 'evidence' that Bankers' activities were damaging their lives rather than benefiting them. Even though communities had no access to scientific support that could validate their experiences, they used their bodily sensations in their argumentation with Bankers' experts in dialogue groups and community meetings. In addition, the times when the community mobilised larger protests in the area were characterised by moments when the bodies of community neighbours were equally impacted by earth movements or gas releases. In using their own bodies as well as other exterior discourses, they could frame the relationship between Bankers and local communities as a relation of oppression (an 'invasion'). Thus, local residents had taken the first step to mobilise an antagonistic frontier against the 'oppressors'.

'Political' versus 'reformist' struggles

Laclau and Mouffe emphasise that resistance takes on very different forms in different contexts. Only some acts of resistance can be defined as, what they call, 'political', meaning "struggles directed towards putting an end to relations of subordination as such".[481] What they mean with the 'political' has thus nothing to do with party politics or demands on the level of the state but "a type of action whose objective is the transformation of a social relation which constructs a subject in a relationship of subordination".[482] Accordingly, one can look at the various forms of resistance in Patos-Marinza and ask if they can be characterised as 'political' or if they were 'reformist' struggles, aimed at improving conditions within a particular regime.

Some of the grievances and demands in Patos-Marinza can be seen as arising from the limits of the hegemonic discourse, the 'outside' where some residents were excluded from the proclaimed 'benefits for all'. These 'losers' claimed that Bankers' hegemonic project was failing; it was not been able to fulfil its promises. The demands from communities can thus be seen as built on the lack that the hegemonic discourse itself produces. When Bankers was stating that there should be only winners, employment, wealth, and an improved environment, Patos-Marinza residents could use their own bodily experiences of 'lack' to demand that the hegemonic narrative should be fulfilled. The 'investment' thus created room for opposition to arise; *I did not win*, one resident said, *neither did I*, another

[481] Laclau & Mouffe (1985/ 2014), p. 136.
[482] Laclau & Mouffe (1985/ 2014), p. 137.

answered. However, rather than creating an antagonistic frontier linked to the discursive formation of the 'invasion', these demands were often directed towards reforming the hegemonic regime, improving the conditions in which subordination is experienced but without changing the regime and the social relations within it. These are thus not 'political' demands as defined by Laclau and Mouffe; they are not demands that aim to *change* a relationship of 'subordination' to one defined as 'oppression' but resistance that aim to *improve* the conditions for those who remain in positions of subordination.

The fantasmatic ideal of the 'good corporation', which I embraced as a CSR professional, was part of maintaining demands in this 'non-political' format. In many interviews, residents expressed the view that the company could be good, that it was the government, the media, the corrupt individuals' fault that it did not work properly. Bankers' CSR practices sustained these fantasmatic ideals about the 'good corporation' and that everyone could win. Community demands, verbalised in satiric posts on social media, as well as in grievances and protests, sometimes maintained this ideal rather than challenged it. Consequently, many residents did not protest to change the system but to claim their right within the 'ideal'. Sustainability standards were part of introducing the idea of 'the good corporation' to the context – they produced an ideal to which the company could be held responsible and, even if this ideal was never achieved, its mere introduction meant that a fantasmatic narrative exercised its grip over the context. The promise of wealth from the company made residents pay money to 'middle men' to be part of the corporate alliance, and loud complaints went quiet when grievances were 'solved' through individual solutions.

Mats Lindqvist argues that when the capitalist discourse fails to materialise the equal and free individuals about which it speaks, the possibility for resistance and change opens up and alternative discourses can gain momentum.[483] Stavrakakis partially agrees with this argument but also emphasises the risk that resistance to a particular hegemonic order can work as a way to strengthen it. He writes:

> It is in the traumatic fact that the Other cannot fully determine the subject that a space for freedom starts to emerge. But this is a freedom that the subject has learned to fear. As Judith Butler has formulated it,

[483] Lindqvist (2012), p. 19.

> this predicament of the subject is usually resolved with the adoption of the following stance: 'I would rather exist in subordination than not exist'.[484]

According to Stavrakakis argument, subjects may rather see themselves as subordinated than in a situation where they are excluded from the hegemonic order. This means that once a fantasmatic narrative of the 'good corporation' has taken hold over a context, there is a risk that subjects, rather than forming opposition, turn to this 'ideal' to be part of the 'winning' side. The discourse of the 'investment' offered an opportunity for subjects in Patos-Marinza to identify with the project of the corporation in which they could become an employee, a contractor, a landowner or a collaboration partner. The alternative discourse of the 'invasion' offered subjects a negative identity of the victim, making the subject position in subordination to the company more desirable than its alternative. To be part of Bankers' project, however marginal and subordinate this participation may have been, was to exist in the hegemonic order as a 'winner'; to oppose Bankers' project was to become a 'victim' or to not exist at all.

Opposition but a missing hegemonic project

Laclau and Mouffe distinguish between a project of opposition and a hegemonic project. They argue that a hegemonic project cannot be built on a 'negative logic' focused on "the elimination of relations of subordination and of inequalities"[485]. A 'strategy of opposition' can be based on such logic since the goal is the "negotiation of a certain social and political order". However, such strategy can never become a strategy to construct a new hegemonic order since it is missing "a nodal point of any kind around which the social fabric can be reconstituted".[486] In Patos-Marinza the various forms of resistance can be viewed as strategies of opposition but since there was no "real attempt to establish different nodal points from which a process of different and positive reconstruction of the social fabric could be instituted",[487] an alternative hegemonic project was missing. The nodal point of the 'invasion' was thus a negation of Bankers' hegemonic order rather than an alternative social order with which subjects could identify.

[484] Stavrakakis (2010), p. 65.
[485] Laclau & Mouffe (2014), p. 171.
[486] Laclau & Mouffe (2014), pp. 172-173.
[487] Laclau & Mouffe (2014), p. 172.

Laclau and Mouffe describe the "disappearance of the political" and the "implosion of the social" as a risk in modern societies where plurality is combined with an "absence of any common point of reference" and "an absence of those articulations which allow the establishment of meanings common to the different social subjects".[488] In Patos-Marinza, this lack of mobilising articulations, which gather subjects with different claims against the company, is what may have hindered further collective action to appear. Bankers' hegemony was shown in the 'neutral' and 'objective' status, which the corporate articulation of reality enjoyed. Few actors in the context questioned the description of Patos-Marinza as an 'oilfield', and alternative articulations of Patos-Marinza as a 'home' or an 'agricultural area' did not gain momentum. Instead community members articulated solutions that involved the continuous operations of the company. These solutions perceived the area as an 'oilfield' and Bankers' operations as an 'investment' that could be beneficial if just some changes could be made. The company investment thus represented a potential fullness for residents, an ideal that could have been achieved, as well as an antagonistic 'other' which hindered this ideal reaching its full realisation.

What was missing in Patos-Marinza was what Laclau and Mouffe call an empty signifier, a symbolic concept that could link residents' bodies together and make their experience valid on a 'community' level. In relation to local demands that never reach a higher level of mobilisation, Laclau underlines that:

> If we remain for a moment at the local level, [...] we can clearly see how these equivalences could be consolidated only when some further steps are taken, both trough the expansion of the equivalential chains and through their symbolic unification.[489]

The demands in Patos-Marinza were brought together in opposition to the Bankers' regime, chains which were created through the description of Bankers' operations as an 'invasion'. However, this was a 'negative logic' since it opposed something but did not present an alternative vision for society. The equivalential links between demands in Patos-Marinza thus lacked an empty signifier that could raise them to form a hegemonic project of their own; they were joined together via what they opposed rather than what they wanted. The lack of an empty signifier also meant

[488] Laclau & Mouffe (2014), p. 172.
[489] Laclau (2005), p. 74.

that the affective dimension of collective identities could not be mobilised, as there was no 'new symbolic order' in which residents could exist in positive subject positions. The project of opposition joined them together as 'victims' while an alternative hegemonic project would create a positive collective identity through which a 'community' could be mobilised, and an alternative order articulated.

Radical democracy and conflict encouraged

The lack of an alternative hegemonic project in Patos-Marinza can through Mouffe's concept of *agonistics* be described as a democratic lack since it closes the social to a particular order and does not provide alternatives for the formation of collective identities. My analysis of Patos-Marinza above has shown how this lack of alternatives was reinforced by sustainability activities; these were directed at amending the dominant system while keeping its fundamental regime and subject positions intact. As emphasised by Stavrakakis:

> Every effective hegemony has to operate on all these levels, co-opting opposition and neutralizing its radical potential – and undergoing, in the process, gradual shifts that, however, do not threaten the reproduction of hierarchical order (the basic parameters of domination).[490]

Sustainability activities aim to reach the goal of consensus between all actors, a consensus that may involve some compromises but at the same time ends up buttressing corporate articulations of society through satisfying and incorporating demands. This stands in sharp contrast to the idea of *radical democracy* for which Laclau and Mouffe argue, a project that acknowledges the impossibility of ever reaching a final consensual agreement. Mouffe underlines that: "What characterises democratic politics is the confrontation between conflicting hegemonic projects, a confrontation with no possibility of final reconsolidation"[491]. In a radical democracy, an alternative hegemonic project is a necessary component for a vital democratic debate. Mouffe defines 'antagonism' as struggles between enemies and 'agonism' as struggles between adversaries. According to Mouffe, agonistic politics means that agonism takes the place of antagonism and 'we' are created in opposition to a 'they' that are not seen as

[490] Stavrakakis (2010), p. 69.
[491] Mouffe (2013), p. 17.

enemies but as legitimate adversaries. An adversary is according to Mouffe "the opponent with whom one shares a common allegiance to the democratic principles of 'liberty and equality for all', while disagreeing on their interpretation"[492]. Radical democracy is thus not a place where consensus is the goal; rather the goal is to establish institutions that can harbour adversaries who fight in order to make their interpretations of the democratic principles hegemonic. Contrary to deliberative democracy where the goal is consensus, radical democracy starts from the assumption that conflicting interpretations cannot be consolidated and thus conflict and struggle become the core feature of how democracy can be understood. Burchell and Cook explain:

> Whereas deliberative democracy identifies consensual decision-making as a significant end point in the political process, Mouffe identifies 'conflictual consensus' as the starting point from which the discussion begins.[493]

'Conflictual consensus' is thus the very goal of the democratic process, a conflict that is never finalised or consolidated. Such conflictual consensus, in which new visions of society encounter each other, is vital in the quest for a definition of 'sustainability' that goes beyond amendments to the current system. Sustainability, in this view, necessarily means different things to different groups and it is this formulation of alternative visions of the future that is important in a democratic sense, not consensus agreements. *What definition/ definitions of 'sustainability' would actors in Patos-Marinza articulate, if they had the opportunity to formulate alternative visions for the area instead of just accepting a corporate ideal?* That is a question that could be a starting point for the construction of alternative futures.

Agonistic pluralism as a way forward

If we start with radical democracy as a desired situation for Patos-Marinza and society at large, what role does the corporation and the activities linked to corporate sustainability and CSR have in creating of agonistic pluralism? And what other practices can be imagined to encourage an agonistic relationship between actors?

[492] Mouffe (2013), p. 7.
[493] Burchell & Cook (2013), p. 749.

Scherer and Palazzo underline that postmodern and poststructuralist philosophy, such as Political Discourse Theory, "provides an excellent starting point for the critique of established management theories because it reveals the unspoken and suppressed, and it tries to discover and criticise power relationships" but then disregard it as "a problematic source for the definition of the role of business firms in society" because of its non-foundational character.[494] Contrary to the understanding of 'sustainability' and 'CSR' as ideally deliberative, where common solutions and an ideal role for the corporation can be found, I have through my analysis of Patos-Marinza highlighted how corporate-community conflicts are built on different understandings of reality and are therefore fundamentally incompatible. In line with the thinking of agonistic pluralism, my analysis highlights how the corporate presence is always defining society in one determinate way, thus hegemonising and structuring the social in a way that is beneficial to its own interest. This underlines how 'solutions' to corporate-community conflicts should not be based on 'redefining' the role of business in society, as Scherer and Palazzo argue, but to underline that corporations always represent one interest and one hegemonic formation of the world. The presence of community resistance and counter-hegemonic movements show how corporate hegemonic articulations need to be continuously criticised and resisted, in order to prevent a closure of the social and a neutralisation of the corporate narrative of 'sustainability'. While deliberative CSR scholarship is based on the idea that the role of businesses should be defined by businesses in interaction with other stakeholders, the agonistic viewpoint acknowledge conflict as an important part of a democratic society and thus underlines the need for a stronger role of alternative actors, such as unions, social movements and civil society organisations, as a counter-balance to state and corporate narratives. As formulated by Dawkins:

> because agonism encourages dissensus as a check on hegemony, there is a clear need for countervailing voices that represents disparate stakeholder views and balances the influence of one group with that of others.[495]

In line with Mouffe, Dawkins thus emphasises that deliberative CSR initiatives can be understood as hegemonic articulations from corporate

[494] Scherer & Palazzo (2007), p. 1103.
[495] Dawkins (2015), p. 11.

actors and that conflict (rather than consensus) should be held as the ideal. Dawkins concludes that:

> stakeholders need the capacity to explicitly contest the content of CSR [and sustainability], and unless they appreciate the conflictual context of their relations with corporations, they mischaracterise their condition.[496]

According to Dawkins, local stakeholders should thus acknowledge that they always have a conflictual relationship with corporations and therefore should focus on contesting corporate definitions of 'sustainability' and 'CSR' rather than participating in consensus-finding activities. Barthold and Bloom argue in a similar vein that "dissensus offers the possibility for continually experiencing our environment in ever new and exciting counter-hegemonic ways".[497] What is at stake in the struggle between corporations and communities is thus the very definition of 'sustainability', that is, what this empty signifier is filled with, and what this filling operation will do for the re-configuration of the social field.

Dawkins agrees with Mouffe that the ideal of agonistic pluralism requires a strengthened role of NGOs, unions and other actors in civil society to reframe and rearticulate the current hegemonic order formed by corporate interests. Similarly, Rhodes et al. emphasise that "business ethics needs to take seriously the lives and voices of those who have been excluded from the neo-liberal consensus" and engage "with the social movements and political activists that struggle through and for radical democracy".[498] Similarly, Colin Crouch emphasises that pressure on corporations needs to be organised. He writes that the:

> pressure on firms [...] to treat CSR as more than a PR exercise has not resulted from the uncoordinated responses of millions of consumers. [...] pressure comes from several elements in a firm's social and political context. At one level, it has to be organized. [...] This marks a shift from corporate social responsibility in an agenda framed by firms themselves to corporate social accountability framed by groups of citizens.[499]

[496] Dawkins (2015), p. 5.
[497] Barthold and Bloom (2020), p. 679.
[498] Rhodes et al. (2020), p. 628.
[499] Crouch (2011).

Corporate social accountability is thus a term that captures a relationship between corporations and society where corporations do not have the power to formulate what responsibility or sustainability are. It is a term that is closer to the idea of agonistic pluralism than the CSR concept. This focus on civil society may appear as a paradox in light of Gramsci's thoughts about civil society as the main apparatus that keeps the hegemonic order in place though the creation of consent. As Malin Gawell points out, when we discuss civil society it is important to recognise that it is comprised of a variety of interests and actors, sometimes conservative, neoliberal or even violent in character.[500] Afrim, a Bankers representative, discussed the role of civil society in Patos-Marinza and the issues connected to the lack of funding for such organisations. He mentioned one specific organisation and added:

> they did something for Bankers and I saw that they were more, how to say, in line with the interest of Bankers because the company financed the service for them. In fact, they should be the opponents and to ask private companies how they spend their money and how they fulfil their obligation to the community. This is the risk of civil society; the lack of funds creates a lot of problems and they lose their independence. And now in Fier, civil society is very weak. We have no [independent] organisation. Bankers are working with another organisation which previously was the strongest voice of the community, but now we are paying them. Hahaha, can you imagine? Okay. We are a private company and we use every type of instrument in order to keep calm the community because we don't want the community to increase the voice for different problems. And this is the way. And people in the area know about this and they will not trust this organisation now. If the people have real problems with Bankers, because now it's a Chinese company and they will face many problems in the field with dust, with many environmental issues. But who will they trust, who will be their representative? From this perspective I can say that civil society it's not stronger than before [after communism]. Because it is dependent on money.[501]

Afrim thus confirms that civil society organisations, instead of taking the role of company opponents, risks becoming part of the corporate hegemonic regime. Caution should thus be taken when proposing a strength-

[500] Gawell (2016).
[501] Interview, Bankers representative, September 2018.

ened role for such organisations. To nuance the role of civil society, Gawell uses the concept of 'activist entrepreneurship' to describe a process in which non-profit organisations are formed that attack norms and articulate new stories about the social; for example in the case of Attac that Gawell studies in detail.[502] What those stories are is, of course, dependent on the parties involved, but this concept may be useful to better understand the type of civil society action needed as a counter-point to corporate hegemonic norms.

Other authors have pointed to the vital role that state institutions have in enforcing democratic demands. Fleming and Spicer argue that:

> Misunderstanding the nature of the corporation and the limits of its ability to 'do good' has resulted in CSR activists being diverted from the more realistic and important task of getting governments to solve social problems.[503]

Fleming and Spicer thus suggest fostering civil society initiatives that work to strengthen the role of state institutions rather than being "diverted" by CSR activities. Similarly, Fooks et al. conclude in their study of the tobacco industry:

> that stakeholder dialogue (and, therefore, social reporting) is primarily a defensive practice aimed at preventing stakeholders from forcing change on companies through formal government intervention.[504]

Corporate sustainability activities can thus be seen as working against an agonistic politics, because they undermine the state as the main arena for agonistic demands and struggles. What these authors emphasise is that activist efforts should be focused on influencing state regulation in a way that benefits social welfare over corporations, rather than trying to make corporations 'behave' voluntarily. However, just as in the discussion about civil society, there is a need to be cautious about the role of the state as an agent for change. As Crouch points out:

> The state, seen for so long by the left as the source of countervailing power against markets and corporations, is today likely to be the com-

[502] Gawell (2006).
[503] Fleming & Spicer (2013), p. 35.
[504] Fooks, Gilmore, Collin, Holden & Lee(2013), p. 294.

> mitted ally of giant corporations, whatever the ideological origins of the parties governing the state.[505]

What Crouch emphasises is that the state, instead of being a counterbalance to corporate power, in many instances rather functions as one side of a corporate-state power complex. However, he too recognises that civil society action directed towards the state can lead to increased regulation of corporate activities, such as in the case of pollution control.

A stronger role for anti-corporate forces within the state and civil society, rather than CSR activities, thus seems to be the road to nurture agonistic pluralism in general. While there is a constant need to be cautious of personal agendas and corrupt practices also within these sectors, they nevertheless represent places for hope in the articulation of counter-hegemonic discourses against sustainability agendas formulated in corporate boardrooms. As formulated by Crouch: "All we can hope for is that there will be scope for diversity, and a constant supply of critical, questioning, quarrelsome voices and practical projects resulting from these".[506] Accordingly, as I have shown in the previous chapters, corporate sustainability and CSR activities is not a solution to context specific (un)sustainability issues but an inherent part of the problem linked to corporate hegemony.

So, what can be done in contexts like Patos-Marinza, and in general, to enhance agonistic pluralism and strengthen the creation of 'sustainability movements'? Dawkins emphasises that the aim is to transform antagonistic places, characterised by violence and intimidation, into places of agonistic pluralism by strengthening the powerless in their negotiation and formulation capacity. Dawkins emphasises that the key for such transformation is to mitigate power asymmetries so that subordinated actors can protect their own interests. This is hardly a task for corporations to assume as it is not in their interest to strengthen their opponents' negotiation and formulation skills. Instead such mitigation of power asymmetries requires that civil society organisations, that are not connected to corporations, step in to provide information about citizens' rights, collect data about corporate activities and create opportunities for residents to legally challenge company activities. In addition, civil society initiatives should be directed at strengthening the ties between various community

[505] Crouch (2011), p. 145.
[506] Crouch (2011), p. 160.

members in order to formulate a joint ideal, an empty signifier, under which community demands can be mobilised. As expressed by Afrim, quoted above:

> In Albania the citizen culture is very weak. So more should be done in order to create a culture of citizens so that they can come together for problems that are concerns for their communities.[507]

Afrim, who otherwise paints a very bleak picture of civil society in Albania still points to the creation of a citizen culture as the only hope for an improved situation for local communities. As should be clear by now, this is not something that can be organised by corporations under the 'sustainability' flag nor something I could assume as a CSR professional. Nevertheless, this is what is needed for an opposing hegemonic project to be articulated, an articulation of sustainability that corporate representatives can never be a part of carrying out. The business of business is business, as the thoughts of Milton Friedman are often summarised. While not agreeing with his vision of society, I am prepared to agree with him on that.

Money as hegemonic articulations and bodies as places of resistance

In my analysis of hegemony and resistance in this and the previous chapters, I have applied Political Discourse Theory as an analytical frame. From this exercise, of comparing theory and a specific empirical context, theory has informed my understanding of Patos-Marinza and shaped the way I have analysed the events I was part of in the past. However, the empirical context has also spoken back to theory; it has posed new questions to this theoretical frame. In this section I will dwell upon two such questions that I came back to over and over again as I proceeded in this dissertation project. The first is the understanding of money as a hegemonic articulation; the second is the understanding of bodies as places of resistance. Sofi Gerber underlines the importance of considering the material aspects of how hegemony is maintained:

> In the perspective of discourse theory we can see how objects not only gain new meanings but also how material objects can be understood as

[507] Interview, Bankers representative, September 2018.

> articulations which contribute to solidifying or transforming discursive structures.[508]

According to Jenny Gunnarsson Payne, the material aspect of the discursive is still relatively unexplored within Political Discourse Theory.[509] My analysis of Patos-Marinza contributes to this theoretical field with an empirical exploration of how materiality in a discursive structure works to strengthen one specific hegemonic configuration at the expense of alternatives. In Patos-Marinza, corporate allies were included into the hegemonic bloc, not only by verbal articulations but also through the dispersion of money to people who rented out land, worked as contractors or were employed. In this way, hegemonic articulations taking the form of money united a broad alliance of actors in the region and beyond; politicians receiving taxes, careerists dreaming of working for an international corporation, small entrepreneurs who saw future income streams, local families who saw opportunities to rent out that piece of land or for their children to get a job. By understanding the streams of money that travelled from Bankers to various actors as chains of equivalence, I want to highlight that the discursive struggle in Patos-Marinza was not only a verbal struggle but a material struggle as well. This material struggle also took the form of concrete practices and materialisations, such as air monitoring systems and the construction of wells and leases. In Patos-Marinza the construction of new wells solidified the 'objective' view of the area as an 'oilfield', Bankers' clean-up activities strengthened the idea of the 'clean investment' and the transfer of money promoted the view of the 'investment' as beneficial to local 'development'. While local residents blocked roads and filed grievances, these corporate material and monetary articulations worked against their counter-hegemonic perspective, enforcing the idea of the 'investment' as beneficial through concrete practices and material objects. The analysis of Patos-Marinza thus underlines the importance of understanding how rhetorical struggles are backed up by organisational, monetary and material means. This analysis highlights the benefits of using Political Discourse Theory as a lens to understand social struggles; not only do verbal arguments become visible but also articulations in the form of actions, organisational forms, money and infrastructure, forcing us to see how these materialities make possible a specific version of the social.

[508] Gerber (2012), p. 57, my translation.
[509] Gunnarsson Payne (2017), p. 256.

If we consider Patos-Marinza as a miniature of society at large, what can the dynamic there tell us about how we relate to sustainability and corporations in general? While Political Discourse Theory emphasises affect as the force that makes actors relate to a specific vision of society, Patos-Marinza highlights the need to add money as another force to be considered. In Patos-Marinza, as well as in many other instances when 'sustainability' is applied by corporations, money is used to cover over holes in the neoliberal hegemonic project. Money makes us all dependent on corporate willingness in various ways and thus makes us less interested to imagine an alternative economic order. Just as residents in Patos-Marinza, we are all dependent on the current economic system, which makes it hard to move over to the other side of the antagonistic frontier, imagining a new society. The affective dimension can explain how our subject positions, as employees, consumers and producers are linked to the current order while an alternative order leave such identities uncertain. Money, as another force, ensure that we remain isolated and satisfied, drawing us into the alliance that advocates for 'sustainability' within the current order, for 'transformism' instead of 'revolution'. As corporations today have the resources to articulate their hegemonic version of 'sustainability' by verbal, monetary and material means, a counter-hegemonic project is struggling on a platform where means are more limited. 'Sustainability', as it is often articulated today, is an empty signifier that unites a broad range of actors into an alliance, but this alliance is often formed on the corporate side, it does not require change but advocates for maintenance.

As I pointed out above, Bankers' hegemonic discourse was enforced by verbal, organisational, material and monetary articulations while local residents had little more than their own words and bodies to use in the struggle. In this uneven struggle, where science, experts, money, standardisations and technology was used to enforce the corporate side, residents had to find other sources as points of rupture where the corporate narrative could be broken. In addition to the external discourses that residents in Patos-Marinza referred to in order to criticise Bankers activities, residents used their bodily experiences as base for their resistance acts. They claimed that they got sick from the air emissions; they expressed fears when the ground was shaking; and they complained that noise from drilling rigs kept them awake at night. The bodies of residents were thus places where the hegemonic discourse of the 'sustainable oil company' was broken. The examples of these bodily references may work as an addition to Laclau and Mouffe's argument that only exterior discourses may alter relations of subordination to relations of oppression. The examples point to that the human body may work as an 'exterior discourse' which opposes a hegemonic way of describing a social relation as 'natural' subordination, framing it instead as an 'oppressive' and damaging relation. The body may function as a starting point for alternative ways of imagining the social, for alternative ways of defining 'sustainability', ways that may create agonistic hegemonic projects. While corporate versions of 'sustainability', as in Patos-Marinza, often dismiss bodily experiences as 'unscientific', 'lazy' or 'ignorant', chains of equivalence between bodies may be formed based on common experiences of physical suffering as a starting point for resistance movements.

Reflections on autoethnography

The movement of 'writing differently' is continuing to blossom within management and organisation studies providing a counter-hegemonic space for poetic, emotional and personal ways of writing academic texts. As Nancy Harding inspiringly writes:

> Each academic text 'written differently' is a micro-revolution. Micro-revolutions add up, overturning dysfunctional, perhaps rotten, sometimes corrupt, practices that inhibit knowledges and understanding. Writing differently revolutionaries want to influence the world. [510]

Even though this text is arranged according to a classic dissertation structure, I hope that some of its sections may encourage, in a 'micro-revolutionary' sense, new ways of thinking about what a dissertation may be and look like. Writing this text has for me been a true revolutionary experience that has changed my way of seeing and being in the world. Even though I have surrendered to some of the hegemonic academic conventions that have told me what dissertation should look like, I have through this process come to discover in what way I learn the best (through stories and feelings) and how much I love to read and write. Those are life-long gifts that I hope I can share with others in the future and autoethnographic writing, I believe, is a beautiful place to begin such journeys.

As capitalism continues to change its face it is important to investigate how new forms of hegemonic articulations are performed. While some disregard corporate 'sustainability' and 'CSR' as mere window dressing,

[510] Harding in Pullen, Helin and Harding (2020), p. 2.

scholars interested in questioning the power of corporations need to investigate what the concepts of 'sustainability' and 'CSR' do in practice, how they are implemented and who gains from this implementation. I hope that this dissertation can work as an inspiration for such studies in other contexts, applying the concepts of transformism, corporatisation and depoliticisation to deconstruct hegemonic articulations. In such research, autoethnographic methodologies can be a way for scholars to analyse their own practices related to the concept of sustainability and how they are part of reproducing or resisting corporate hegemony. Autoethnographic methodologies prevent scholars from picturing themselves as distant or 'objective' observers of reality by placing the researcher in the middle of 'the social' in which she is an active part. As we are all active reproducers of the current unsustainable ways of living, that is a methodology particularly suitable to uncover constraints to sustainability revolutions. Starting with the researcher's own body, chains of equivalence can be formed to other bodies and research can in this way resist hegemonic ways of describing the social by putting bodily experiences of unsustainable social configurations first. As I walked the gravel paths of Patos-Marinza with gas emission filling my nose and with dust from heavy traffic in my eyes, I could feel my own body resisting the corporate 'sustainability' regime that I was part of promoting. Similar experiences can be the starting points for other autoethnographic explorations of hegemonic narratives that ignore the harm being done to subordinate bodies.

There are several subject positions that the researcher may relate to when adopting an autoethnographic approach to uncover and question sustainability regimes and corporate hegemonic orders; the sustainability professional and the community representative are two of these. The sustainability professional is a position that anyone who addresses the concept of sustainability in their workplace can relate to. In this subject position, you may ask yourselves which side of the antagonistic frontier you are strengthening by your work; are you contributing to new sustainability visions and realities or to continuous corporate hegemony by transgressive acts that hinder the lack and contradictions in neoliberal orders from being disclosed? The community representative is a position available to those who live in local contexts impacted by corporate operations. In this subject position you may ask yourself if corporate power is increasingly legitimised by discourses linked to 'CSR' and 'sustainability'. You may come in contact with persons calling themselves a CSR professsional, community liaison officer, social compliance ombudsman, or any other intricate formulation implying that they are reaching out to you with good intentions. You may even be offered a generous compensation for negative impacts from corporate operations or you may be invited to community dialogues or stakeholder groups to 'influence' corporate practices. In that case you may ask yourself what happens if you refuse that open hand that is stretched out in front of you, if you turn your back on their smile and tell them to go back to where they came from. You may compare your options between negotiating with the company as an individual and responding as a 'community'. Finally, you may question whether corporate 'sustainability' activities represent a revolutionary change away from damaging business models or if they merely function as legitimising mechanisms that allow corporate power to grow stronger.

References

Aguinis, H. (2011). Organizational responsibility: Doing good and doing well. In S. Zedeck (Ed.), *APA handbook of industrial and organizational psychology*, 3 (pp. 855–879). Washington, DC: American Psychological Association.

Aguinis, H. & Glavas, A. (2012). What We Know and Don't Know About Corporate Social Responsibility: A Review and Research Agenda. *Journal of Management*, 38, 932–968.

Alamgir, F. & Banerjee, S. B. (2019). Contested compliance regimes in global production networks: Insights from the Bangladesh garment industry. *Human Relations*, 72(2), 272–297.

Alvesson, M. & Sköldberg, K. (1994). *Tolkning och reflektion: vetenskapsfilosofi och kvalitativ metod*. Lund: Studentlitteratur.

Alvesson, M., Bridgman, T., & Willmott, H. (2009). *The Oxford handbook of critical management studies* (Eds.). Oxford: Oxford University Press.

Alvesson, M. & Kärreman, D. (2011). *Qualitative Research and Theory Development – Mystery as Method*. London: Sage.

Alvesson M. & Sandberg J. (2013). *Constructing Research Questions – Doing Interesting Research*. London: Sage.

Amnesty International (2013). *Submission to the World Bank Safeguard Policies Review and Update, April 2013*. Available at: https://www.amnesty.org/download/Documents/16000/ ior800022013en.pdf (accessed February 2017).

Anderson, P. (1976). The antinomies of Gramsci. *New Left Review*, 1(100), 5–78.

Aneesh, A. (2017). 'Relocating Global Assemblages': An Interview with Saskia Sassen. *Science, Technology and Society*, 22(1), 128–134.

Banerjee, S. B. & Linstead, S. (2001). Globalization, multiculturalism and other fictions: Colonialism for the new millennium? *Organization*, 8, 683–722.

Banerjee, S. B. (2008) Corporate Social Responsibility: The Good, the Bad and the Ugly. *Critical Sociology*, 34(1), 51–79.

Banerjee, S. B., Carter, C. & Clegg, S (2009). Managing Globalization. In M. Alvesson, T. Bridgman, and H. Willmott (Eds.), *The Oxford handbook of critical management studies* (pp.186–212). Oxford University Press.

Banerjee, S. B. (2018). Markets and Violence. *Journal of Marketing Management*, 34(11–12): 1023–1031.

Barinaga, E. (2015). Att skriva fram den andra. In B. Borgström, J. Helin, M. Norbäck, & E. Raviola (Eds.), *Skrivande om skrivande* (pp. 161–176). Lund: Studentlitteratur AB.

Barthold, C. & Bloom, P. (2020). Denaturalizing the Environment: Dissensus and the Possibility of Radically Democratizing Discourses of Environmental Sustainability, *Journal of Business Ethics*, 164(4), 671–681.

Bauman, Z. (1998). *Globalization: The human consequences* (European perspectives). New York: Columbia University Press.

Brewis, J. (2005). Signing My Life Away? Researching Sex and Organization. *Organization,* 12(4), 493–510.

Burawoy, M. (1979). *Manufacturing consent: Changes in the labor process under monopoly capitalism.* Chicago: University of Chicago Press.

Burchell, J. & Cook, J. (2013). CSR, Co-optation and Resistance: The Emergence of New Agonistic Relations Between Business and Civil Society. *Journal of Business Ethics,* 115, 741–754.

Business and Human Rights Resource Centre (2018). *Sweden authorises indictment of Lundin Oil executives over alleged complicity in war crimes in So. Sudan; co. denies allegations.* Available at: https://www.business-humanrights.org/en/swedish-prosecutors-to-question-lundin-petroleums-ceo-for-companys-possible-complicity-in-south-sudan-war-crimes-company-comments (accessed 20 May 2019).

Buttigieg, J. A. (1992). Chronology. In J. A. Buttigieg (Ed.), *Prison Notebooks – Volume I* (pp. 65-94). New York: Columbia University Press.

Böhm, S., Spicer, A. & Fleming, P. (2008). Infra-political dimensions of resistance to international business: A Neo-Gramscian approach. *Scandinavian Journal of Management,* 24, 169–182.

Carpentier, N. (2005). Identity, contingency and rigidity – The (counter-) hegemonic constructions of the identity of the media professional. *Journalism,* 6(2), 199–219.

Carroll, A. (2015). Corporate social responsibility. *Organizational Dynamics, 44*(2), 87–96.

Cederström, C. & Hoedemaekers, C. (Eds.) (2010). *Lacan and Organization.* London: MayFlyBooks.

Cederström, C. & Hoedemaekers, C. (2010). Preface. In Cederström, C. & Hoedemaekers, C. (Eds), *Lacan and Organization (pp. xiii–xviii).* London: MayFlyBooks.

Cederström, C. & Marinetto, M. (2013). Corporate Social Responsibility á La the Liberal Communist. *Organization,* 20(3), 416–32.

Cernea, M. (2003). For a New Economics of Resettlement: A Sociological Critique of the Compensation Principle. *International Social Science Journal,* 175, 1–27.

Chakrabarty, D. (1992). Postcoloniality and the Artifice of History: Who Speaks for "Indian" Pasts? *Representations,* 37, 1–26.

Choi, N. (2015). Reinvigorating a critical discussion on 'development' in development-induced displacement and resettlement. In I. Satiroglu, & N. Choi (Eds.), *Development-Induced Displacement and Resettlement: New perspectives on persisting problems* (pp. 41–55). London: Routledge.

Contu, A., Michaela D., & Campbell J. (2010). Editorial: Jacques Lacan with Organization Studies. *Organization,* 17(3), 307–15.

Contu, A., Florence P., & Nicolas B. (2013). Multinational Corporations' Politics and Resistance to Plant Shutdowns: A Comparative Case Study in the South of France. *Human Relations,* 66 (3), 363–84.

Crane, A., Palazzo, G., Spence, L. & Matten, D. (2014). Contesting the Value of "Creating Shared Value". *California Management Review,* 56(2), 130–53.

Crouch, C. (2011). *The strange non-death of neoliberalism,* Polity, Cambridge.

Czarniawska, B. (2014). *Social Science Research: From Field to Desk.* London: Sage Publications.

Dawkins, C. (2015). Agonistic Pluralism and Stakeholder Engagement. *Business Ethics Quarterly,* 25(1), 1–28.

Denzin, N. K. (2013/2016). Interpretive Autoethnography. In S. Holman Jones, T. E. Adams & C. Ellis (Eds.), *Handbook of Autoethnography* (pp. 123–142). New York: Routledge.

Dobers, P. (2010). The Many Faces of Corporate Social Responsibility. In P. Dobers (Ed.), *Corporate Social Responsibility – Challenges and* Practices (pp. 7–17). Stockholm: Santérus Academic Press.

Doloriert, C. & Sambrook, S. (2011). Accommodating an Autoethnographic PhD: The Tale of the Thesis, the Viva Voce, and the Traditional Business School. *Journal of Contemporary Ethnography*, 40 (5), 582–615.

Elkington, J. (1994). Towards the Sustainable Corporation: Win-Win-Win Business Strategies for Sustainable Development. *California Management Review, 36*(2), 90–100.

Elkington, J. (1997). Cannibals with Forks: The triple bottom line of 21st century business. Capstone: Oxford.

Elkington, J. (2004). Enter the triple bottom line, The Triple Bottom Line: Does it All Add Up? In A. Henriques and J. Richardson, *Assessing the Sustainability of Business and CSR* (pp. 1–16). Earthscan: London

Ellis, C.; Adams, T. E. and Bochner, A. P. (2011). Autoethnography: An Overview. *Forum: Qualitative Social Research,* 12 (1), Art. 10.

Ellis, C. (2013/2016). Preface: Carrying the Torch for Autoethnography. In Holman Jones, S.; Adams, T. E.; Ellis, C. (Eds.), *Handbook of Autoethnography* (pp. 9–12). New York: Routledge.

Environmental Justice Altas (2020). *EJAtlas – Global Altlas on Environmental Justice.* Available at: https://ejatlas.org, (accessed 8 October 2020).

Fleming, P., & Spicer, A. (2003). Working at a Cynical Distance: Implications for Power, Subjectivity and Resistance. *Organization, 10*(1), 157–179.

Fleming, P. and Jones, M. T. (2013). *The End of Corporate Social Responsibility – Crisis and Critique.* London: Sage Publications Ltd.

Fooks, G., Gilmore, A., Collin, J., Holden, C. & Lee, K. (2013). The Limits of Corporate Social Responsibility: Techniques of Neutralization, Stakeholder Management and Political CSR. *Journal of Business Ethics*, 112, 283–299.

Fotaki, M., Long, S., & Schwartz, H. (2012). What Can Psychoanalysis Offer Organization Studies Today? Taking Stock of Current Developments and Thinking about Future Directions. *Organization Studies, 33*(9), 1105–1120.

Friedman, M. (1970). The social responsibility of business is to increase its profits. *New York Times Magazine*, 32(13), 122–124.

Frynas, J. G. and Stephen, S. (2015). Political Corporate Social Responsibility: Reviewing Theories and Setting New Agendas. *International Journal of Management Reviews*, 17, 483–509.

Gabriel, Y. (2013). Researchers as Storytellers: Storytelling in Organizational Research. In M. Gotti & C. S. Guinda (Eds.), *Narratives in Academic and Professional Genres* (pp. 105–122). Berne: Peter Lang.

Garriga, E. and Melé, D. (2004). Corporate social responsibility theories: mapping the territory. *Journal of Business Ethics*, 53, 51–71.

Gaventa, J. (1982). *Power and Powerlessness. Quiescence and Rebellion in an Appalachian Valley.* Illinois: University of Illinois Press.

Gawell, M. (2006). Activist Entrepreneurship: Attac'ing Norms and Articulating Disclosive Stories. Doctoral dissertation, Business studies. Stockholm: Stockholm University.

Gawell, M. (2016). ”Illusionen Om Det Goda Civilsamhället.” *Kurage: Idétidskrift För Det Civila Samhället*, 20, 20–22.

Gilberthorpe, E. & Banks, G. (2012). Development on whose terms?: CSR discourse and social realities in Papua New Guinea's extractive industries sector. *Resources Policy*, 37, 185–193

Gilmore, S., Harding, N., Helin J., & Pullen, A. (2019). “Writing Differently.” *Management Learning*, 50(1), 3–10.

Gerber, S. (2012). Det materiella i fokus. *Kulturella perspektiv*, 3–4, 50–58.

Gerber, S., Gunnarson Payne, J. & Lundgren, A. S. (2012). Diskursetnologi. *Kulturella perspektiv*, 3–4, 2–6.

Glynos, J. & David H. (2007). *Logics of Critical Explanation in Social and Political Theory*. Abingdon: Routledge.

Glynos, J., Klimecki, R., & Willmott, H. (2015) Logics in Policy and Practice: A Critical Nodal Analysis of the UK Banking Reform Process. *Critical Policy Studies*, 9(4), 1–23.

Gramsci, A. (1929–1933/1999). *Notebooks*. In Q. Hoare and G. Nowell-Smith (Eds. and Trans.). *Selections from the Prison Notebooks*. London: ElecBook.

Gramsci, A. (1929–1930/1992). First Notebook. In J. A. Buttigieg (Ed.), *Prison Notebooks – Volume I* (pp. 99–236). New York: Columbia University Press.

Gramsci, A. (1930–1932/2007). Eighth Notebook. In J. A. Buttigieg (Ed.), *Prison Notebooks – Volume III* (pp. 229–383). New York: Columbia University Press.

Grant, D., Iedema, R. and Oswick, C. (2009). Discourse and Critical Management Studies. In M. Alvesson, T. Bridgman & H. Willmott (Eds.), *The Oxford handbook of critical management studies* (pp. 213–231). Oxford University Press.

Green, P. (2003). Albanien: Miljö och miljörörelse. In T. Lundén & T. Book (Eds.), *Det bergiga Balkan – konflikternas halvö* (pp. 63–72). Svenska Sällskapet för Geografi och Antropologi: Visby.

Gunnarsson Payne, J. (2017). Från politisk diskursteori till etnologiska diskursanalyser. In J. Gunnarsson Payne & M. Öhlander, *Tillämpad Kulturteori* (pp. 251–272). Lund: Studentlitteratur AB.

Halme, M. (2010). Something good for everyone? Investigation of three corporate responsibility approaches. In P. Dobers (Ed.), *Corporate Social Responsibility – Challenges and Practices* (pp. 217–239). Stockholm: Santérus Academic Press.

Hedlund, H. and Sjöberg, Ö. (2003). I skuggan av en myt: livet i en syd-albansk by. In T. Lundén & T. Book (Eds.), *Det bergiga Balkan – konflikternas halvö* (pp. 73–91). Svenska Sällskapet för Geografi och Antropologi: Visby.

Hilson, G. (2012). Corporate Social Responsibility in the extractive industries: Experiences from developing countries. *Resources Policy*, 37, 131–137.

Holstein, J. A. & Gubrium, J. F. (1995). *The Active Interview – Qualitative Research Methods Series, 37*. London: Sage Publications Ltd.

Ho, K. (2009). *Liquidated: An Ethnography of Wall Street*. Durham: Duke University Press.

Holman Jones, S., Adams, T. E. & Ellis, C. (2013/2016). Introduction: Coming to Know Autoethnography as More than a Method. In S. Holman Jones, T. E. Adams & C. Ellis (Eds.), *Handbook of Autoethnography* (pp. 17–48). New York: Routledge.

Islam, G. (2015). Practitioners as Theorists: Para-ethnography and the Collaborative Study of Contemporary Organizations. *Organizational Research Methods,* 18(2), 231–251.

Joutsenvirta, M. & Vaara, E. (2015). Legitimacy Struggles and Political Corporate Social Responsibility in International Settings: A Comparative Discursive Analysis of a Contested Investment in Latin America. *Organization Studies,* 36(6), 741–777.

Kallio, T. J. (2007). Taboos in Corporate Social Responsibility Discourse. *Journal of Business Ethics,* 74 (2), 165–175.

Kourula, A. & Delalieux, Guillaume (2016). The Micro-level Foundations and Dynamics of Political Corporate Social Responsibility: Hegemony and Passive Revolution through Civil Society. *Journal of Business Ethics,* 135, 769–785.

Kuhlman, J. W., & Farrington, J. (2010). What is sustainability? *Sustainability,* 2(11), 3436–3448.

Kvarnström, E. (2016). *Institutionella samspel. Om möten mellan en kommersiell och en ideell logik.* Doctoral dissertation, Business studies, Uppsala universitet.

Laclau, E. & Mouffe, C. (1985/2014). *Hegemony and Socialist Strategy. Towards a Radical Democratic Politics.* 2nd Edition. London: Verso.

Laclau, E. (1997). The Death and Resurrection of the Theory of Ideology. *The Johns Hopkins University Press, MLN,* 112(3), 297–321.

Laclau, E. (2005). *On Populist Reason.* London: Verso.

Laclau, E. (2006). Ideology and post-Marxism, *Journal of Political Ideologies,* 11(2), 103–114.

Levy, D. L. (2008). Political contestation in global production networks. *Academy of Management Review,* 33, 943–963.

Levy, D. L. & Egan, D. (2003). A Neo-Gramscian Approach to Corporate Political Strategy: Conflict and Accommodation in the Climate Change Negotiations. *Journal of Management Studies,* 40(4), 803–829.

Lindqvist, M. (2012). Klasskamrater revisited. *Kulturella perspektiv.* 3–4, 15–24.

Luning, S. (2012). Corporate Social Responsibility (CSR) for exploration: Consultants, companies and communities in processes of engagements. *Resources Policy,* 37, 205–211.

Madison, D. S. (2005). *Critical Ethnography. Method, Ethics and Performance.* London: Sage.

Matten, D. and Crane, A. (2005). Corporate Citizenship: Towards an Extended Theoretical Conceptualization, *Academy of Management Review,* 30(1), 166–179.

Marchart, O. (2007). *Post-foundational Political Thought: Political Difference in Nancy Lefort, Laclau and Badiou.* Edinburgh: Edinburgh University Press.

Mouffe, C. (2013). *Agonistics: Thinking the World Politically.* London: Verso.

NASA (2018). *What is a black hole?* Available at: https://www.nasa.gov/audience/forstudents/k-4/stories/nasa-knows/what-is-a-black-hole-k4.html (accessed 20 August 2020).

Nilsson, G. (2012). Att analysera sanningens rörlighet – Objektivitet, politik och fält. Diskursetnologi. *Kulturella perspektiv,* 3–4, 41–49.

Nyberg, D., Wright, C. & Kirk, J. (2018). Dash for Gas: Climate Change, Hegemony and the Scalar Politics of Fracking. *UK British Journal of Management,* 29, 235–251.

O'Doherty, D., Vachhani, S. J. & De Cock, C. (2019) *Rethinking Politics in Organization, EGOS 2020 Track.* Available at: https://www.egosnet.org/jart/prj3 /egos/main.jart?rel=de&reservemode=reserve&contentid=1566433211083&subtheme_id=1542700474415 (accessed 13 December 2019).

Persson, S. (2019). Spotlight on Sara Persson. In *AOM CMS Division Newsletter*, June 2019 (pp. 12–13). Available at: https://higherlogicdownload.s3.amazonaws.com/AOM/6f82acc5-5f6b-41fb-a485-f1639ebcf18c/UploadedImages/2019_June_AOM-CMS_Division_Newsletter-pages-12-13.pdf (accessed June 2019).

Porter, M. E. & Kramer, M. R. (2011). Creating Shared Value. *Harvard Business Review*, 89(1–2), 62–77.

Prasad, A. (2013). Playing the Game and Trying Not to Lose Myself: A Doctoral Student's Perspective on the Institutional Pressures for Research Output. *Organization*, 20(6), 936–48.

Pullen, A., Helin, J., & Harding, N. (2020). Introducing. In A. Pullen, J Helin & N Harding (Eds.), *Writing differently* (pp. 1–12). Dialogues in critical management studies, 4. Bingley: Emerald Publishing Limited.

Rhodes, C., Iain M., & Pullen, A. (2020). Dissensus! Radical Democracy and Business Ethics. *Journal of Business Ethics*, 164(4), 627–32.

Rodriguez, P., Siegel, D.S., Hillman, A. & Eden, L. (2006). Three lenses on the multinational enterprise: politics, corruption, and corporate social responsibility. *Journal of International Business Studies*, 37, 733–746.

Satiroglu, I. & Choi, N. (2015). Editors' introduction: reflections on development induced displacement and resettlement research and practice for renewed engagement. In I. Satiroglu, & N. Choi (Eds.), *Development-Induced Displacement and Resettlement: New perspectives on persisting problems* (pp. 1–16). London: Routledge.

Scherer, A. G. & Palazzo, G. (2007). Toward a Political Conception of Corporate Responsibility: Business and Society Seen from a Habermasian Perspective. *The Academy of Management Review*, 32(4), 1096–1120.

Scherer, A. G., Palazzo G. & Matten D. (2014). The Business Firm as a Political Actor: A New Theory of the Firm for a Globalized World. *Business & Society*, 53(2), 143–156.

Scherer, A. G. (2018). Theory Assessment and Agenda Setting in Political CSR: A Critical Theory Perspective. *International Journal of Management Reviews*, 20, 387–410.

Schwartz, B. & Tilling, K. (2009). 'ISO-lating' Corporate Social Responsibility in the Organizational Context: A Dissenting Interpretation of ISO 26000. *Corporate Social Responsibility and Environmental Management*, 16, 289–299.

Schwartz, B. & Tilling, K. (2010). Standardizing Sustainability: A Critical Perspective on ISO 14001 and ISO 26000. In P. Dobers (Ed.), *Corporate Social Responsibility – Challenges and Practices* (pp. 71–93). Stockholm: Santérus Academic Press.

Spence, C. (2007). Social and environmental reporting and hegemonic discourse. *Accounting, Auditing & Accountability Journal*, 20(6), 855–882.

Stavrakakis, Y. (2010). Symbolic Authority, Fantasmatic Enjoyment and the Spirits of Capitalism: Genealogies of Mutual Engagement. In C. Cederström & C. Hoedemaekers (Eds.), *Lacan and Organization* (pp. 59–100). London: MayFlyBooks.

Svensson, P. (2017). Debatt: Samverkan får inte hota fri kritisk forskning. *Dala-Demokraten*, 13 July 2017.

Thanem, T. & Knights, D. (2012). Feeling and speaking through our gendered bodies: Embodied self-reflection and research practice in organisation studies. *International*

Journal of Work Organisation and Emotion, 5(1), 91–108.

Thomas, P. D. (2009/2010). *The Gramscian moment: philosophy, hegemony and Marxism.* Chicago, Ill.: Haymarket.

Toyosaki, S. & Pensoneau-Conway, S. L. (2013/2016). Autoethnography as a Praxis of Social Justice. In S. Holman Jones, T. E. Adams & C. Ellis (Eds.), *Handbook of Autoethnography* (pp. 557–575). New York: Routledge.

Ulus, E., & Gabriel, Y. (2018). Bridging the contradictions of social constructionism and psychoanalysis in a study of workplace emotions in India. *Culture and Organization, 24*(3), 221–243.

Ulus, E. (2019). Transferential loss: Unconscious dynamics of love, learning and grieving. *Academy of Management Learning and Education.* In press.

UNDP Sverige (2019). *För företag.* Available at: https://www.globalamalen.se/for-foretag (accessed 20 November 2019).

Vaara, E. & Tienari, J. (2008). A Discursive Perspective on Legitimation Strategies in Multinational Corporations. *The Academy of Management Review*, 33(4), 985–993.

Vachhani, S. (2012). The Subordination of the Feminine? Developing a Critical Feminist Approach to the Psychoanalysis of Organizations. *Organization Studies,* 33(9), 1237–255.

Van Maanen, J. (1988/2011). *Tales of the field: on writing ethnography. 2nd edition.* Chicago: The University of Chicago Press.

Vickers, D. A. (2019). At-home Ethnography: A Method for Practitioners. *Qualitative Research in Organizations and Management: An International Journal,* 14(1), 10–26.

Wall, S. (2006). An Autoethnography on Learning about Autoethnography. *International Journal of Qualitative Methods,* 5(2), 146–160.

Werther, W. B & Chandler D. (2005). Strategic Corporate Social Responsibility as Global Brand Insurance. *Business Horizons,* 48(4), 317–24.

Whelan, G. (2013). Corporate Constructed and Dissent Enabling Public Spheres: Differentiating Dissensual from Consensual Corporate Social Responsibility. *Journal of Business Ethics*, 115, 775–769.

Wilke, H. & Wilke, G. (2007). Corporate Moral Legitimacy and the Legitimacy of Morals: A Critique of Palazzo/Scherer's Communicative Framework. *Journal of Business Ethics*, 81, 27–38.

Willmott, H. (2005). Theorizing Contemporary Control: Some Post-structuralist Responses to Some Critical Realist Questions. *Organization*, 12(5), 747–80.

Winter Jørgensen, M. & Phillips, L. (1999/2000). *Diskursanalys som teori och metod.* (S. E. Torhell, trans.). Lund: Studentlitteratur AB.

Woolf, V. (1928/2012). A Room of One's Own. In *Wordsworth Classics. A Room of One's Own & The Voyage Out* (pp. 29–108). Hertfordshire: Wordsworth Editions Limited.

Yengoh, G.T. & Armah, F.A. (2015). Effects of Large-Scale Acquisition on Food Insecurity in Sierra Leone. *Sustainability*, 7, 9505–9539.

Zickar, M. J. & Carter N. T. (2010). Reconnecting With the Spirit of Workplace Ethnography. *Organizational Research Methods,* 13(2), 304–319.

Zguri, R. (2017). *Relations between media and politics in Albania.* Tirana: Albanian Media Insitute & Friedrich Ebert Foundation. Available at: https://library.fes.de/pdf-files/bueros/albanien/14001.pdf (accessed 10 November 2019).

Empirical material

Participant observation – working experience in Albania

(Extract from my CV as written in January 2016)

08.2012–12.2015	**Community Relations Coordinator**, Bankers Petroleum, Albania Experience in: consultation and disclosure activities with local stakeholders such as residents in the project area, local authorities and NGOs; planning, implementing and monitoring community development projects within the fields of local infrastructure, agriculture, livelihood assistance and vocational training; monitoring and evaluation of community investments including household surveys, focus groups, interviews and cost-benefit evaluations of finalized projects; development of various databases in access for budget planning and monitoring, stakeholder engagement and grievance management; support in the process to receive and address grievances from communities; advising on and implementing social compliance and impact mitigation activities related to construction, drilling and operations; drafting of various reports such as Social Management Plans, Evaluation Reports and yearly reports to international finance institutions IFC and EBRD.
11.2011–07.2012	**Resettlement Action Plan Manager**, Devoll Hydropower, Albania Manager with responsibility to form a team of field workers and start the planning process for physical and economic resettlement of project impacted communities. Experience in: Planning and implementing socio-economic census and asset inventory with project affected households; Development and

	management of working methods for team of field workers; Verification and quality control of data collection; Conducting meetings with impacted communities and local officials; Producing public information material. Gained understanding of: Drafting a Resettlement Action Plan; IFC Performance Standard 5; Entitlement criteria for compensation of lost assets; Land-based livelihood restoration; Expropriation; Albanian immovable property rights issues.
11.2010 -10.2011	**Social Research Officer**, Bankers Petroleum, Albania Experience in: Planning and implementing Social Impact Assessments (for Bridge, Oil Wells and Pipeline) and Quantitative and Qualitative Social Baseline Assessment in project affected communities; Drafting and monitoring Social Action Plans; Public Consultation and Disclosure. Gained understanding of: IFC/EBRD Performance Standards; Land Acquisition; Grievance Redress Mechanism; Management of social impacts in private sector.
05.2010–09.2010	**ESIA Assistant,** Statkraft, Albania Assistant during the Social Impact Assessment for Devoll Hydropower Project in a rural mountain area of Albania. Experience in: Rapid Rural Assessment Baseline; Mapping of project affected Socio-Cultural Sites; Implementing Impact Consultations with local communities; and Drafting of Social Impact Assessment Report.

Reports and webpages

Albpetrol (no date). *Patos Marinza.* Available at: http://www.albpetrol.al/prodhimi-i-naftes/vendburimet/patos-marinza/ (accessed 20 February 2018).

Bankers Petroleum (2009). *Bankers Petroleum Finalizes US$110 million debt financing.* Available at: http://www.bankerspetroleum.com/investing/news-releases/ bankers-petroleum-finalizes-us110-million-debt-financing (accessed 12 July 2016).

Bankers Petroleum (2010). *Unlocking Patos-Marinza – Annual Report 2010.* Available at: https://www.bankerspetroleum.com/sites/default/files/2010_ar.pdf (accessed 26 April 2018).

Bankers Petroleum (2011a). *Project Information Document – Land Access at Bankers.*

Bankers Petroleum (2011b). *Draft Social Baseline of Patos-Marinza Project Affected Communities.*

Bankers Petroleum (2012a). *Environmental and Social Management Report: For Public Disclosure.*

Bankers Petroleum (2012b). *Project Information Document – Geology and Earthquakes in Fier and Albania.*

Bankers Petroleum (2015a). *Patos-Marinza Oil Industry and Communities.* Communication material summarizing Bankers' Community Survey disclosed in November 2015.

Bankers Petroleum (2015e). *Participatory Air Monitoring Programme 2015.*

Bankers Petroleum (2016a). *History/Timeline.* Available at: http://www.bankers petroleum.com/about/historytimeline (accessed 11 July 2016).

Bankers Petroleum (2016b). *Responsibility/Philosophy.* Available at: http://www.ban kerspetroleum.com/responsibility/philosophy (accessed 11 July 2016).

Bankers Petroleum (2016d). *Bankers in Albania.* Available at: http://www.bankers petroleum.com/albania/bankers-albania (accessed 14 July 2016).

Bankers Petroleum (2016f). *Bankers Petroleum Announced Closing of Plan of Arrangement Transaction.* Available at: http://www.bankerspetroleum.com /investing/news-releases/bankers-petroleum-announces-closing-plan-arrangement-transaction (accessed October 2016).

Bankers Petroleum (2016g). *Public Grievance Mechanism.* Available at: http:// www.bankerspetroleum.al/en/node/154 (accessed 27 October 2016).

Bankers Petroleum (2016h). *Environment.* Available at: https://wwwbankers petro leum.al/en/node/117 (accessed 11 July 2016).

Bankwatch Network (2014). *The long shadow of an oil legacy – Fact finding mission report from the Bankers Petroleum oil fields at Patos Marinza, Albania.* Available at: https://bankwatch.org/sites/default/files/Bankers-Petroleum-report-Feb14.pdf (accessed 30 March 2018).

CAO (2013a). *CAO Assessment Report.* Available at: http://www.cao-ombudsman.org/ cases/casedetail.aspx?id=197 (accessed 1 November 2016).

CAO (2013b). *Summary Report – November 2013.* Available at: http://www.cao-ombudsman.org/cases/case_detail.aspx?id=197 (accessed 19 July 2016).

CAO (2016). *CAO Case Progress Report. Albania – Bankers Petroleum Complaint.* Available at: http://www.cao-ombudsman.org/cases/case_detail.aspx?id=197 (accessed 1 November 2016).

CAO (2017). *About the CAO: Who We Are.* Available at: http://www.cao-ombudsman .org/about/whoweare/ (accessed 17 June 2017).

EBRD (2008). Environmental and Social Policy. Available at: http://www.ebrd.com/downloads/about/policies/environmental_policy/2008-05-14,_Environmental_and_Social_Policy-_Publication.pdf (accessed 6 April 2016).

EBRD (2009). *Patos-Marinza Environmental Remediation and Development.* Available at: http://www.ebrd.com/work-with-us/projects/psd/patosmarinza-environmental-remediation-and-development.html (accessed 31 October 2016).

EBRD (2014). *Environmental and Social Policy.* Available at: http://www.ebrd.com/who-we-are/our-values/environmental-and-social-policy/performance-requirements.html%20 (accessed 21 November 2016).

EBRD (2014b). EBRD: Financial Intermediates. Guides Notes for Category A Projects. Available at: http://www.ebrd.com/cs/Satellite?c=Content&cid=1395247833140&pagename=EBRD%2FContent%2FDownloadDocument (accessed 6 April 2018).

IFC (2002). *Handbook for Preparing a Resettlement Action Plan.* Washington DC: International Finance Corporation.

IFC (2007). *Stakeholder Engagement: A Good Practise Handbook for Companies doing Business in Emerging Markets.* Washington DC: International Finance Corporation.

IFC (2009a). *Environmental and Social Action Plan, Bankers Petroleum Albania Limited (Project #27306).* Available at: http://ifcext.ifc.org/ifcext/spiwebsite1.nsf /0/A6D5BBB1BD8CE5D6852576BA000E2D19/$File/Bankers%20ESAP%20022509%20Final%20for%20disclosure.pdf (accessed 11 July 2016).

IFC (2009b). *Good Practice Note – Addressing Grievances from Project-Affected Communities.* Washington DC: International Finance Corporation.

IFC (2012a). *International Finance Corporation's Policy on Environmental and Social Sustainability.* https://www.ifc.org/wps/wcm/connect/7141585d-c6fa-490b-a81 2-2ba87245115b/SP_English_2012.pdf?MOD=AJPERES&CVID=kiIrw0g (accessed 11 July 2016).

IFC (2012b). *Performance Standards of Environmental and Social Sustainability.* Available at: https://www.ifc.org/wps/wcm/connect/24e6bfc3-5de3-444d-be9b-226188c95454/PS_English_2012_Full-Document.pdf?MOD=AJPERES&CVID=jkV-X6h (accessed 11 July 2016).

IFC (2012c). *IFC's Sustainability Framework: From Policy Update to Implementation.* Available at: https://www.scribd.com/document/118011305/IFC-s-Sustainability – Framework-From-Policy-Update-to-Implementation#fullscreen (accessed 11 July 2016).

IFC (2013). *Environmental and Social Review Summary.* Available at: http://ifcext.ifc.org /ifcext/spiwebsite1.nsf/DocsByUNIDForPrint/CB12EB27CE63A56B85257B0A005CE573?opendocument (accessed 11 July 2016).

Institute of Geosciences, Energy, Water and Environment (2016). *Department of Seismology.* Available at: http://www.geo.edu.al/newweb/?fq=brenda&kid=13&gj=gj2 (accessed 10 September 2016).

Proactiveinvestors (2009). *Bankers Petroleum: Developing Europe's largest onshore oilfield.* Available at: http://www.proactiveinvestors.co.uk/companies/ news/ 70480/bankers-petroleum-developing-europes-largest-onshore-oilfield-1683.html (accessed 21 February 2018).

UNEP (2000). *Post-conflict Environmental Assessment – Albania.* Available at: https://postconflict.unep.ch/publications/albaniafinalasses.pdf (accessed 24 April 2018).

Facebook posts

Alba Leaks (2015, May 11). *Picture without comment.* [Facebook post] Available at: https://www.facebook.com/photo.php?fbid=1427074164277655&set=a.1427074174277654.1073741828.100009252564546&type=3&theater (accessed 26 April 2018).

@nopetroleum (2015, April 28). *Picture without comment.* [Facebook post] Available at: https://www.facebook.com/nopetroleum/photos/a.1442603346037403.107371826.1439881802976224/1442603349370736/?type=3&theater (accessed 27 March 2018).

@nopetroleum (2015, August 7). *Picture without comment.* [Facebook post] Available at: https://www.facebook.com/nopetroleum/photos/a.1446325938998477.107 3741827.1439881802976224/1480923618872042/?type=3&theater (accessed 26 April 2018).

@vetvetdyhere (2014a, July 23). *Po qenke balle kazani moj e uruar* [Facebook post] Available at: https://www.facebook.com/VetVetDyHere/photos/a.569508713089750.1073741828.569423539764934/805612186146067/?type=3&theater (accessed 10 September 2016).

@vetvetdyhere (2014b, March 20). *Picture without comment.* [Facebook post] Available at: https://www.facebook.com/VetVetDyHere/photos/a.569508713089750.1073 741828.56 9423539764934/737577916282828/?type=3&theater (accessed 10 September 2016).

@vetvetdyhere (2014c, March 20). *Picture without comment.* [Facebook post] Available at: https://www.facebook.com/VetVetDyHere/photos/a.569508713089750.1073741828.569423539764934/737583596282260/?type=3&theater (accessed 10 September 2016).

@vetvetdyhere (2014d, April 15). *Picture without comment.* [Facebook post] Available at: https://www.facebook.com/Naftetaret/photos/a.569508713089750/751258254914794/?type=3&theater (accessed 22 May 2019).

@vetvetdyhere (2014e, March 31). *Picture without comment.* [Facebook post] Available at: https://www.facebook.com/Naftetaret/photos/a.569508713089750/7437326 15667358/

@vetvetdyhere (2014f, May 19). *Picture without comment.* [Facebook post] Available at: https://www.facebook.com/Naftetaret/photos/a.569508713089750/769845566389396/

@vetvetdyhere (2015a, September 10). *Picture without comment.* [Facebook post] Available at: https://www.facebook.com/VetVetDyHere/photos/a.569508713089750.1073741828.569423539764934/1034839703223313/?type=3&theater (accessed 27 March 2018).

@vetvetdyhere (2015b, September 25). *Bankers demton rende shendetin.* [Facebook post] Available at: https://www.facebook.com/Naftetaret/photos/a.569508713089750/1043471582360125/?type=3&theater (accessed 22 May 2019).

YouTube videos

Albania Oilfield (2014, January 24). *Awakening the giant.* Available at: https://www.youtube.com/watch?v=Ob7mfb1ftgQ (accessed 19 July 2016).

Kanali Shtate (2013, November 22). *Proteste ne Zharrez Shpertimet Nuk Ndalen Banoret Bllokojne Rrugen Lajm.* Available at: https://www.youtube.com/watch?v=fUkDLCdjvXY (accessed 12 April 2018).

Nick Carlson (2013, December 14). *Commute to work....in Albania.* Available at: https://www.youtube.com/watch?v=2lNNcuqMpl0 (accessed 2 February 2018).

Oil & Gas Council (2015, December 6). *David French Bankers Petroleum 1.* Available at: https://www.youtube.com/watch?v=4kSNCyHjzPI. (accessed 19 November 2017).

Ora News Emisione (2015, December 2). *Bankers, nje koncesion i arte ne Republiken e Bananeve- Të Paekspozuarit – 12/ 02/ 2015 – Ora News.* Available at: https://www.youtube. com/watch?v=DHRczmt8pX0 (accessed 25 April 2018).

Top Channel (2013, November 22). *Protestë pas një tërmeti – Top Channel Albania – News – Lajme.* Available at: https://www.youtube.com/watch?v=JtMGJJwneew (accessed 12 April 2018).

Top Channel (2014, March 3). *Fier, protestë për tërmetin – Top Channel Albania – News – Lajme.* Available at: https://www.youtube.com/watch?v=4v60-HgMhYs (accessed 12 April 2018).

VizionPlusAlbania (2013, September 13). *Proteste kundër "Bankers..." – News, Lajme – Vizion Plus.* Available at: https://www.youtube.com/watch?v=BsmlzhWz_Rg (accessed 6 April 2018).

VizionPlusAlbania (2013, December 9). *Fier, sërish protesta ndaj "Bankers" – News, Lajme – Vizion Plus.* Available at: https://www.youtube.com/watch?v=vuemOxMsxIU (accessed 12 April 2018).

VizionPlusAlbania (2015, March 16). *Protesta e familjes në Fier nga dëmet e "Bankers Petrolium" – News, Lajme – Vizion Plus.* Available at: https://www.youtube.com/watch?v=fCTALXjvUeY (accessed 18 April 2018).

Interviews with corporate representatives and partners

Interviews include Bankers' staff, Bankers' former staff, Bankers' managers, representatives or former representatives from Bankers' contractors, government representatives and representatives from organizations collaborating with Bankers. Quoted interviewees have been given the fictive names: Afrim, Artur, Gezim, Klodian, Gramos, Ditjon, Ediona, Rezart, Jonida, Ervis and Lidia. Dates and positions are not referred to in order to protect identities.

Date	Position	Organization	Location	Length	Recorded
31/10/17	Manager	Bankers' contractor	Contractor office	01:37:82	Audio Transcr.
01/11/17	Former employee	Bankers' contractor	Café	01:24:65	Audio Transcr.
01/11/17	Manager	Bankers	Bankers' office	00:57:92	Audio Transcr.
02/11/17	Senior representative	Local government	Government office	45 min	Notes
02/11/17	Manager	Bankers	Bankers' office	00:42:71	Audio Transcr.
02/11/17	Employee	Bankers	Restaurant	00:27:18	Audio Transcr.
03/11/17	Employee	Bankers	Bankers' office	00:29:31	Audio Part Trans.
03/11/17	Manager	Bankers	Bankers' office	00:56:10	Audio Part Trans.
03/11/17	Senior representative	Local government	Government office	45 min	Notes
05/11/17	Manager	Bankers' partner organization	Café	00:49:55	Audio Part Trans.
05/11/17	Former employee	Bankers	Café	01:03:41	Audio Part Trans.
13/09/18	Former employee	Bankers	Café	01:09:42	Audio Part Trans.
14/09/18	Employee	Bankers	Café	01:40:28	Audio Part Trans.

Interviews with Patos-Marinza residents

Quoted interviewees have been given the fictive names: Shkelqim, Artan, Lisa, Ergys, Berti, Edison, Armand, Alkeida, Flamur, Ermal, Fatmir, Alban, Taulant, Florenc, Besa and Fatjon. Dates and village names are not referred to in order to protect identities.

Date	Village	Type of meeting	Location	Participants	Length	Recorded
04/09/18	Belina	Group interview	Restaurant	8 men (age 30–70)	01:41:25 + 00:14:35	Audio Transcr.
05/09/18	Belina	Chat	Gate	1 man (50)	5 min	Notes
05/09/18	Belina	Family visit	Yard	2 women & 4 men (age 20–50)	01:15:51	Audio Transcr.
05/09/18	Belina	Family visit	Land	2 men (20–50)	20 min	Notes
06/09/18	Marinza	Group interview	Café	7 men & 1 woman (40–70)	01:41:56	Audio Transcr.
06/09/18	Marinza	Family visit	Living room	2 men & 1 woman (50–60)	00:24:51	Audio Transcr.
07/09/18	Marinza	Chat	Gate	1 woman (40)	15 min	Notes
07/09/18	Marinza	Chat	Street	1 man (60)	15 min	Notes
07/09/18	Marinza	Chat	Yard	2 men (60) & 1 woman (60)	15 min	Notes
07/09/18	Marinza	Family visit	Yard	2 women (20, 60)	45 min	Notes
07/09/18	Marinza	Family visit	Living room	1 woman (50)	30 min	Notes
10/09/18	Zharrza	Group interview	Café		01:32:56	Audio Transcr.
11/09/18	Zharrza	Family visit	Veranda	2 men & 2 women (60–20)	00:29:31	Audio Transcr.
11/09/18	Zharrza	Chat	Yard	Woman (50)	15 min	Notes
11/09/18	Zharrza	Family visit	Yard	Woman (50)	15 min + 00:14:46	Notes + Audio Transcr.
12/09/18	Belina	Chat	Kindergarten	2 women (30–40)	15 min	Notes
12/09/18	Belina	Family visit	Restaurant	1 woman & 1 man (40–50)	45 min	Notes
12/09/18	Belina	Chat	Gate	1 woman & 1 man (50)	5 min	Notes
12/09/18	Belina	Chat	Gate	1 woman (20)	5 min	Notes
12/09/18	Belina	Family visit	Veranda	2 women & 3 men (20–65)	1 h and 15 min	Notes

Annex 1: Introductory letter to interview participants

PhD Research Project:
Company – Community Relations in Patos-Marinza Oilfield
November 2017

You have received this letter as part of your participation in the PhD Research Project *Corporate- Community Relations in Patos-Marinza Oilfield*. The project focus on the operations of the Canadian oil and gas company Bankers Petroleum Ltd. and the company's community relations programmes in Patos-Marinza during the years 2009–2016. The aim of this research project is to develop general knowledge about company-community relations in the extractive industries using Patos-Marinza as an example.

In September 2016, I was employed by *Södertörn University* as a PhD Candidate and will spend the next four years on this research project. The project is fully funded by *Södertörn University*. Your participation in this research project is fully confidential which means that your name, position or personal details will not be disclosed to any external parties. The comments and opinions that you express during this interview will be used to get a broad picture about company-community relations in Patos-Marinza. The final product of this research project will be a book published by *Södertörn University* and scientific articles in journals within the area of business studies.

For additional questions or comments please do not hesitate to contact me.

Sincerely,

Sara Persson
PhD Candidate in Business Studies
School of Social Sciences
Baltic and East European Graduate School (BEEGS)

SÖDERTÖRN UNIVERSITY | Stockholm, Sweden
+46 (0)739 25 78 98 | sara.persson@sh.se

Annex 2: Interview guide

Introduction

First, I want to thank you for your participation in my PhD Research Project *Corporate- Community Relations in Patos-Marinza Oilfield*. The project focus on the operations of the Canadian oil and gas company Bankers Petroleum Ltd. and the company's community relations programmes in Patos-Marinza during the years 2009–2016. The aim of this research project is to develop general knowledge about company-community relations in the extractive industries using Patos-Marinza as an example.

In September 2016, I was employed by *Södertörn University* as a PhD Candidate and will spend the next four years on this research project. The project is fully funded by *Södertörn University*. Your participation in this research project is fully confidential which means that your name, position or personal details will not be disclosed to any external parties. The comments and opinions that you express during this interview will be used to get a broad picture about company-community relations in Patos-Marinza. The final product of this research project will be a book published by *Södertörn University* and scientific articles in journals within the area of business studies.

When I worked for Bankers I was constantly confused about the various opinions that people has about how community relations should be managed. That is why I am doing this project and why I hope to get your view on this issue.

History

Tell me about your background, where are you from originally and where did you study?
Can you tell me about when you first came in contact with the oil industry and Patos-Marinza?
Can you tell me about how you first started working for Bankers?
Were you part of the transformation from Anglo Albanian Petroleum (AAP) to Bankers? Can you tell me about that process?
What was your impression of Bankers when you started? How was it different from today?

Can you describe how Patos-Marinza looked like during communism and later during AAP? How was it different from today?
Can you tell me about when IFC became involved in 2009? How did that change Bankers?

Company-Community Relationship
How would you describe Bankers reputation in Albania in general?
What are the positive things people say about Bankers? What are the negative things?
What do the media write about Bankers?
What do the central and local politicians say about Bankers?
Which are the main supporters of the company?
How was the relationship between Albpetrol and communities during communism?
How is the relationship different today?
How would you describe the relationship between Bankers and the communities?
What are the main issues between Bankers and the communities?
What is the company strategy to handle these issues?
How does media write about these issues?
What do the politicians say about these issues?
What strategy would you use to improve company- community relationships if you could decide?

Specific
Can you tell me about your experience from the earthquake conflict and the protests that have happened during the years?
Can you tell me about your experience from the conflict over air quality and the many grievances related to this?
Can you tell me about your experience from the gas accident in Marinza?
Can you tell me about your experience from the thefts from the oil field?
What is your experience from Bankers implementing a community investment programme? What are the best types of investments according to you?
What is your experience from Bankers hiring policies and complaints about unemployment?
What is your experience from land acquisition and issues with land borders and registration?

Cultural

How do you feel being an Albanian but working in a Canadian company?

Is there an Albanian way of working that Canadians did not agree with or understand?

Is there a Canadian way of working that you think Albanian staff did not agree with?

Have you been in any situation where you have experienced a conflict between working for a foreign company in Albania?

Do you feel that actors in the Albanian society expect things from you that foreign managers do not understand?

What was the difference between Canadian and Chinese management?

What are the main changes that has happened after the Chinese took over?

Final

Is there anything else you want to tell me that you think is important for this topic?

Is there anyone you think I should talk to?

Are there any written sources you think I should consult?

What are your thoughts about this interview and my project?

What kind of book about Patos-Marinza would you like it to be? What would you read?

Annex 3: IFC's performance standards

Performance Standards on Environmental and Social Sustainability[511]
January 1, 2012

1. IFC's Sustainability Framework articulates the Corporation's strategic commitment to sustainable development, and is an integral part of IFC's approach to risk management. The Sustainability Framework comprises IFC's Policy and Performance Standards on Environmental and Social Sustainability, and IFC's Access to Information Policy. The Policy on Environmental and Social Sustainability describes IFC's commitments, roles, and responsibilities related to environmental and social sustainability. IFC's Access to Information Policy reflects IFC's commitment to transparency and good governance on its operations, and outlines the Corporation's institutional disclosure obligations regarding its investment and advisory services. The Performance Standards are directed towards clients, providing guidance on how to identify risks and impacts, and are designed to help avoid, mitigate, and manage risks and impacts as a way of doing business in a sustainable way, including stakeholder engagement and disclosure obligations of the client in relation to project-level activities. In the case of its direct investments (including project and corporate finance provided through financial intermediaries), IFC requires its clients to apply the Performance Standards to manage environmental and social risks and impacts so that development opportunities are enhanced. IFC uses the Sustainability Framework along with other strategies, policies, and initiatives to direct the business activities of the Corporation in order to achieve its overall development objectives. The Performance Standards may also be applied by other financial institutions.

2. Together, the eight performance standards establish standards that the client is to meet throughout the life of an investment by IFC:

Performance Standard 1:	Assessment and Management of Environmental and Social Risks and Impacts

[511] IFC (2012b, p. i)

Performance Standard 2:	Labor and Working Conditions
Performance Standard 3:	Resource Efficiency and Pollution Prevention
Performance Standard 4:	Community Health, Safety, and Security
Performance Standard 5:	Land Acquisition and Involuntary Resettlement
Performance Standard 6:	Biodiversity Conservation and Sustainable Management of Living Natural Resources
Performance Standard 7:	Indigenous Peoples
Performance Standard 8:	Cultural Heritage

Södertörn Doctoral Dissertations

1. Jolanta Aidukaite, *The Emergence of the Post-Socialist Welfare State: The case of the Baltic States: Estonia, Latvia and Lithuania*, 2004
2. Xavier Fraudet, *Politique étrangère française en mer Baltique (1871–1914): De l'exclusion à l'affirmation*, 2005
3. Piotr Wawrzeniuk, *Confessional Civilising in Ukraine: The Bishop Iosyf Shumliansky and the Introduction of Reforms in the Diocese of Lviv 1668–1708*, 2005
4. Andrej Kotljarchuk, *In the Shadows of Poland and Russia: The Grand Duchy of Lithuania and Sweden in the European Crisis of the mid-17th Century*, 2006
5. Håkan Blomqvist, *Nation, ras och civilisation i svensk arbetarrörelse före nazismen*, 2006
6. Karin S Lindelöf, *Om vi nu ska bli som Europa: Könsskapande och normalitet bland unga kvinnor i transitionens Polen*, 2006
7. Andrew Stickley. *On Interpersonal Violence in Russia in the Present and the Past: A Sociological Study*, 2006
8. Arne Ek, *Att konstruera en uppslutning kring den enda vägen: Om folkrörelsers modernisering i skuggan av det Östeuropeiska systemskiftet*, 2006
9. Agnes Ers, *I mänsklighetens namn: En etnologisk studie av ett svenskt biståndsprojekt i Rumänien*, 2006
10. Johnny Rodin, *Rethinking Russian Federalism: The Politics of Intergovernmental Relations and Federal Reforms at the Turn of the Millennium*, 2006
11. Kristian Petrov, *Tillbaka till framtiden: Modernitet, postmodernitet och generationsidentitet i Gorbačevs glasnost' och perestrojka*, 2006
12. Sophie Söderholm Werkö, *Patient patients? Achieving Patient Empowerment through Active Participation, Increased Knowledge and Organisation*, 2008
13. Peter Bötker, *Leviatan i arkipelagen: Staten, förvaltningen och samhället. Fallet Estland*, 2007
14. Matilda Dahl, *States under scrutiny: International organizations, transformation and the construction of progress*, 2007
15. Margrethe B. Søvik, *Support, resistance and pragmatism: An examination of motivation in language policy in Kharkiv*, Ukraine, 2007
16. Yulia Gradskova, *Soviet People with female Bodies: Performing beauty and maternity in Soviet Russia in the mid 1930–1960s*, 2007

17. Renata Ingbrant, *From Her Point of View: Woman's Anti-World in the Poetry of Anna Świrszczyńska*, 2007
18. Johan Eellend, *Cultivating the Rural Citizen: Modernity, Agrarianism and Citizenship in Late Tsarist Estonia*, 2007
19. Petra Garberding, *Musik och politik i skuggan av nazismen: Kurt Atterberg och de svensk-tyska musikrelationerna*, 2007
20. Aleksei Semenenko, *Hamlet the Sign: Russian Translations of Hamlet and Literary Canon Formation*, 2007
21. Vytautas Petronis, *Constructing Lithuania: Ethnic Mapping in the Tsarist Russia, ca. 1800–1914*, 2007
22. Akvile Motiejunaite, *Female employment, gender roles, and attitudes: The Baltic countries in a broader context*, 2008
23. Tove Lindén, *Explaining Civil Society Core Activism in Post-Soviet Latvia*, 2008
24. Pelle Åberg, *Translating Popular Education: Civil Society Cooperation between Sweden and Estonia*, 2008
25. Anders Nordström, *The Interactive Dynamics of Regulation: Exploring the Council of Europe's monitoring of Ukraine*, 2008
26. Fredrik Doeser, *In Search of Security After the Collapse of the Soviet Union: Foreign Policy Change in Denmark, Finland and Sweden, 1988–1993*, 2008
27. Zhanna Kravchenko. *Family (versus) Policy: Combining Work and Care in Russia and Sweden*, 2008
28. Rein Jüriado, *Learning within and between public-private partnerships*, 2008
29. Elin Boalt, *Ecology and evolution of tolerance in two cruciferous species*, 2008
30. Lars Forsberg, *Genetic Aspects of Sexual Selection and Mate Choice in Salmonids*, 2008
31. Eglė Rindzevičiūtė, *Constructing Soviet Cultural Policy: Cybernetics and Governance in Lithuania after World War II*, 2008
32. Joakim Philipson, *The Purpose of Evolution: 'struggle for existence' in the Russian-Jewish press 1860–1900*, 2008
33. Sofie Bedford, *Islamic activism in Azerbaijan: Repression and mobilization in a post-Soviet context*, 2009
34. Tommy Larsson Segerlind, *Team Entrepreneurship: A process analysis of the venture team and the venture team roles in relation to the innovation process*, 2009
35. Jenny Svensson, *The Regulation of Rule-Following: Imitation and Soft Regulation in the European Union*, 2009
36. Stefan Hallgren, *Brain Aromatase in the guppy, Poecilia reticulate: Distribution, control and role in behavior*, 2009
37. Karin Ellencrona, *Functional characterization of interactions between the flavivirus NS5 protein and PDZ proteins of the mammalian host*, 2009

38. Makiko Kanematsu, *Saga och verklighet: Barnboksproduktion i det postsovjetiska Lettland*, 2009
39. Daniel Lindvall, *The Limits of the European Vision in Bosnia and Herzegovina: An Analysis of the Police Reform Negotiations*, 2009
40. Charlotta Hillerdal, *People in Between – Ethnicity and Material Identity: A New Approach to Deconstructed Concepts*, 2009
41. Jonna Bornemark, *Kunskapens gräns – gränsens vetande*, 2009
42. Adolphine G. Kateka, *Co-Management Challenges in the Lake Victoria Fisheries: A Context Approach*, 2010
43. René León Rosales, *Vid framtidens hitersta gräns: Om pojkar och elevpositioner i en multietnisk skola*, 2010
44. Simon Larsson, *Intelligensaristokrater och arkivmartyrer: Normerna för vetenskaplig skicklighet i svensk historieforskning 1900–1945*, 2010
45. Håkan Lättman, *Studies on spatial and temporal distributions of epiphytic lichens*, 2010
46. Alia Jaensson, *Pheromonal mediated behaviour and endocrine response in salmonids: The impact of cypermethrin, copper, and glyphosate*, 2010
47. Michael Wigerius, *Roles of mammalian Scribble in polarity signaling, virus offense and cell-fate determination*, 2010
48. Anna Hedtjärn Wester, *Män i kostym: Prinsar, konstnärer och tegelbärare vid sekelskiftet 1900*, 2010
49. Magnus Linnarsson, *Postgång på växlande villkor: Det svenska postväsendets organisation under stormaktstiden*, 2010
50. Barbara Kunz, *Kind words, cruise missiles and everything in between: A neoclassical realist study of the use of power resources in U.S. policies towards Poland, Ukraine and Belarus 1989–2008*, 2010
51. Anders Bartonek, *Philosophie im Konjunktiv: Nichtidentität als Ort der Möglichkeit des Utopischen in der negativen Dialektik Theodor W. Adornos*, 2010
52. Carl Cederberg, *Resaying the Human: Levinas Beyond Humanism and Antihumanism*, 2010
53. Johanna Ringarp, *Professionens problematik: Lärarkårens kommunalisering och välfärdsstatens förvandling*, 2011
54. Sofi Gerber, *Öst är Väst men Väst är bäst: Östtysk identitetsformering i det förenade Tyskland*, 2011
55. Susanna Sjödin Lindenskoug, *Manlighetens bortre gräns: Tidelagsrättegångar i Livland åren 1685–1709*, 2011
56. Dominika Polanska, *The emergence of enclaves of wealth and poverty: A sociological study of residential differentiation in post-communist Poland*, 2011

57. Christina Douglas, *Kärlek per korrespondens: Två förlovade par under andra hälften av 1800-talet*, 2011

58. Fred Saunders, *The Politics of People – Not just Mangroves and Monkeys: A study of the theory and practice of community-based management of natural resources in Zanzibar*, 2011

59. Anna Rosengren, *Åldrandet och språket: En språkhistorisk analys av hög ålder och åldrande i Sverige cirka 1875–1975*, 2011

60. Emelie Lilliefeldt, *European Party Politics and Gender: Configuring Gender-Balanced Parliamentary Presence*, 2011

61. Ola Svenonius, *Sensitising Urban Transport Security: Surveillance and Policing in Berlin, Stockholm, and Warsaw*, 2011

62. Andreas Johansson, *Dissenting Democrats: Nation and Democracy in the Republic of Moldova*, 2011

63. Wessam Melik, *Molecular characterization of the Tick-borne encephalitis virus: Environments and replication*, 2012

64. Steffen Werther, *SS-Vision und Grenzland-Realität: Vom Umgang dänischer und „volksdeutscher" Nationalsozialisten in Sønderjylland mit der „großgermanischen" Ideologie der SS*, 2012

65. Peter Jakobsson, *Öppenhetsindustrin*, 2012

66. Kristin Ilves, *Seaward Landward: Investigations on the archaeological source value of the landing site category in the Baltic Sea region*, 2012

67. Anne Kaun, *Civic Experiences and Public Connection: Media and Young People in Estonia*, 2012

68. Anna Tessmann, *On the Good Faith: A Fourfold Discursive Construction of Zoroastripanism in Contemporary Russia*, 2012

69. Jonas Lindström, *Drömmen om den nya staden: Stadsförnyelse i det postsovjetisk Riga*, 2012

70. Maria Wolrath Söderberg, *Topos som meningsskapare: Retorikens topiska perspektiv på tänkande och lärande genom argumentation*, 2012

71. Linus Andersson, *Alternativ television: Former av kritik i konstnärlig TV-produktion*, 2012

72. Håkan Lättman, *Studies on spatial and temporal distributions of epiphytic lichens*, 2012

73. Fredrik Stiernstedt, Mediearbete i mediehuset: Produktion i förändring på MTG-radio, 2013

74. Jessica Moberg, *Piety, Intimacy and Mobility: A Case Study of Charismatic Christianity in Present-day Stockholm*, 2013

75. Elisabeth Hemby, *Historiemåleri och bilder av vardag: Tatjana Nazarenkos konstnärskap i 1970-talets Sovjet*, 2013

76. Tanya Jukkala, *Suicide in Russia: A macro-sociological study*, 2013
77. Maria Nyman, *Resandets gränser: svenska resenärers skildringar av Ryssland under 1700-talet*, 2013
78. Beate Feldmann Eellend, *Visionära planer och vardagliga praktiker: postmilitära landskap i Östersjöområdet*, 2013
79. Emma Lind, *Genetic response to pollution in sticklebacks: natural selection in the wild*, 2013
80. Anne Ross Solberg, *The Mahdi wears Armani: An analysis of the Harun Yahya enterprise*, 2013
81. Nikolay Zakharov, *Attaining Whiteness: A Sociological Study of Race and Racialization in Russia*, 2013
82. Anna Kharkina, *From Kinship to Global Brand: the Discourse on Culture in Nordic Cooperation after World War II*, 2013
83. Florence Fröhlig, *A painful legacy of World War II: Nazi forced enlistment: Alsatian/Mosellan Prisoners of war and the Soviet Prison Camp of Tambov*, 2013
84. Oskar Henriksson, *Genetic connectivity of fish in the Western Indian Ocean*, 2013
85. Hans Geir Aasmundsen, *Pentecostalism, Globalisation and Society in Contemporary Argentina*, 2013
86. Anna McWilliams, *An Archaeology of the Iron Curtain: Material and Metaphor*, 2013
87. Anna Danielsson, *On the power of informal economies and the informal economies of power: rethinking informality, resilience and violence in Kosovo*, 2014
88. Carina Guyard, *Kommunikationsarbete på distans*, 2014
89. Sofia Norling, *Mot "väst": om vetenskap, politik och transformation i Polen 1989–2011*, 2014
90. Markus Huss, *Motståndets akustik: språk och (o)ljud hos Peter Weiss 1946–1960*, 2014
91. Ann-Christin Randahl, *Strategiska skribenter: skrivprocesser i fysik och svenska*, 2014
92. Péter Balogh, *Perpetual borders: German-Polish cross-border contacts in the Szczecin area*, 2014
93. Erika Lundell, *Förkroppsligad fiktion och fiktionaliserade kroppar: levande rollspel i Östersjöregionen*, 2014
94. Henriette Cederlöf, *Alien Places in Late Soviet Science Fiction: The "Unexpected Encounters" of Arkady and Boris Strugatsky as Novels and Films*, 2014
95. Niklas Eriksson, *Urbanism Under Sail: An archaeology of fluit ships in early modern everyday life*, 2014
96. Signe Opermann, *Generational Use of News Media in Estonia: Media Access, Spatial Orientations and Discursive Characteristics of the News Media*, 2014

97. Liudmila Voronova, *Gendering in political journalism: A comparative study of Russia and Sweden*, 2014

98. Ekaterina Kalinina, *Mediated Post-Soviet Nostalgia*, 2014

99. Anders E. B. Blomqvist, *Economic Natonalizing in the Ethnic Borderlands of Hungary and Romania: Inclusion, Exclusion and Annihilation in Szatmár/Satu-Mare, 1867–1944*, 2014

100. Ann-Judith Rabenschlag, *Völkerfreundschaft nach Bedarf: Ausländische Arbeitskräfte in der Wahrnehmung von Staat und Bevölkerung der DDR*, 2014

101. Yuliya Yurchuck, *Ukrainian Nationalists and the Ukrainian Insurgent Army in Post-Soviet Ukraine*, 2014

102. Hanna Sofia Rehnberg, *Organisationer berättar: narrativitet som resurs i strategisk kommunikation*, 2014

103. Jaakko Turunen, *Semiotics of Politics: Dialogicality of Parliamentary Talk*, 2015

104. Iveta Jurkane-Hobein, *I Imagine You Here Now: Relationship Maintenance Strategies in Long-Distance Intimate Relationships*, 2015

105. Katharina Wesolowski, *Maybe baby? Reproductive behaviour, fertility intentions, and family policies in post-communist countries, with a special focus on Ukraine*, 2015

106. Ann af Burén, *Living Simultaneity: On religion among semi-secular Swedes*, 2015

107. Larissa Mickwitz, *En reformerad lärare: Konstruktionen av en professionell och betygssättande lärare i skolpolitik och skolpraktik*, 2015

108. Daniel Wojahn, *Språkaktivism: Diskussioner om feministiska språkförändringar i Sverige från 1960-talet till 2015*, 2015

109. Hélène Edberg, *Kreativt skrivande för kritiskt tänkande: En fallstudie av studenters arbete med kritisk metareflektion*, 2015

110. Kristina Volkova, *Fishy Behavior: Persistent effects of early-life exposure to 17α-ethinylestradiol*, 2015

111. Björn Sjöstrand, *Att tänka det tekniska: En studie i Derridas teknikfilosofi*, 2015

112. Håkan Forsberg, *Kampen om eleverna: Gymnasiefältet och skolmarknadens framväxt i Stockholm, 1987–2011*, 2015

113. Johan Stake, *Essays on quality evaluation and bidding behavior in public procurement auctions*, 2015

114. Martin Gunnarson, *Please Be Patient: A Cultural Phenomenological Study of Haemodialysis and Kidney Transplantation Care*, 2016

115. Nasim Reyhanian Caspillo, *Studies of alterations in behavior and fertility in ethinyl estradiol-exposed zebrafish and search for related biomarkers*, 2016

116. Pernilla Andersson, *The Responsible Business Person: Studies of Business Education for Sustainability*, 2016

117. Kim Silow Kallenberg, *Gränsland: Svensk ungdomsvård mellan vård och straff*, 2016

118. Sari Vuorenpää, *Literacitet genom interaction*, 2016

119. Francesco Zavatti, *Writing History in a Propaganda Institute: Political Power and Network Dynamics in Communist Romania*, 2016

120. Cecilia Annell, *Begärets politiska potential: Feministiska motståndsstrategier i Elin Wägners 'Pennskaftet', Gabriele Reuters 'Aus guter Familie', Hilma Angered-Strandbergs 'Lydia Vik' och Grete Meisel-Hess 'Die Intellektuellen'*, 2016

121. Marco Nase, *Academics and Politics: Northern European Area Studies at Greifswald University, 1917–1992*, 2016

122. Jenni Rinne, *Searching for Authentic Living Through Native Faith – The Maausk movement in Estonia*, 2016

123. Petra Werner, *Ett medialt museum: Lärandets estetik i svensk television 1956–1969*, 2016

124. Ramona Rat, *Un-common Sociality: Thinking sociality with Levinas*, 2016

125. Petter Thureborn, *Microbial ecosystem functions along the steep oxygen gradient of the Landsort Deep, Baltic Sea*, 2016

126. Kajsa-Stina Benulic, *A Beef with Meat: Media and audience framings of environmentally unsustainable production and consumption*, 2016

127. Naveed Asghar, *Ticks and Tick-borne Encephalitis Virus – From nature to infection*, 2016

128. Linn Rabe, *Participation and legitimacy: Actor involvement for nature conservation*, 2017

129. Maryam Adjam, *Minnesspår: Hågkomstens rum och rörelse i skuggan av en flykt*, 2017

130. Kim West, *The Exhibitionary Complex: Exhibition, Apparatus and Media from Kulturhuset to the Centre Pompidou, 1963–1977*, 2017

131. Ekaterina Tarasova, *Anti-nuclear Movements in Discursive and Political Contexts: Between expert voices and local protests, 2017*

132. Sanja Obrenović Johansson, *Från kombifeminism till rörelse: Kvinnlig serbisk organisering i förändring, 2017*

133. Michał Salamonik, *In Their Majesties' Service: The Career of Francesco De Gratta (1613–1676) as a Royal Servant and Trader in Gdańsk*, 2017

134. Jenny Ingridsdotter, *The Promises of the Free World: Postsocialist Experience in Argentina and the Making of Migrants, Race, and Coloniality*, 2017

135. Julia Malitska, *Negotiating Imperial Rule: Colonists and Marriage in the Nineteenth century Black Sea Steppe*, 2017

136. Natalya Yakusheva, *Parks, Policies and People: Nature Conservation Governance in Post-Socialist EU Countries*, 2017

137. Martin Kellner, *Selective Serotonin Re-uptake Inhibitors in the Environment: Effects of Citalopram on Fish Behaviour*, 2017

138. Krystof Kasprzak, *Vara – Framträdande – Värld: Fenomenets negativitet hos Martin Heidegger, Jan Patočka och Eugen Fink*, 2017

139. Alberto Frigo, *Life-stowing from a Digital Media Perspective: Past, Present and Future*, 2017

140. Maarja Saar, *The Answers You Seek Will Never Be Found At Home: Reflexivity, biographical narratives and lifestyle migration among highly-skilled Estonians*, 2017

141. Anh Mai, *Organizing for Efficiency: Essay on merger policies, independence of authorities, and technology diffusion*, 2017

142. Gustav Strandberg, *Politikens omskakning: Negativitet, samexistens och frihet i Jan Patočkas tänkande*, 2017

143. Lovisa Andén, *Litteratur och erfarenhet i Merleau-Pontys läsning av Proust, Valéry och Stendhal*, 2017

144. Fredrik Bertilsson, *Frihetstida policyskapande: Uppfostringskommissionen och de akademiska konstitutionerna 1738–1766*, 2017

145. Börjeson, Natasja, *Toxic Textiles – Towards responsibility in complex supply chains*, 2017

146. Julia Velkova, *Media Technologies in the Making – User-Driven Software and Infrastructures for computer Graphics Production*, 2017

147. Karin Jonsson, *Fångna i begreppen? Revolution, tid och politik i svensk socialistisk press 1917–1924*, 2017

148. Josefine Larsson, *Genetic Aspects of Environmental Disturbances in Marine Ecosystems – Studies of the Blue Mussel in the Baltic Sea*, 2017

149. Roman Horbyk, *Mediated Europes – Discourse and Power in Ukraine, Russia and Poland during Euromaidan*, 2017

150. Nadezda Petrusenko, *Creating the Revolutionary Heroines: The Case of Female Terrorists of the PSR (Russia, Beginning of the 20th Century)*, 2017

151. Rahel Kuflu, *Bröder emellan: Identitetsformering i det koloniserade Eritrea*, 2018

152. Karin Edberg, *Energilandskap i förändring: Inramningar av kontroversiella lokaliseringar på norra Gotland*, 2018

153. Rebecka Thor, *Beyond the Witness: Holocaust Representation and the Testimony of Images - Three films by Yael Hersonski, Harun Farocki, and Eyal Sivan*, 2018

154. Maria Lönn, *Bruten vithet: Om den ryska femininitetens sinnliga och temporala villkor*, 2018

155. Tove Porseryd, *Endocrine Disruption in Fish: Effects of 17α-ethinylestradiol exposure on non-reproductive behavior, fertility and brain and testis transcriptome*, 2018

156. Marcel Mangold, *Securing the working democracy: Inventive arrangements to guarantee circulation and the emergence of democracy policy*, 2018

157. Matilda Tudor, *Desire Lines: Towards a Queer Digital Media Phenomenology*, 2018

158. Martin Andersson, *Migration i 1600-talets Sverige: Älvsborgs lösen 1613–1618*, 2018

159. Johanna Pettersson, *What's in a Line? Making Sovereignty through Border Policy*, 2018

160. Irina Seits, *Architectures of Life-Building in the Twentieth Century: Russia, Germany, Sweden*, 2018

161. Alexander Stagnell, *The Ambassador's Letter: On the Less Than Nothing of Diplomacy*, 2019

162. Mari Zetterqvist Blokhuis, *Interaction Between Rider, Horse and Equestrian Trainer – A Challenging Puzzle*, 2019

163. Robin Samuelsson, *Play, Culture and Learning: Studies of Second-Language and Conceptual Development in Swedish Preschools*, 2019

164. Ralph Tafon, *Analyzing the "Dark Side" of Marine Spatial Planning – A study of domination, empowerment and freedom (or power* in, of *and* on *planning) through theories of discourse and power*, 2019

165. Ingela Visuri, *Varieties of Supernatural Experience: The case of high-functioning autism*, 2019

166. Mathilde Rehnlund, *Getting the transport right – for what? What transport policy can tell us about the construction of sustainability*, 2019

167. Oscar Törnqvist, *Röster från ingenmansland: En identitetsarkeologi i ett maritimt mellanrum*, 2019

168. Elise Remling, *Adaptation, now? Exploring the Politics of Climate Adaptation through Post-structuralist Discourse Theory*, 2019

169. Eva Karlberg, *Organizing the Voice of Women: A study of the Polish and Swedish women's movements' adaptation to international structures*, 2019

170. Maria Pröckl, *Tyngd, sväng och empatisk timing – Förskollärares kroppsliga kunskaper*, 2020

171. Adrià Alcoverro, *The University and the Demand for Knowledge-based Growth: The hegemonic struggle for the future of Higher Education Institutions in Finland and Estonia*, 2020

172. Ingrid Forsler, *Enabling media: Infrastructures, imaginaries and cultural techniques in Swedish and Estonian visual arts education*, 2020

173. Johan Sehlberg, *Of Affliction – The Experience of Thought in Gilles Deleuze by way of Marcel Proust*, 2020

174. Renat Bekkin, *People of reliable loyalty…: Muftiates and the State in Modern Russia*, 2020

175. Olena Podolian, *The Challenge of 'Stateness' in Estonia and Ukraine: The international dimension a quarter of a century into independence*, 2020

176. Patrick Seniuk, *Encountering Depression In-Depth: An existential-phenomenological approach to selfhood, depression, and psychiatric practice*, 2020

177. Vasileios Petrogiannis, *European Mobility and Spatial Belongings: Greek and Latvian migrants in Sweden*, 2020

178. Lena Norbäck Ivarsson, *Tracing environmental change and human impact as recorded in sediments from coastal areas of the northwestern Baltic Proper*, 2020

179. Sara Persson, *Corporate Hegemony through Sustainability - A study of sustainability standards and CSR practices as tools to demobilise community resistance in the Albanian oil industry*, 2020

www.ingramcontent.com/pod-product-compliance
Ingram Content Group UK Ltd.
Pitfield, Milton Keynes, MK11 3LW, UK
UKHW041635190726
13854UKWH00006B/2508

9 789189 109315